# DEMOCRATIC ARTWORKS

SUNY Series, Interruptions:
Border Testimony(ies) and Critical Discourse/s
Henry A. Giroux, Editor

# DEMOCRATIC ARTWORKS

## *Politics and the Arts from Trilling to Dylan*

Charles Hersch

State University of New York Press

*To my father, Robert Hersch,*
*and in memory of my mother, Joan Hersch*

*Cover photograph by Helen Liggett.*

Published by
State University of New York Press



Printed in the United States of America



For information, address the State University of New York Press, State University Plaza, Albany, NY 12246

Production by Bernadine Dawes • Marketing by Fran Keneston

**Library of Congress Cataloging-in-Publication Data**

Hersch, Charles, 1956–
Democratic artworks : politics and the arts from Trilling to Dylan / Charles Hersch.
p. cm. — (SUNY series, interruptions — border testimony(ies) and critical discourses)
Includes bibliographical references and index.
ISBN 0-7914-3801-5 (hc : alk. paper). — ISBN 0-7914-3802-3 (pb : alk. paper)
1. Arts—Political aspects—United States. 2. Arts, Modern—20th century—United States. I. Title. II. Series.
NX180.P64H47 1998
700'.973'09045—dc21 97-47022
CIP

1 2 3 4 5 6 7 8 9 10

# *Contents*

Preface ix

Introduction 1

1. Literature and Democracy: The New York Intellectuals 17
2. Liberalism, the Novel, and the Self: Lionel Trilling and the Dilemmas of Political Action 53
3. The Sixties: Politics, Aesthetics, and Everyday Life 77
4. "Let Freedom Ring!": Jazz and African American Politics, 1950–1970 95
5. Authenticity and Surreality: Bob Dylan, the New Left, and the Counterculture 127

Conclusion 163

Notes 173

Index 221

# *Preface*

This book brings together two of my passions in life: political theory and the arts, particularly music. My interest in politics came to the fore during early adolescence, while the Vietnam War was in full swing. Too young and too ensconced in suburbia to join the huge demonstrations taking place an hour's drive north in Berkeley, my political consciousness nevertheless developed under the influence of "the sixties." During the following years that consciousness was nurtured in conversations with friends and family. I recall with particular fondness ongoing debates with my grandfather, the late Bert C. Hersch. My interest in the arts dates back as far as I can remember. I have played one musical instrument or another since childhood, from clarinet to rock guitar to jazz saxophone.

Michael Rogin first showed me that my two interests could be brought together in a course at Berkeley entitled "Cultural Symbols and Human Bonds in Feudal and Early Modern Europe." Much of the course consisted of tracing the development of medieval and Renaissance society and politics by examining a succession of paintings from the period. I was hooked, and when I returned to Berkeley a few years later as a graduate student, Rogin became my dissertation advisor, along with another inspiring teacher, Hanna Pitkin, and the late James E. B. Breslin. That dissertation, after much rethinking, reshaping, and rewriting, eventually became this book. Fortunately, the finished product is a substantially different work than the rough draft that earned me a doctorate.

A book with such a long gestation accumulates many debts. Joshua Miller and Brian Weiner, in addition to their sustaining and rewarding friendship, provided invaluable criticism of virtually the entire manuscript over a period of years. My colleagues in the political science department at Cleveland State University, particularly present and former chairs Robert Charlick and John Holm, have offered encouragement and support despite my research's distance from mainstream political science. Craig Werner and Norman Jacobson helped shape the book with incisive criticism. I also owe a debt of gratitude to an anonymous reader who, very early in this book's life, wrote four single spaced pages of helpful comments in a review for another press; though his or her name is lost, the influence is not. Rachel Carnell and Daniel Melnick also contributed thoughtful suggestions concerning parts of the book; they and other members of the Theory Reading Group provided intellectual stimulation and great cooking. Linda Manning and Patty Taylor supplied secretarial help and various graduate assistants cheerfully graded my constitutional law briefs. Additional thanks go to jazz greats Max Roach and Marion Brown for interviews and, in the case of the latter, inspiring saxophone lessons.

I am grateful for the love and encouragement of my father Robert Hersch and my late mother Joan Hersch. I am also thankful for the emotional support of my sister Julie Hersch, my parents-in-law Leo and the late Ita Glueckselig, Joanne Hersch, and John Gerring, and the professional support of Wilson Carey McWilliams, Nicholas Xenos, and Wendy Brown. Finally, I thank my wife Nina Glueckselig for being my best friend and soulmate, and my sons Max and Gabriel for their inspiring energy, curiosity, and humor.

Portions of chapters 2 and 4 have previously been published, in different form; I am grateful to the publishers' permission to reprint them in this book. The previous versions are "Liberalism, the Novel, and the Self: Lionel Trilling on the Political Functions of Literature," *Polity* 24, no. 1 (fall 1991): 91–106; and "'Let Freedom Ring!': Free Jazz and African-American Politics," *Cultural Critique* 32 (winter

1995–96): 97–123, by permission of Oxford University Press. Finally, for permission to quote from the lyrics to their songs, I thank the following copyright holders:

"Driva' Man" and "Freedom Day" by Max Roach and Oscar Brown Jr., used by permission of Max Roach/Milma Publishing.
"Fables of Faubus" by Charles Mingus, used by permission of Sue Mingus/Jazz Workshop, Inc.
"Blowin' in the Wind," copyright © 1962 by Warner Bros. Music, renewed 1990 by Special Rider Music
"Masters of War," copyright © 1963 by Warner Bros. Music, renewed 1991 by Special Rider Music
"Ballad of Hollis Brown," copyright © 1963 by Warner Bros. Music, renewed 1991 by Special Rider Music
"The Lonesome Death of Hattie Carroll," copyright © 1964, 1966 by Warner Bros. Music, renewed 1992 by Special Rider Music
"Joan Baez in Concert, Part 2" (jacket notes), copyright © 1973 by Special Rider Music
"11 Outlined Epitaphs" (liner notes), copyright © 1964 by Special Rider Music
"My Back Pages," copyright © 1964 by Warner Bros. Music, renewed 1992 by Special Rider Music
"A Hard Rain's A-Gonna Fall," copyright © 1963 by Warner Bros. Inc., renewed 1991 by Special Rider Music
"Talkin' World War III Blues," copyright © 1963, 1966 by Warner Bros. Music, renewed 1992 by Special Rider Music
"It's Alright, Ma (I'm Only Bleeding)," copyright © 1965 by Warner Bros. Music, renewed 1993 by Special Rider Music
"Ballad of a Thin Man," copyright © 1965 by Warner Bros. Inc., renewed 1993 by Special Rider Music
"Desolation Row," copyright © 1965 by Warner Bros. Music, renewed 1993 by Special Rider Music
"Subterranean Homesick Blues," copyright © 1965 by Warner Bros. Music, renewed 1993 by Special Rider Music
"Tombstone Blues," copyright © 1965 by Warner Bros. Inc., renewed 1993 by Special Rider Music
"Stuck Inside of Mobile with the Memphis Blues Again," copyright © 1966 by Dwarf Music
"I Shall Be Free No. 10," copyright © 1971, 1973 by Special Rider Music
"Only a Pawn in Their Game," copyright © 1963, 1964 by Warner Bros. Music, renewed 1991 by Special Rider Music
"Bob Dylan's 115th Dream," copyright © 1965 by Warner Bros. Music, renewed 1993 by Special Rider Music

# *Introduction*

*[I]n Old Time* Poets *were the Lights and Instructors of the World, and gave Laws to Men in their Conduct in their several Relations and Affairs of Life.*

—John Bulkey, American Puritan (1725)

## I

On August 28, 1963, Martin Luther King stood before 250,000 Americans and proclaimed, "Let freedom ring!," urging citizens to "transform the jangling discords of our nation into a beautiful symphony of brotherhood." In his writings King envisioned a "beloved community" in which "mutual regard" and equality would replace racial hierarchy and distrust. In this community, argued King, cohesiveness would not hamper, but instead would enhance, individuality.

Three years earlier such a community had been symbolically created by eight musicians in a recording studio. If the result was not a "symphony" per se, Ornette Coleman and his fellow musicians nevertheless created music called "free jazz" that expressed some of the ideas about equality and freedom that were becoming prominent in the struggles of African Americans for justice. In particular, they explored the notion, central to both the civil rights movement and the emerging New Left, that a coherent, "harmonious" group can result from the free interaction of equal individuals. "Free jazz" musicians hoped that the enactment of freedom in a musical context would educate people about, and thus contribute to, political freedom.

Drawing on such examples, this book argues that artworks can politically educate citizens and thus contribute to democracy. I take as my material writings and musical performances from the 1950s and 1960s, an era when Americans debated about the meaning and practice of democracy in intellectual journals, in novels and songs, and in the streets. I hope to clarify the variety of ways works of art can act as vehicles for political education and to suggest some limitations on their ability to do so.

From the nation's inception Americans have looked to the arts for political education. As early as 1795, the poet Timothy Dwight conveyed his wish to improve the country's "economical, political, and moral sentiments," arguing that poetry is uniquely suited to such a task because it is "more deeply felt and more lastingly remembered" than philosophy.[1] The impulse to use the arts for political change has come to the fore periodically in American history, often during times of crisis like the Depression.

Rarely in our history has the arts' political role seemed as central as in the 1950s and 1960s. Of course, on some level all artworks are "political" in that they are created by individuals or groups who exist in a particular society at a specific historical moment; to varying degrees such works will accept or reject that society's dominant values.[2] But the statement that all art is political obscures as much as it illuminates, because it ignores the extent to which a particular work is political in a narrower sense of the word. In this book I am interested in political art in this narrower sense—that is, in artworks that implicitly or explicitly comment on social and political arrangements. It is true that many works implicitly do this, but it would be difficult to argue that all works do so, or do so equally.

This book focuses on what I call "democratic artworks"—works that support democracy. In the fifties, many writers and critics argued that in the face of the totalitarian threat artworks, novels in particular, taught citizens values essential to liberal democracy. In the sixties, rock music with political lyrics was played at political demonstrations, "freedom songs" accompanied civil rights actions, and jazz performances musically enacted a vision of equality.

How exactly might works of art have contributed to politics in these two decades, and what does this tell us about art's capacity for political education? This book addresses these questions through case studies of important critics and artists in this twenty-year period: in the fifties, the New York Intellectuals, a group of writers and critics who took as their central concern literature's political role; in the sixties, jazz musicians and the singer-songwriter Bob Dylan. Although there have been many treatments of these figures, rarely have they been considered from the perspective of political theory, and never as a group. My purpose is to construct from a detailed examination of a variety of sources in the fifties and sixties—Lionel Trilling's essays in literary criticism, avant-garde jazz performances, Dylan's songs—a theoretical account of some of the means by which artworks educate for democracy.

My purpose is not exclusively theoretical, however. I also intend to call into question conservative attacks on political art and sixties art in particular. Conservatives contend that sixties art rejected reason in favor of an anarchic celebration of the irrational that undermines democracy.[3] In attacks on NEA grants to political artists and the analysis of art in terms of race and gender, they also make the larger claim that when an artwork serves political purposes, political ideas become reduced to clichés and the aesthetic quality of the work suffers.[4] Through my examination of art and criticism from the fifties and sixties I show that politically engaged artworks can embody complex political ideas and support democracy by educating citizens.

## II

The key terms of this book—art, democracy, and political education—are themselves contested. What follows consists of a series of definitions appropriate for this study; I do not aim to contribute to the perennial debates about their "real" meaning.[5]

*Art* is a highly contested concept. Common, everyday understanding excludes from the term objects that serve concrete functions. A photograph by Ansel Adams is "art" while a Chanel No. 5 advertisement is not; a beautifully designed chair falls under the rubric of "craft," but is not art per se.

Yet challenges to this conception of art have arisen as well. As we shall see, African American aesthetic theory and practice reject the separation of art from the rest of life that has been central to the European conception. Even within the European tradition some artworks from Duchamp's inverted umbrella stand onward have questioned the distinction between art and functional, everyday objects. Indeed, the period encompassed by this book produced many such works, from "happenings" and restaurants functioning as works of art to Warhol's paintings of Campbell's soup cans.[6] The incorporation of the arts in the political movements of the sixties called into question the idea that practical use, particularly political use, threatens the integrity of aesthetic endeavors.

*Democracy* is a concept with no accepted single definition. Indeed, rather than being one concept, it consists of a few core postulates and a number of related ideas, many of which are in tension with one another. Definitions of democracy give differing emphases to these competing ideas. To the extent that societies have emphasized various aspects of democracy, there are different kinds of democracies.

Certain core values stand at the center of all conceptions of democracy: popular control of government; respect for individuality; civil rights and liberties; and dialogue about ideas. More generally, democratic theory emphasizes the ability of citizens to actively shape themselves and their society through political action, to be subjects rather than objects. Beyond these central values, two models of democracy can be singled out: liberal and participatory.[7] Liberal democracy emphasizes individual rights. In classical liberal theory, these rights are mostly negative, in essence "the right to be left alone"; politics consists of the government's attempts to make sure that individuals and groups pursuing their self-interest compete fairly. Later liberal theorists deviate from this classical model. While stressing negative liberty, John Stuart Mill emphasizes the need for participation and solidarity, at least by a certain portion of the population.[8] And while classical liberals tend to see individuals as driven by a single, unitary self-interest, more recent liberal theorists have stressed individuals' capacities for inner conflict and moral deliberation.[9] However, common to all of liberalism is the notion that everyday policy decisions should be made by leaders and elites rather than the citizenry as a body, and the belief that politics consists of the adjustment of private interests rather than the expression of a common interest.

Participatory democracy, as the name suggests, emphasizes citizen participation. From this perspective, it is not enough that people have the right to be involved in politics; in a true democracy citizens must take an active part in creating the conditions that control their lives. Dialogue should take place not only among elites or at election times, but among the vast body of citizens at many times during the year. Participatory democrats also emphasize the need for solidarity and community among citizens, often created by common culture and common values; for them, politics embodies the search for a public interest, however tentative, not just the clash among private interests.

Finally, another view of democracy comes from its critics. For these critics, from Plato to the present, democracy represents a radical leveling process that does not allow those who are meritorious to develop their talents and attain influence.[10] As Plato put it, democracy "dispenses 'equality' equally to equals and unequals alike."[11] From this perspective, democracy means the end of all standards of excellence, from aesthetics to morality. Defenders of democracy have sought in various ways to show that it is consistent with excellence and individuality.

*Political education* is the process by which citizens acquire the knowledge and sensibility necessary to participate in politics, including familiarity with politics or one's political system, the ability to think critically and imaginatively, and the capacity to consider the effects of one's actions on the public interest rather than just on one's private interest. Anything that encourages these abilities can be considered a source of political education—a book, a theory, an institution, or a practical experience. As opposed to the social science term "political socialization," which stresses the passive absorption of values, political education emphasizes citizens' ability to shape the political system in which they participate.[12]

Thus, an important part of political education involves getting people to think critically about political practices and institutions. According to Sheldon Wolin, the political theorist as a political educator

> chang[es] the political perceptions of his readers. He wants to alter the accepted way of viewing politics, to change the familiar appearance of politics. As commentator, the theorist is engaged in the politics of perception.[13]

Wolin defines perception broadly to include "thinking, evaluating, intuiting and feeling."[14]

This change in perception has two aspects. First, political educators criticize society and politics, and even individual ways of being, often by exposing as conventional what appears to be natural. This denaturalization of the political order empowers human beings to take control of their collective existence. In the words of John Schaar: "Political theory constantly reminds us that the world we live in is a human construction, that we are creatures who in a significant degree choose and produce our own worlds."[15] Political educators also criticize society in the name of nature, as when the existence of "natural rights" is used to oppose social conventions or government power. Second, political education encourages people to envision alternatives to existing political and social arrangements, practices, and values. Although the political theory texts discussed by Wolin and Schaar have a small audience, more popularly accessible works can politically educate as well.

Because of its effect on perception, vision or imagination is central to political education. The engagement of the playful imagination allows us to see the familiar in new ways and to envision alternatives.[16] Wittgenstein made a similar point about the role of the imagination when he said that philosophy gives us "a new way of looking at things. As if you had invented a new way of painting, or, again, a new metre, or a new kind of song."[17]

## III

If imagination is central to political education, then artworks are ideal teachers. Not that works of art are themselves political theory per se. They can rarely if ever convey ideas with the same depth or as systematically as, let's say, the *Republic.* Yet artworks can do something that works of philosophy or theory do only secondarily: engage the emotions. It is true that different art media, and different individual works, have varying degrees of emphasis on the emotions; however, as a general rule, the arts more directly reach the feelings than do works of philosophy or theory. This is not to say that Plato or Marx never causes readers joy, sorrow, and fear—each uses rhetoric and images to appeal to the emotions of readers—but only that such effects are secondary to presenting an intellectually persuasive argument.

It is because of their effect on the feelings that artworks have the ability to alter our values and perceptions more effectively than a political tract alone. (We shall see how the arts' effect on the emotions creates dangers as well.) Indeed, what is crucial for the artworks and critical theories chronicled in this book is the ability of the arts to connect thoughts and feelings, mind and body. Thus artworks at their best engage the whole individual, touching what might be called his or her "sensibility," a sense of self and world that encompasses both ideas and emotional (or even bodily) perceptions. In the words of Clifford Geertz,

> If there is a commonality [among all the arts in all the places that one finds them] it lies in the fact that certain activities everywhere seem specifically designed to demonstrate that ideas are visible, audible, and—one needs to make up a word here—tactible, that they can be cast in forms where the senses, and through the senses the emotions, can reflectively address them.[18]

Thus the playwright Amiri Baraka tells how bebop jazz changed him because it "suggested *another* mode of being. Another way of living. Another way of perceiving reality. . . ."[19] For Baraka, jazz encouraged values and ways of living different from those of mainstream America.

The political power of the arts rests upon this connection with sensibility. Works of art can help individuals consider political issues while avoiding intellectualization, or the partitioning off of one's political ideas from the rest of one's life.[20] Democracy itself requires a particular kind of sensibility. This concept of a "democratic sensibility" assumes that democracy requires, in addition to formal mechanisms for popular control of government, a particular stance on the part of citizens toward themselves and other members of the polity. In relation to oneself, this attitude encompasses terms like thoughtfulness, critical thinking, and the acceptance of complexity; in relation to others, solidarity, tolerance, respect, and receptivity. Calling such an attitude or stance "sensibility" indicates a utilization of both thought and feeling. Having a democratic sensibility goes beyond holding a set of ideas; rather, citizens must allow such ideas to become part of their mode of perceiving and experiencing the world. (It is possible to treat someone respectfully out of an intellectual attitude of obligation or out of fear of punishment, but the results are likely to be less complete and not as lasting.)

An explanation of exactly how works of art encourage a democratic sensibility emerges in my case studies, but in general there are three modes of political education by works of art. First, some artworks allow people to more fully experience social and political conditions as they are. A more accurate view of social reality allows citizens, if circumstances are right, to bring about positive change. Second, works of art can create the experience of questioning oneself and society. At their best, democratic artworks create a sense of discomfort and inner conflict that leads to a reconsideration of previously held views. Such texts can promote the kind of inner dialogue that James Boyd White describes as "a perpetual interchange between the person that a text asks you to become and the other things you are."[21]

Finally, democratic artworks let citizens experience, in a preliminary and incomplete manner, ways of being appropriate to a new society, what Raymond Williams calls "emergent" "structures of feeling"—that is, new social "meanings and values as they are actually lived and felt."[22] Though citizens might easily dismiss perceptions of alternatives as fanciful or purely personal, artworks affirm their possibility by bringing them into material existence and making them public.

Artworks' educative role in the fifties and sixties varied depending upon the kind of democracy envisioned by artists and theorists as well as on the perceived threats to it. In the fifties, many intellectuals and politicians saw as their central task the preservation of liberal democracy against communism and mass culture. In their view, communism endangered liberty and diversity, while mass culture threatened the individuality and rationality necessary for responsible liberal citizenship.[23] Chapter 1 traces the New York Intellectuals' argument that in the face of such threats the arts, primarily literature, play an important role in preserving liberal democracy. In chapter 2 I discuss the view of the New York Intellectual Lionel Trilling that literature can encourage inner moral and political deliberation, strengthening citizens' judgment, individuality, and sense of tolerance for others.

By the sixties, liberalism itself was under attack from the other democratic tradition: participatory democracy. As I show in chapter 3, black and white activists saw the individualism, competitiveness, and inequality in liberal society as a threat to the solidarity, participation, and equality necessary for democracy. Activists sought to free individuals from established social roles that were rooted in liberal values and create an alternative community based on solidarity and mutual respect. In chapters 4 and 5 I elucidate the arts' contribution to participatory democracy in the sixties by examining several jazz and rock performances.[24] While jazz musicians constructed political narratives and created works that modeled an egalitarian community, Bob Dylan used folk music to unmask political deception and celebrate authenticity. Consistent with the counterculture's "politics of experience" Dylan's later rock songs employed surrealistic techniques to loosen the hold of the rational mind. Thus did artists and critics in the fifties and sixties shed light on how artworks can contribute to liberal and participatory democracy.

## IV

A number of caveats and clarifications are in order here. The first concerns the book's central division between "the fifties" and "the sixties."

"Decade thinking" has obvious flaws: the world did not change at the stroke of midnight, January 1, 1960. It is possible to overstate the differences between the two decades, as have many commentators on both ends of the political spectrum. Art and art criticism in the fifties is sometimes seen as detached and apolitical, as opposed to the "political" art and criticism of the decade that followed. Depending upon the commentator's political perspective, this absence of politics is seen as positive or negative. Thus, in a book on the culture of the sixties, Morris Dickstein presents fifties writers and critics as escapists: "The literary intellectuals [of the fifties] . . . simply abandoned politics to pursue private myths and fantasies, to devote their work to the closet intensities of the isolated self or isolated personal relationships."[25] Conservatives, on the other hand, praise intellectuals of the fifties for their avoidance of ideology, painting the decade as a golden age when "[t]here was . . . a fairly simple division of writers, or at any rate only one division that mattered: good writers and bad."[26]

A more complex understanding of the relationship between the fifties and the sixties would need to take into account statements like the following by Lionel Trilling, the New York Intellectual par excellence:

> Literature in its relation to life is polemical. . . . I can't think of literature or any art without supposing that it has an axe to grind, that it is arguing or urging or bullying or tempting or seducing me into certain ways of being which have inevitable reference to ways of acting. That is, for me, . . . a work of literature, or of any art, has ultimately a moral and even a political relevance.[27]

Cultural and political activists of the sixties, whether they were aware of it or not, drew upon important intellectual currents from the 1950s.

Yet one must not overstate the continuities between the two decades, either. As Todd Gitlin puts it, "History rarely follows the decimal system as neatly as it did in 1960."[28] Although leading figures in both decades promoted "political" art, they had radically different understandings of the nature of politics, democratic politics in particular, and of art. We shall see that in the context of these two very different decades, political artworks embodied and evoked very different sensibilities.

Why, the reader may wonder, in moving from the fifties to the sixties do I shift from critics (the New York Intellectuals) to practitioners (jazz and rock musicians)? This shift has the disadvantage of asymmetry but, as far as the sixties are concerned, examining works of art themselves yields more insight into the ways art during that decade contributed to political education than looking at theory or criticism might. This is primarily because neither critics nor artists in the decade did a very good job of articulating theories about the political functions of the arts in the sixties. Sometimes art in the sixties was so obviously political, or tied to political movements, that criticism seemed less crucial.[29]

The change of focus from literature to music also requires some explanation. This shift does not imply that music was insignificant in the fifties and literature unimportant in the sixties, nor that literature always supports liberal democracy and music participatory democracy. Rather, my choices reflect the priorities of each decade. Though abstract expressionist painting was prominent in the 1950s, literature and literary criticism overwhelmingly predominated the pages of *Partisan Review,* the most important political and cultural journal of the decade. However, in the sixties the political art that was the most prominent took the form of music. While *Catch-22* and the novels of Vonnegut and Mailer helped create the culture of the sixties, literature did not become central to the daily life, and political life, of most young people the way music did.

More importantly, the shift in predominance from literature to music reflected changes in the nature of politics. Literature more easily supported the society of reflective liberal individuals envisioned by the New York Intellectuals, while music contributed to the participatory, experiential politics of the sixties in a way that literature could not. This difference between music and literature has much to do with the differences between sound and sight. Sound flows into and takes over spaces, penetrating listeners; visual objects are more easily held at a distance. Whereas sound tends to unite people by creating an encompassing environment, a written text encourages individuality.[30] In addition, sounds often affect the body in a more forceful way than visual stimuli. Sound vibrations can be felt in the whole body, and beyond this music provokes bodily sensation and reaction (swaying, dancing) by its very nature. Sound can evoke a direct, "primitive" response, tapping into early, basic associations. After all, infants strongly react to sounds, whether a soothing voice or a loud noise, before they respond to visual stimuli.

Because of these differences between sound and sight, listening to music and reading are very different activities. Reading isolates the individual. It is true that if many people read the same book a kind of community is created, yet people at a concert become united in a more direct and emotional way than a community of readers.[31] Popular music in particular, often speaking as it does to everyday, personal concerns, has a particular ability to create emotional resonance among a group of people.[32]

Of course, a recording of music can function much like a written text, isolating the individual in his or her room or car, or even (with a Walkman) in his or her mind. It was a different experience to hear Bob Dylan at a coffeehouse or concert than on a stereo in suburbia. At the same time, listening to recorded music in the sixties was often (as it is now) a communal affair, with a stereo playing at a meeting or party.

Because of its communal nature and its effect on the body and even the unconscious, then, music was more suited to the participatory nature of politics in the sixties. It, more than literature, could help create the kind of emotional ties that sixties activists sought for themselves and society. Literature, on the other hand, was well suited for the society of reflective individuals envisioned by theorists of liberalism like Trilling.

It should be noted that my aim is not to try to prove that these works were successful in actually realizing their potential to politically educate. Rather, I try to illustrate artworks' resources for democratic political education. Individual artworks may or may not succeed in this task; much depends upon the preconceptions of the audience and the climate of the times.

I am also not attributing a single, fixed meaning to a work of art. "Cultural studies" theorists have shown how readers and listeners actively *use* works of art in a variety of ways, depending upon their values and lifestyles, sometimes even ignoring or contradicting parts of their overt content.[33] The enthusiastic response to Bob Dylan at a West Point concert in 1990 would seem to confirm such views.[34]

Yet artworks are not blank slates. Consumers' ability to use a work of art for their own purposes does not mean it has no meaning in itself.[35] Listeners focus on different facets of a work, often receiving different messages, but those different facets revolve around a core set of meanings that are "in" the work itself. The meaning of a work of art consists of an interaction between its content and its context. Theorists and activists in the fifties and sixties found in artworks meanings that could be used for political education in the context of the politics of their respective decades. This book makes explicit the connections between those works and the politics of their times.

My analysis of such connections does not rest on "reflection theory," the idea that works of art passively mirror other, presumably more primary, political and social processes.[36] Rather, both art and politics are part of a larger process, in which neither realm has priority. As Williams puts it, "If the art is part of the society, there is no solid whole, outside it, to which . . . we concede priority."[37] Another way of saying this is that since art is created by people whose thoughts and feelings are affected by their society and its political system, one would expect to see similar ideas and values expressed through culture and politics.[38]

Such a notion of a social whole does not imply that every part of it has equal influence; not all groups of people have the same ability to shape it.[39] Artworks in our society are commodities, produced, marketed, and sold by large corporations; this is particularly true of rock songs. Left critics of rock focus on its mass cultural status to denigrate its potential for political education. Other more sympathetic rock critics and fans distinguish between "authentic" rock and more "commercial" rock musicians who "sell out," drawing implicitly on Frankfurt School critiques of mass culture.[40]

Rather than denying rock's commercial status or using it to negate any emancipatory potential, I would (with Simon Frith) notice the tension between rock's countercultural claims and its commercial reality. As Frith puts it, "Rock is a mass-produced music that carries a critique of its own means of production. . . ."[41] While acknowledging the corporate and economic power behind the production, distribution, and reception of artworks, I seek to shed light on the resources of such works for democratic political education.

While this book rejects reflection theory, neither does it focus on the intention of the artist. I am not claiming that the artists analyzed here would recognize or admit the politically educative function and methods I find in their works. The perspective and concerns of the artist and the analyst are often different. Although the intention of the artist influences the work's spectrum of possible significations, my emphasis is on the work's meaning in the context of its time, a meaning partly a function of the work itself and partly of its audience.

Finally, in choosing to focus on the New York Intellectuals, Dylan, and free jazz, I am not suggesting that they were the only important critics and artists, politically speaking, during the fifties and sixties. Nor am I implying that Dylan represents rock music as a whole during the sixties, although he was one of the most influential artists. Though there were many other musicians performing during the decade, my aim is not to present a representative sample, but to look at performances that illustrate a number of different ways artworks can act as vehicles for political education. I also wish to connect these performances with the political ideas of their times, showing how they might have contributed to the struggle for democracy in ways that theories alone could not have.

## V

I have argued that what gives artworks a unique capacity for democratic political education is their engagement of the senses. Yet this engagement carries the potential to undermine democracy as well, encouraging the submergence of the individual into the collective at the expense of democratic values, or pulling citizens away from politics, leaving the political realm to an elite. Ironically, artworks may undermine democracy precisely because of their ability to create shared experience. One thinks here of Hitler's use of aesthetics to create compliant masses, as can be seen in Leni Riefenstahl's film *Triumph of the Will*. For those opposed to democracy, the well-constructed artwork serves as a model for an orderly society, one free from the messiness and imperfections of popular rule. If art creates community, such communities can preserve (or even enhance) individuality, but they may also threaten it.

Art also may undermine democracy by drawing its audience away from politics. While artworks have the ability to connect politics with experience, experience can become an end in itself, an escape from public life. That is, while artworks can spur people to action, art and aesthetic experience can come to constitute a kind of substitute action, thought to be sufficient in itself. Here one is reminded of members of the sixties counterculture who described playing the guitar as a revolutionary act. One must differentiate between cultural action for its own sake and art that is more truly tied to politics.

Many have argued that popular culture encourages unthinking conformity and thus discourages political action. Diverse critics from Eliot to Adorno have argued that mass-market films, novels, songs, and television programs contain predigested, clichéd ideas that foreclose independent thought. Indeed, this book will look closely at the New York Intellectuals' version of this view in postwar America. Others reject this critique of "mass culture," emphasizing popular art's emancipatory potential.[42] However, even critics of the argument against mass culture recognize that while popular culture has the capacity to provoke thought and empower citizens, it also can reinforce conformity, passivity, and antipolitical consumerism. That is, popular culture's ability to reach millions of citizens gives it both the capacity to encourage democracy and to subvert it.

Applied to critics and artists of the fifties and sixties, these concerns raise two sets of questions. First, what can we learn about the relationship between art's ability to encourage democracy and its capacity to help create order and community destructive of individuality? Were the New York Intellectuals right to see mass culture as totalitarian? Was the community called for by Dylan's folk and rock music democratic or one that submerged individuality? Did free jazz musicians' and Dylan's creation of new musical structures reflect and encourage democracy or hierarchy?

Second, what light do these artists and critics shed on the dual capacity of artworks to create political engagement and to draw citizens away from politics? Do the New York Intellectuals' writings on literature's evocation of experience help us understand the way artworks support political engagement? Did Dylan's music call for political action or serve as a diversion from politics? As part of popular culture, did it encourage unthinking conformity and clichéd thought as the New York Intellectuals predicted? So many resources for democratic education, yet so many paths away from democracy: such is my central theme in this examination of the arts' political role in the fifties and sixties.

# 1
# LITERATURE AND DEMOCRACY
## The New York Intellectuals

The idea that the arts can strengthen democracy arose out of an ambivalence about democracy itself. This ambivalence, born out of the democratization of the nineteenth century, can be seen in one of the seminal modern theorists of the arts' political role and the most important thinker for the New York Intellectuals of the 1950s: Matthew Arnold.[1] Arnold posed the questions and dilemmas that would occupy these American writers and critics nearly a hundred years later.

Arnold's writings, particularly *Culture and Anarchy* (1869), represent a reaction to democratization in England. He sees efforts to include the working class in politics, culminating in the extension of the franchise in the Reform Bill of 1867, as a cause for concern.[2] Democracy, Arnold believes, is "natural and inevitable," a consequence of the human drive toward freedom and self-realization.[3] Yet he worries that democracy's support for that drive will lead to its undoing, creating anarchy. Liberty, carried too far, will lead to the destruction of guiding social rules and values; an excess of individualism will tear apart the bonds holding the body politic together.

For Arnold, the solution to the dangers posed by the spread of democracy can be summed up in a single word: culture. (By "culture" Arnold refers to art as well as to works of criticism and history.) Democracy spreads a zeal for absolute freedom; culture teaches values that limit behavior and shape individuals according to social ideals. Whereas democracy sets the passions in motion, culture encourages rational thought; works of culture ask individuals to put aside their own prejudices and appreciate form and meaning in a disinterested manner. In the face of democracy's tendency to promote individualism, culture creates solidarity by uniting all citizens in a shared appreciation of beauty and truth. In short, the arts take us out of our "every day selves," which keep us "separate, personal, at war," and promote what Arnold calls our "best self," by which "we are united, impersonal, at harmony."[4] The sensibility encouraged by culture prevents democracy's collapse from its own excesses.[5]

But how democratic is the community held together by culture? Does Arnold believe everyone can acquire a cultured sensibility? Here one finds a central ambiguity. On the one hand, everyone seems capable of benefiting from culture; Arnold praises culture's role in creating equality by raising up the lower classes rather than speaking down to them.

> [Culture] is not satisfied till we *all* come to a perfect man; it knows that the sweetness and light of the few must be imperfect until the raw and unkindled masses of humanity are touched with sweetness and light. . . . [W]e must have a broad basis, must have sweetness and light for as many as possible.[6]

Culture here is a kind of democratic political education, empowering all citizens by teaching them to think in a flexible, critical manner. Democracy seems to be defined as collective self-governance, the shaping of society by all, utilizing the human capacity for reason and choice.

At other times, however, Arnold seems to suggest that only the few can be truly "cultured"; lamenting the majority's "ignorance and prejudice" and "natural taste for the bathos," he urges politicians not to pander to them.[7] Here the problem is too much democracy, with democracy being defined from the critic's perspective as absolute freedom and equality. From this point of view, Arnold fears that the "multitude" (the working class), "persons who need to follow an ideal, not to set one," will become dominant; what is needed is to make sure that democracy does not consist of a vulgar mass with no ideals to guide them.[8]

> [T]his and that man, and this and that body of men, all over the country, are beginning to assert and put in practice an Englishman's right to do what he likes; his right to march where he likes, meet where he likes, hoot as he likes, threaten as he likes, smash as he likes. All this, I say, tends to anarchy. . . .[9]

In this second view of Arnold, intellectuals act critically, reasonably, and flexibly *for* others; the majority benefits, but most are followers rather than thinkers.

The antidemocratic Arnold emphasizes another theme as well: the distinction between culture and its popular imitations, or as the dichotomy would come to be called, "high" and "low" culture. "Popular literature" encourages passion and prejudice; only high culture can keep society politically healthy.[10] Thus intellectuals not only need to assure the spread of culture but constantly distinguish and separate it from its popular imitations.

In the end, Arnold's unflattering view of the "mass," based on the kind of prejudice he elsewhere criticizes, undermines his apparent embrace of democracy. Democracy, in which (as he sees it) leaders must do what voters want rather than what is best, is precisely the problem for Arnold. Under such conditions, he asserts, the government can never be anything but a vehicle for various class interests.[11]

Is a more centralized, less responsive government the answer? Arnold expresses admiration for the healthy control over education by the Prussian sovereign, yet he then disavows foreign governments as models for England.[12] Such intellectual dancing about leads to the conclusion that Arnold ultimately condemns politics itself except as embodied in an abstract, idealized State. Though culture appears at first to constitute a program for political action, it is in fact a repudiation of politics in favor of intellectual and aesthetic pursuits, a preference for knowing over doing.[13] Thus an embrace of the arts that purports to support democratic politics ends up rejecting democracy and even politics itself.

Arnold's work leaves us with three sets of questions. Are the arts an aid to democracy, helping citizens to be active and responsible political actors, or a solution to the dangers of democracy, a means to preserve political and aesthetic excellence from leveling by the people?[14] Second, what is the political role of popular culture? Is it, as Arnold suggests, a threat to healthy politics, or can it encourage responsible democratic citizenship? Finally, to what extent does a reliance on culture as a political ideal risk rejecting politics altogether in favor of the aesthetic realm?

These questions run through the work of the New York Intellectuals, a group of writers, most of them Jewish, who began as Marxists in the 1930s but as anticommunist liberals in the 1950s came to dominate American critical discourse.[15] Present in all their work is the notion that literature can contribute to democracy by helping readers grapple with political ideas and see society as it really is, thus facilitating more effective action. In the thirties, they argued that modernism helped educate people in the service of democratic, non-Stalinist Marxism; in the fifties, they promoted realism and its beneficial effects on liberal democracy.[16] In both their Marxist and liberal phases, their thought was shaped by their opposition to critics who called for simpler, more "popular," and seemingly more "democratic" art—"proletarian literature" and "Popular Front" art in the thirties, "mass culture" in the fifties. In each case, the Intellectuals suggested that modernism, or realist literature that encompasses political complexity, is more truly democratic.

True inheritors of Arnold's complex legacy, their ideas about who literature could empower—an elite or the citizenry as a whole—varied in response to their shifting views of democracy, views that tended to mirror the country's political climate. Their trajectory from the thirties to the late fifties is a movement away from the idea that the arts can or should educate the populace for political action, with democracy increasingly seen less as popular rule than as a set of values (tolerance, rationality, individuality) that need the elite's protection from the majority.

In addition to its focus on these questions, the work of the New York Intellectuals is a response to their contemporaries. In the Thirties, they reacted primarily against Stalinism, but also against T. S. Eliot and conservatism. By the fifties, they defined themselves against communism, McCarthy and the "radical right," and the New Critics. Yet they were influenced, sometimes consciously and sometimes against their explicit intentions, by their opponents as well.

Primarily working in the essay form in the journal *Partisan Review*, these intellectuals did not create fully developed theories but a set of intriguing suggestions about the arts' political role. My goal in this chapter is to create out of these suggestions coherent accounts of the arts' function as a vehicle for democratic political education. (The work of New York Intellectual Lionel Trilling, who developed a unique and powerful account of literature's relationship to liberalism while avoiding some of the problems of his peers, merits separate analysis, and is largely reserved for chapter 2.) I also ask whether the New York Intellectuals, like Arnold, in their embrace of culture ultimately rejected democracy or even politics itself.

## I

The conversation about the arts' political role that culminated in the 1950s and 1960s began during the Depression. It was then that a group of writers and critics who would become known as the New York Intellectuals began their careers. Like many intellectuals in the Thirties, they drew on Marxism, but they sought to develop an understanding of the arts' political role that differed from that of the Communist Party. What distinguished the New York Intellectuals from other Marxists was their embrace of the early, humanistic Marx and Leon Trotsky and their rejection of artworks favored by the American Communist Party: "proletarian literature" and "Popular Front" art. In opposition to what they saw as the deterministic Marxism and constricting aesthetics of the Party, they developed the outlines of a rich Marxist understanding of literature's politically educative role, an understanding neglected by recent commentators.

Proponents of "proletarian literature" believed that "art, an instrument of the class struggle, must be developed by the proletariat as one of its weapons."[17] Literature should reflect the experience of the proletariat and those who have been forced into proletarian-like circumstances by events like the Depression. Such art, though particular to the proletariat, reveals the true nature of modern society, because only the oppressed can see capitalism as it really is.[18]

How does "proletarian literature" help bring about socialism? According to one of its main proponents, Michael Gold, working-class literature should describe its society; facts are the "new poetry" of the modern world. Individual emotions and stories are not as important as the "large objective pattern." Authors should be optimistic, inciting their readers to action rather than discouraging them with modernist nihilism. Simplicity in form and in content is crucial, so proletarian novels and stories can be understood by workers. Out of this, Gold and others hoped, would come a new working-class culture. The writer would likewise have a new role in politics, radicalizing the masses and preparing them for socialism.[19]

Though the first half of the decade saw proletarian literature ascendant, with the rise of fascism in Europe the Communist Party changed its approach. In 1935, the Communist International called for a "Popular Front" to fight fascism. In the name of unity, Marxist writers toned down criticism of the United States, celebrating American virtues and culture. Writers who embraced aesthetic detachment and looked to European values were criticized as elitist, un-American, overly individualistic, and therefore delinquent in the fight against fascism. Critics called for art that would represent America and its people; proletarian literature was replaced by a literature of "democratic affirmation" in which "progressive" artists illustrated their unity with the American people.[20]

The New York Intellectuals rejected both proletarian literature and Popular Front art, yet remained Marxists who saw an important political role for the arts.[21] They noted that in Marx's few writings about the arts he rejected propagandistic, tendentious novels and poems, seeing conservatives like Balzac as more revealing of the nature of capitalist society than many "socialist" novelists.[22] The New York Intellectuals sought to develop out of Marx's early work a more democratic model of the arts' political function.

Marx's early writings come out of the German humanistic tradition and its view that the essence of being human is the ability to create. In the words of Friedrich Schiller, one of the founders of this tradition, a human being "does not rest satisfied with what Nature has made of him" but has the capacity to consciously change the conditions that govern him, "remodelling the work of need into a work of his free choice."[23] By his choice of words ("work," "remodel," "make"), Schiller argues here that there is a connection between the capacity to create works of art and the human ability for choice and control over life; this suggests a connection between the arts and democracy, although Schiller himself does not go this far.[24] Marx argues that whereas animals are part of nature and their activity totally conditioned by biological instincts and physical needs, humans create their own environment, even their own nature. Free, "self-conscious" production means that instead of producing only out of necessity, humans produce according to "the laws of beauty."[25]

In Marx's view, it is precisely this capacity for creativity, so tied up with freedom, that capitalism stifles, impoverishing the experience of life. In capitalist society, the senses only perceive what serves individuals' egoistic needs; the jeweler sees in a stone only monetary value. We cannot really hear beautiful music or appreciate beautiful art, nor see other people as unique individuals.[26]

Marx argued that under communism our perceptions of the world, and especially of other people, would undergo a kind of revolution, an "*emancipation* of all the human qualities and senses." In an emancipated society, the senses "relate themselves to the thing for the sake of the thing."[27] Human beings would perceive the world in all its variety and plenitude rather than only seeing in things and persons what can fulfill their egoistic needs. At the same time, the world itself would be more human and less alien, because it would be freely produced and adorned by humans.

Aesthetics for Marx, then, represents the human ability to freely create, to shape the conditions that govern us, and to see others as subjects instead of objects. It is this potentially democratic aspect of Marx that the New York Intellectuals sought to build on. They acknowledged that some of Marx's writings sound deterministic: the proletariat is inevitably carried along by impersonal historical forces. This was the notion adopted by modern communism, with the Party becoming the interpreter of history's laws.[28] Marx's deterministic side was predominant in "proletarian literature"—characters seemed less like individuals than pawns in a preconceived historical game. The New York Intellectuals sought to build a theory of the political function of the arts based on Marx's writings that present workers as creators, as heroes in the drama of history.[29]

The side of Marx that gives citizens a more active and creative role, in opposition to the perceived determinism of proletarian literature and the Communist Party, was embodied for many Intellectuals in Leon Trotsky. Most of the leading New York Intellectuals were not Trotskyites per se, and indeed, there were tensions between the Russian revolutionary and *Partisan Review*.[30] Despite the existence of these tensions, Trotsky contributed to the New York Intellectuals' search for a Marxist literary theory, partly by allowing them to repudiate Stalinism without rejecting Marxism.[31] More importantly, Trotsky provided justification for the Intellectuals' attempt to combine Marxism with modernism. Trotsky, like the early Marx, sees socialism as part of a larger aesthetic emancipation; after the revolution, he argues, not only will the arts advance tremendously but existence will become more beautiful.[32] More significantly for the Intellectuals, though Trotsky believes that the arts can play an important revolutionary role, he rejects "proletarian literature" because of its restrictiveness and narrow view of politics.

> Art, like science, does not only not seek orders, but by its very essence, cannot tolerate them. . . . Art can become a strong ally of revolution only insofar as it remains faithful to itself.[33]

Trotsky goes further: not only must art be independent, but good art is by its nature radical—"[P]rotest against reality . . . always forms part of a really creative piece of work."[34] As he puts it in a manifesto written with André Breton and Diego Rivera, "The independence of art—for the revolution; the revolution—for the complete liberation of art."[35]

This formulation is vague, if not circular. It does not justify the claim that all creative work is a "protest against reality." But it gave the Intellectuals the freedom to pursue their ideas about the radical role of modernist art. In addition, Trotsky represented a model of the revolutionary intellectual, combining theory and practice.[36]

What the New York Intellectuals added to the early Marx and Trotsky was a focus on experience, influenced by Deweyan pragmatism.[37] The Intellectuals argued that art can only effectively politically educate if it comes out of and reaches experience. Art can neither accurately portray political reality nor educate its audience without drawing on and evoking experience and emotions.

In the New York Intellectuals' view, it was proletarian literature's distance from the experience of the artist and audience that made it a poor vehicle for political education. Advocates of proletarian literature saw a focus on experience as decadent and "bourgeois," a means of avoiding the "real" historical and political forces behind life. For William Phillips and Philip Rahv, two prominent New York Intellectuals, the result was that too much of what passed for literature among the Left consisted of "editorial write-ups"—abstract doctrine unconnected with emotions or experience.[38] Similarly, in an early anticipation of the argument against "mass culture," Clement Greenberg argued that "kitsch" shared with communist-approved art a divorce from authentic experience. In addition, according to Greenberg, both kinds of art, while seemingly democratic—that is, representative of "the people"—were actually products of small, powerful elites: manufacturers and business executives in the one case, Party leaders in the other.[39]

In addition to their opposition to the putative Left, the Intellectuals criticized conservatives who believed that the arts can or should only portray the private experience of the artist. They sought instead to promote political novels with the richness of experience of the greatest, sometimes apolitical, literature. Sketching such an alternative to both the Communist Party and conservatism required an expanded understanding of experience, one that takes into account political ideas. Transcending the dichotomization of inner, personal life and political ideas and events, Phillips and Rahv emphasize that the values and ideologies of the artist's time form part of his or her personal experience.[40] For artists to sever experience from its social context is to reject life's richness.[41] "To see oneself truly is to see oneself in relation to the larger social issue, and to see the larger social issue truly is to see oneself in it."[42] They see this as simply a derivative of Marxism and the "materialist view of society which regards ideas and values as historical, on the premise that the way men think and feel is a result of the way they live."[43] Yet the artist does not passively reflect his or her experience in capitalist society, but like Marx himself could subject it to critical evaluation in the service of a new sensibility.[44]

The New York Intellectuals did not have to wait to find the beginnings of such a new sensibility, for modernism came to be seen in the late thirties as the politically progressive art. After 1937, the goal of *Partisan Review* (*PR*) was (in the words of its editors) to bring about a "rapprochement between the radical tradition on the one hand and the tradition of modern literature on the other."[45] In striking contrast to what they saw as the simplistic morality tales advocated by the Communist Party (either in "proletarian literature" or Popular Front works), the New York Intellectuals believed that modernist literature best helped bring about a better society. Such literature critiques current society and points, sometimes against the conscious wishes of the authors, toward a new society with a new sensibility by directly evoking that sensibility in the reader.

Proposing modernist artists as the vanguard of political change appeared perverse. After all, writers like Eliot, Pound, Faulkner, and Lawrence were viewed by many as apolitical at best, near fascists at worst. Some commentators argue that *PR*'s attempt to combine modern literature and radical politics was a failure; they contend that the two paths were pursued simultaneously but never connected.[46] This is mistaken; after all, *PR* writer F. W. Dupee claimed that studying T. S. Eliot helped prepare him for Marxism.[47] A brief look at some of Eliot's early, influential essays illustrates the complex legacy of modernism, a legacy that allowed Marxists to draw on the work of a political reactionary.

Eliot's early essays present a critique of modernity; he praises organic, agrarian virtues, which were under assault by urban industrial society. As political theory, this is unexceptional; what is important is Eliot's argument that literature can compensate for the defects of modernization. For Eliot, the best works of literature, primarily poems, bring together what has been torn asunder in modern society: language and experience, thought and feeling. In his view, the best poets are thinkers, but not in the traditional sense. A poet like Donne does not display ideas per se, but "a direct sensuous apprehension of thought, or a recreation of thought into feeling." The greatest poets "feel their thought as immediately as the odour of a rose"; the thought is an "experience . . . modify[ing] his sensibility."[48] Thus contrary to those who accused him of advocating psychological repression, Eliot here sees poems as revealing and evoking experience—the place where thought and feeling meet. Like the early New York Intellectuals, Eliot seeks to preserve the richness of experience in the face of modern society's tendency to bifurcate it into abstract ideas and unmediated emotion. In this his critique has similarities to Marx and later critical theorists who argued that industrial capitalism narrows the capacity for experience.[49]

Yet there is another, more authoritarian, side to Eliot. Like Matthew Arnold, Eliot sees art as a force for order in the face of the threat of anarchy that democratization brings. Standing against the ceaseless change of industrial society, the canon of works constituting the literary tradition represents a source of permanent, impersonal values, an "ideal order" and authority.[50]

Unlike Arnold, however, Eliot never suggests that culture can help create a better democracy; rather, democracy itself is the problem. He envisions an elite group of critics as moral and spiritual leaders for society; the aesthetic order of great works of art has its political correlate in a society run by an elite.[51] By the mid-forties, Eliot explicitly came to advocate a "superior culture," dominated by a hereditary elite, maintaining a shared religious faith.[52]

If order is the solution to modernity's problems, the danger is self-expression, which Eliot sees as a surrender to uncontrolled passions. The artist unrestrained by tradition hastens the breakdown of order in society. The function of the artist is to let poetry flow through him or her by rejecting the voice of self in favor of the work and the tradition: "The progress of an artist is a continual self-sacrifice, a continual extinction of personality."[53]

Eliot's rejection of artistic self-expression in favor of form, order, and tradition has political implications as well. For him, the artistic expression of an "inner voice" is analogous to an overly democratic society guided by an unruly working class:

> My belief is that those who possess the inner voice are ready enough to harken to it, and will hear no other. The inner voice, in fact, sounds remarkably like an old principle which has been formulated by an elder critic [i.e., Arnold in *Culture and Anarchy*] in the now familiar phrase of "doing as one likes." The possessors of the inner voice ride ten in a compartment to a football match at Swansea, listening to the inner voice, which breathes the eternal message of vanity, fear, and lust.[54]

Eliot's argument for modernist aesthetic order is premised on the vision of a community where an elite restrains the potential chaos of the "masses." The orderliness and harmony of art is recreated in an orderly society. Thus while he presents an inspiring ideal in which art can reflect and evoke experience, potentially helping individuals live more fully, two problems limit its emancipatory potential. First, such experience is confined to the few who are capable of it. Second, Eliot's vision of the self-abnegating artist suggests a rejection of active engagement in the world. Art here is a refuge from society, an alternative source of order and meaning. By the fifties, each of these problems with Eliot's advocacy of a political role for culture, each a part of modernism's legacy, would resurface in American intellectual life.

New York Intellectuals like Phillips and Rahv rejected Eliot's authoritarianism, instead using his insights into the arts' ability to unite thought and feeling, history and experience, to construct a Marxist understanding of the arts' educative role. In the Intellectuals' view, Eliot accurately evoked the experience of life in an oppressive, alienating modern society, even if he saw the cause as existential or religious rather than political. Furthermore, modernist literature's destruction of traditional aesthetic forms reflected and contributed to the breakdown of bourgeois society. Despite Eliot's "reactionary beliefs," "his sensibility . . . produced a trenchant idiom for the dislocation of bourgeois perspectives amidst a tightening commercial way of life."[55] The proletarian literature movement and the Communist Party had rejected modernism as formalistic; but for the New York Intellectuals formal features contain and convey values and political ideas. Echoing Eliot and anticipating the New Critics, Rahv insists that form is a *"mode of perception";* "What we call style is really the writer's instrument for evoking the quality of experience. . . ."[56] Thus Rahv says of Dostoevsky, "Reactionary in its abstract content . . . his art is radical in sensibility and subversive in performance."[57]

Modernist literature does not simply subvert existing society, however; the Intellectuals' reading of Marx suggests that such art also helps prepare for a new one. After all, although the bourgeoisie creates misery, it also prepares the ground for socialism by its revolutionary modernization:

> All fixed, fast-frozen relations, with their train of ancient and venerable prejudices and opinions, are swept away, all new-formed ones become antiquated before they can ossify. All that is solid melts into air, all that is holy is profaned, and man is at last compelled to face with sober senses, his real conditions of life, and his relations with his kind.[58]

For Marx, modern art is part of the same transformation of society that produces the proletariat, which Marx designated the first modern class.[59] By reflecting and encouraging modern sensibility, modern art brings us closer to socialism. Some New York Intellectuals saw this idea confirmed in the early, government-supported, avant-garde Soviet cinema.[60] When Stalin betrayed the revolution and set up a reactionary bureaucracy, modernist film and modern art in general were denounced as formalistic and bourgeois, and the arts lost their revolutionary direction. But the Intellectuals, drawing on Marx and Eliot, sought to keep alive the vision of artworks that evoke the experience of modern capitalist society's dissolution and the beginnings of a new sensibility.

In the end, the Intellectuals in the 1930s failed to produce the kind of complex, experience-based Marxist theory of the arts that they had hoped to. In particular, they needed to tie the sensibility of modernist art much more closely to politics. After all, Marx believed that the emancipation of the senses could only occur after the destruction of capitalism.[61] To develop a fuller theory, they would have had to more explicitly discuss the relationship between modernism and democracy, and analyze the political components of "experience" in more depth.

The New York Intellectuals hoped that modern art was part of a larger emancipatory and democratic political change. Members of the Communist Party accused them of being elitist betrayers of democracy. They implicitly argued that though a T. S. Eliot poem is much more difficult to read than a proletarian novel, the former is more democratic because it puts readers in touch with political reality and encourages critical thought, thus empowering them. Proletarian literature and Popular Front art, though created in the name of democracy, demand subservience of individuals to a party hierarchy, subverting any democratic intentions behind it. However, the New York Intellectuals never explained how modernist art could be part of a political movement.[62] They needed to at least address modernist art's inaccessibility to most citizens.

In terms of the Intellectuals' intriguing suggestions about the way art speaks to people's experience, they might have asked questions like, Under what conditions is a focus on experience political? If experience is shaped by dominant ideologies, focusing on experience would seem to diminish one's ability to criticize society. How, if at all, can experience provide critical detachment rather than passive acceptance? How does experience shape ideas and vice versa? If readers apprehend modernity through literature, how might that lead them to political reflection or political action?

The Intellectuals' failed to develop their early ideas more fully partly because they were not systematic theorists and partly because history turned away from the conditions for the kind of society, and therefore the kind of art, that they wanted. But their attempt at an American Marxist aesthetic theory, although largely unsuccessful, was an admirable alternative to the views of both the Communist Party and conservatives. This work, almost uniformly neglected by historians of the Intellectuals, represents an important lost opportunity in American cultural theory.[63]

As time went on, the New York Intellectuals grew less and less certain that the arts could create a new sensibility and thus politically educate for social change. The intellectual community seemed divided between blind adherence to the Stalinist party line (the Popular Front) and a reactionary worship of the past.[64] In the Intellectuals' view, artists who become appendages to political organizations were almost worse than the "private" artist concerned only with "personal experience."[65]

Under these conditions, the New York Intellectuals rejected political engagement in favor of detachment and shifted their focus from artists to critics. In the absence of a revolutionary movement worthy of the name, Rahv argues, "all [the artist] can do is to utilize the possibilities of individual and group secession from, and protest against, the dominant values of our time."[66]

It is the intellectual rather than the artist, however, who leads the protest against dominant values.[67] According to Rahv, only intellectuals are detached enough from the class system to see "the life of society as a whole," which is expressed in great works of art. He describes the intellectual class as "standing apart from society and as possessing special and superior interests and ideals."[68] This vanguard group has the perspective to criticize what is bad, preserve what is good, and prepare the way for a new, future consciousness.

This new emphasis on detached intellectuals does not so much signal a victory as a new battle, however. Intellectuals have to continuously struggle to avoid absorption into the dominant society, particularly what became known as "mass culture."[69] The Popular Front was seen as an example of the capitulation of the intelligentsia to society.[70]

In the late thirties, this argument for a detached high culture guarded by intellectuals was wedded to Marxism: it ensured that certain values and cultural objects were protected from commodification and would retain their power to critique society.[71] However, although throughout the early forties many New York Intellectuals remained Marxists, the postwar period saw most of them abandon Marxism in favor of liberal anticommunism. The Intellectuals embraced what was called the "new liberalism," which rejected liberalism's conventional form as naive, idealistic, and dogmatic. From this perspective, holding onto traditional liberal assumptions would lead to weak opposition to (or even support for) communist totalitarianism. New liberalism was seen as realistic because it was grounded in an accurate view of human nature as capable of, perhaps even tending toward, great evil. Rejecting the old optimistic liberal view of history as progressive, new liberals saw history as tragic, and fraught with complexity and ambiguity.[72]

In their minds, a rejection of Marxism was not the result of a theoretical reconsidering of position, but rather a "realistic" acknowledgment of the fact that two stark alternatives existed: totalitarian communism and liberal democracy. However imperfect the latter, and however one might ideally favor some form of nontotalitarian socialism, they felt it was their responsibility as critics and artists to help protect the tangible freedoms of American society against elimination by communism. In a famous statement in 1952, *Partisan Review* acknowledged this new political stance and its importance for the arts:

> Politically, there is a recognition that the kind of democracy which exists in America has an intrinsic and positive value: it is not merely a capitalist myth but a reality which must be defended against Russian totalitarianism. . . . For better or for worse, most writers no longer accept alienation as the artist's fate in America; on the contrary, they want very much to be a part of American life. More and more writers have ceased to think of themselves as rebels and exiles. They now believe that their values, if they are to be realized at all, must be realized in America in relation to the actuality of American life.[73]

Ironically, the Intellectuals came to believe that the very democracy they strove to defend had produced a threat to its health and even very existence: "mass culture."[74] This view caused them to rethink what democracy meant and reevaluate art's role in it.

In light of their changed political perspective, the Intellectuals' defense of "high culture" took on a new meaning. Now art's role was not to transform society but to defend liberalism from two threats: mass culture and conservatism. Mass culture breeds conformity and ideological thinking, both of which contribute to the growth of communism. Conservatism was represented in politics by McCarthy and the "radical right." In the realm of criticism, the New York Intellectuals felt compelled to respond to the increasingly influential New Critics. As the Agrarians of the early thirties, this group of writers had staked out a critique of mass culture, though in the service of conservatism, nearly ten years before the Intellectuals began to address the topic. Reconfigured in the forties as the New Critics, they championed formalism, again ultimately with conservative political implications. It is partly in response to the New Critics that the New York Intellectuals in the 1950s developed their own political analysis of the arts' role.

## II

The movement that would become the New Criticism began with Eliot's writings in the 1920s.[75] Unlike the New York Intellectuals, who tried to use these writings for Marxism, the Southern Agrarians in the thirties adopted his work for conservatism, drawing on the connections he created among aesthetic, critical, and political order.

In their seminal work *I'll Take My Stand* (1930), a collection of essays by (among others) future New Critics Allen Tate, John Crowe Ransom, and Robert Penn Warren, the Southern Agrarians criticize mass society and mass culture.[76] They see in mass industrial society a system not designed to make individuals happy, but to fulfill its own imperatives. Although applied science is supposed to make labor easier, they argue, the worker has not benefited. Workers toil harder than ever, yet because of the inevitable crisis of overproduction their jobs are not secure. However, the harmful effects of industrialism extend far beyond workers. Advertising persuades people they want what is produced, whether they need it or not; industrialism destroys nature, and with it any sense of the world's meaning or wonder.[77]

This picture of industrial capitalism brings to mind the *Communist Manifesto* or, from the liberal point of view, later New York Intellectual writings on mass society.[78] Yet while Marx saw capitalism's destruction as a necessary clearing-out process making way for socialism, and the New York Intellectuals wanted to protect liberalism from the forces of reaction, the Agrarians wanted to preserve the values of preindustrial society. In particular, they saw in the preindustrial South a "genuine humanism," a culture that embraced and united all aspects of life rather than fragmenting them.

One of the main concerns of their critique of modern industrial society is its harmful effects on the arts. Only in an agrarian society, Donald Davidson argues, can the arts develop. Industrialism's materialism and distance from nature create a hostile climate for genuine art.[79] In one of the first American critiques of what would come to be called "mass culture," Davidson sees Americans' increasing leisure time filled by inferior, mass-produced art whose primary purpose is to enhance the income of manufacturers and merchants. Proponents of industrialism claim that "the shop girl can get a ten-cent print of Corot to hang above her dressing table, or buy her dollar edition of Shakespeare, with an introduction by Carl Van Doren." Yet, instead what is mass produced and mass marketed prevails. "The shop-girl does not recite Shakespeare before breakfast. . . . Instead the shop-girl reads the comic book with her bowl of patent cereal and puts on a jazz record while she rouges her lips. She reads the confession magazines and goes to the movies."[80]

Davidson claims that by criticizing "mass culture" he is not advocating aristocracy; good art, he argues, has at times been popular.[81] Yet despite this protestation, he champions the preindustrial South without a single mention of slavery, and he praises eighteenth-century society in contrast to the "spiritual disorganization" brought on by democracy and the rise of the middle class:

> Eighteenth Century society, which pretended to classicism artistically and maintained a kind of feudalism politically, was with all its defects a fairly harmonious society in which the artist was not yet out of place, although he was already beginning to be.[82]

At first glance, *I'll Take My Stand* seems anachronistic and quixotic, as it seemed to many at the time. At its best, however, it offers a critique of the dominance of marketplace values similar to that of Marx and the New York Intellectuals. The book also sees in art values like community and nature that would come to be revived by the New Left. However, unlike the New Left, for the Agrarians the community united by culture was not a democratic one. The Agrarians' preference for preindustrial society left them increasingly irrelevant to intellectual and political debates, and the movement ended during the last half of the 1930s. Yet its influence lived on when some of the former Agrarians became the New Critics and dominated the study and teaching of poetry in the postwar period.[83]

On the surface, the New Critics abandon the political program of the Agrarians. They seem to be formalists, rejecting political and social analyses of poetry in favor of close reading focusing on a unified structure. Thus they forcefully reject the idea that a poem has a paraphrasable message or meaning, a belief they call "the heresy of paraphrase."[84] They also dismiss criticism that focuses on authorial intention ("the intentional fallacy"), reader reaction to the work ("the affective fallacy"), or its historical context.[85] Instead, they focus on structure; the poem's structure is its meaning: "'[F]orm' . . . embraces and penetrates 'message' in a way that constitutes a deeper and more substantial meaning than either abstract message or separable ornament."[86]

But although inseparable from a poem's structure, its meaning is not a merely aesthetic or formal one. Rather, through its structure a poem presents a "simulacrum of reality"; the poet impresses upon the reader the unity of life itself.[87] Contrary to those who accused them of focusing on form for its own sake, they believe that the best poems do justice to the complexity of experience in a way that prose statement cannot. Allen Tate argues that although the "truth" of a poem is purely one of internal, aesthetic "coherence" rather than "correspondence" with the world, this coherence mirrors reality, or at least reality at its best.[88]

What kind of reality do the best poems create and reflect? At first, it might seem an anarchic one. Unlike prose, a poem's meaning is necessarily ambiguous: poems often center around words with multiple meanings, and this multiplicity is heightened by the relationships among words in the poem. In *The Well Wrought Urn* Cleanth Brooks speaks of the constant instability of poetic meaning:

> The tendency of science is necessarily to stabilize terms, to freeze them into strict denotations; the poet's tendency is by contrast disruptive. The terms are continually modifying each other, and thus violating their dictionary meanings.[89]

Such multiplicity of meaning creates a work of art whose message cannot be paraphrased, for "whatever statement we may seize upon as incorporating the 'meaning' of the poem, immediately the imagery and the rhythm seem to set up tensions with it, warping and twisting it, qualifying it and revising it."[90] Such language ("disruptive," "violating," "warping," "twisting") seems to cast a poem as a force for questioning, or even subversion; it potentially attacks the idea of order itself, causing a kind of instability in the mind of the reader. Brooks here evokes the radical side of modernism, apparent in surrealism, culminating in deconstruction.

But although the New Critics open the door to (post)modernist disruption, they close it just as quickly through the concept of structure. "Structure" as described by Brooks does not constitute merely formal features (meter, versification) but the "total pattern," particularly the way the poem takes disparate materials and forges them into a "hierarchy subordinated to a total and governing attitude."[91] Thus the tensions that threaten to create chaos are resolved and contained by structure. A typical New Critical reading finds ambiguities and paradoxes in the poem and then shows how the poem's structure ultimately resolves them into a unity.[92]

The New Critics' embrace of coherence as the highest value ultimately makes their work conservative and antidemocratic. As Russell Reising argues, the New Critics' apparent formalism is actually "an aestheticization . . . of a deeply conservative interpretation of history."[93] The continuity between the New Critics' aesthetic and the political conservatism of the Agrarians is apparent in an early essay by John Crowe Ransom entitled "Forms and Citizens." Like Eliot, Ransom explicitly sees aesthetic form as a "technique of restraint," a correlate of a well-ordered society.[94] In an image that betrays a view of human nature as rapacious and dangerous, he compares aesthetic form to codes of manners that dictate courtship rather than rape.[95] Aesthetic forms, like social, political, and religious conventions, impede the direct acting out of the instincts:

> [Aesthetic forms] stand between the individual and his natural object and impose a check upon his action; the reason must have been known well to the governors of old societies, for they honored the forms with unanimity. . . . To the concept of direct action the old society—the directed and hierarchical one—opposed the concept of aesthetic experience, as a true opposite, and checked the one in order to induce the other.[96]

Thus aesthetic disorder, or the breakdown of forms, reflects and hastens social chaos. As Tate put it, "Formal versification is the primary structure of poetic order, the assurance to the reader and to the poet himself that the poet is in control of the disorder both outside himself and within his own mind."[97] Aesthetic form, far from merely a "formal" concern, is a correlate of an ordered society, exemplified by the Old South that had been praised by the Agrarians. The focus on paradox and irony also serve a conservative purpose, suggesting that all action is fraught with difficulties and therefore dangerous.

The early New York Intellectuals also believed that the breakdown of aesthetic form hastened the breakdown of established political structures, but they wholeheartedly approved. In the postwar period, the Intellectuals no longer hoped for radical change, but still did not think of themselves as conservatives. Their task, as they saw it, was in fact to preserve liberalism from the threat of, among other things, the New Critics' conservatism.

## III

Despite the conservative implications of their work, the New Critics rejected an overtly political role for poetry and criticism. New York Intellectuals like Philip Rahv and Lionel Trilling sought to distinguish themselves from the New Critics' conservatism and focus on form by supporting a political approach to literature, in particular realist novels that could aid liberalism. Echoing one of his primary concerns in the thirties, Rahv saw the New Criticism as an avoidance of the full range of experience, a rejection of the particularity and "gross immediacy" that were the novel's strengths.[98] Elsewhere he characterized the New Criticism, and its related field of symbolic criticism, as motivated by a fear of history, a "denial of historical time in favor of mythic, eternal time."[99] As such, it simply capitulates to the status quo; its "traditionalist bias" "align[s] it implicitly with the conservative reaction to which some American intellectuals succumbed under the gross pressures and inducements of the Cold War."[100]

For Rahv, the novel at its best portrays the reality of human beings in history. Style in the novel is, as Proust put it, "essentially a matter not of technique but of vision."[101] And echoing Marx, Rahv argues that since history is the "sphere of freedom," the arena where human beings are actors rather than passive subjects, to banish history from literature and criticism is a form of resignation.[102] Without vision, critics and novelists are trapped in a kind of formalism that refuses to engage the human capacity for active construction of the world. Citing Arnold, Rahv calls for criticism that is "educative and preparative in intent" and engages with the work's historical context.[103] Though thirties critics erred by merging criticism and life, he argues, in the fifties the opposite was true; typically one sees a blindness to the intimate connection between the two.[104] Trilling also issued many calls for literature that would engage with political ideas and move people to action.[105]

The Intellectuals saw one style of novel as particularly encouraging the kind of responsible engagement with the world that they looked for in art: realism. Just as, in their view, the postwar situation demanded political realism and the abandonment of socialist idealism, so literature should portray life as it is rather than spinning hopeful illusions. Rahv called realism "the most valuable acquisition of the modern mind," while Trilling described the novel as "a perpetual quest for reality, the field of its research being always the social world."[106]

What do they mean by realism? They define it in part by distinguishing it from other approaches to literature. They oppose realism to didactic political novels where characters represent social types or tendencies. Writers like Orwell, Malraux, and Silone portray particular characters in unique situations rather than characters as symbols or mere vehicles for ideas.[107]

Despite his praise for what he sees as the realism of Europeans like Orwell, Rahv views this sense of particularity and faithfulness to experience as quintessentially American. Though American literature's concern with experience results in works that lack intellect, this deficiency is compensated for by a fidelity to reality, an ability to convey "the quality of felt life."[108]

The Intellectuals' call for realism seemed to contradict their continual support of modernism. They dealt with this problem by definition, arguing as they had in the thirties that modernism, though it appears to be opposed to realism, actually presents a more "realistic" depiction of modern life than do didactic forms like "socialist realism."[109]

The New York Intellectuals also opposed realism to naturalism. Though realism and naturalism are often closely linked by critics, writers for *PR* sharply distinguished them.[110] The most important difference, they argued, centers on the issue of individual responsibility. Naturalism sees individuals as the passive victims of their natural or political environment. By rejecting naturalism in the 1940s, writers wished to "reestablish focuses of moral responsibility, to be done with the featureless passive sufferer."[111] Realism, while resembling naturalism in its focus on the relationship between individuals and their environment (particularly society), shows individuals struggling to overcome their conditions and take responsibility for their actions.[112]

In the Intellectuals' view, however, writers must not make the opposite mistake of portraying characters as unconditionally free. A good realist novel shows individuals coming up against life's inevitable limitations and irreconcilable conflicts. Like the New Critics, the Intellectuals believed that what literature should show us is that life is ironic, complex, tragic, and incomplete, and therefore one has to be wary of absolutes. What Trilling called "moral realism" teaches that any stance or action is fraught with contradictions and dilemmas and that one should therefore act slowly and prudently. Thus the best realist authors tread a middle path between determinism and the utopian idealism of unlimited freedom, both of which can lead to totalitarianism. The awareness of limited freedom makes one truly free to act in one's best interest and less likely to oppress others in the name of universal ideals and ideologies. In short, realist literature educates readers to be better citizens in a liberal democracy.

## IV

On its face, the Intellectuals' support for realism is a call for political action, action made more responsible by an awareness of reality's complexities and dilemmas. Yet ultimately the shift toward realism represents a rejection of action and an uncritical acceptance of the status quo. First, though realism implies a notion of realistic action, the Intellectuals did not discuss what that action might be or even look like. The Intellectuals believed that they were rescuing true politics—more attuned to the reality of human nature and a complex, evil world—from communism's infantile, fantasy-based pseudopolitics. Yet they created no image of politics or society in its place. Their emphasis was almost entirely on the dangers of political vision and political action, and suggested that it is best to leave things as they are. Thus Trilling argued that those who are dissatisfied with present society underestimate the value of accepting what exists; property and "the stupidity of the old unthinking virtues" are bulwarks against "the danger of the ultimate and absolute power which mind can develop when it frees itself from conditions, from the bondage to things and history."[113] Though the Intellectuals spoke out against irresponsible action and justified traditional arrangements, they did not make the case for tradition in itself, but only as an alternative to change. Rather than defend present social conditions against particular criticisms, they suggested that acceptance is valuable in itself. Thus as social commentary their literary criticism lacks the particularity and engagement with experience that they had demanded in others.

Equally important, in the work of the Intellectuals the concept of realism itself is problematic. Since the character of reality and of human nature was assumed rather than debated, support for realism became a way of removing a whole set of propositions from discussion. The question for them was whether a particular work of literature accurately portrayed reality as they saw it, not whether this view of reality could be rationally defended.

As the New York Intellectuals embraced the status quo, they increasingly saw literature and criticism as alternatives to the dangers of political involvement. Writing shifted from an aid to political action to a symbolic politics that replaced its real life counterpart. As Leslie Fiedler wrote in *PR*,

> It is not . . . our duty *as writers* to deny our vocation for a gun or the O.W.I., or to impugn the autonomy of our fictions with dogmatic assertions or pledges of allegiance. . . . But the absolute claim of freedom in the creative act, in *going on writing* as we understand it, challenges many political systems and is challenged by them, most spectacularly these days the Soviet Communist world-view.[114]

Writing, for Fielder, replaces politics as "our most human of activities."[115] A year later, William Barrett went even further, claiming that the detached writer turns out to be "the most committed at a deeper level." *Finnegans Wake*, for example, shows that the author is so dedicated to language, "literary tradition," and "the most primitive and universal message of familial life" as to make "the absence of a political ideology look like a rather superficial deficiency."[116] Admittedly, Trilling and Rahv probably would have not made such statements, but sentiments such as Fiedler's and Barrett's increasingly permeated *Partisan Review*.

In sum, the New York Intellectuals' writings reveal a growing distrust of political action. In the thirties, and even early forties, although the Intellectuals argued that literature should not be narrowly tied to a political party or narrow program, they believed that it could lead to social transformation by experientially teaching the reader to envision the present more clearly and anticipate the future. By the late forties and fifties, the arts were a refuge from the dangers of society, especially one danger in particular: mass culture.

American intellectuals' fear of mass culture dates back to the last half of the nineteenth century. Just as Arnold's *Culture and Anarchy* was a response to growing democracy in England, American anxieties about mass culture (themselves influenced by Arnold's work) took place in a context of the rising fears of "leveling," particularly by immigrants.[117] George Templeton Strong complained about the streets "absolutely swarming, alive and crawling with the unwashed Democracy," while Henry James said that "the huge democratic broom" had swept away the past and brought about a time of "the new, the simple, the cheap, the common, the commercial, the immediate, and, all too often, the ugly."[118] Lawrence Levine has shown how the separation of "high" from "low" culture, which came into being at this time, was seen as a means both of saving art and enforcing homogeneity (or "purity"), staving off the perceived disorder of racial and ethnic intermixing.[119]

The New York Intellectuals' revival of mass-culture theory in the post-World War II era arose out of similar concerns. Now, however, the threat was not the working class but Soviet communism and the rising "masses." In the Intellectuals' view, both threats to liberal democracy were reflected in and spread by the arts: "mass culture" was symptomatic of both threats, and "high culture" was the cure. Arnold's doubts that high culture can empower the whole citizenry rather than an elite recur, then, in the work of the Intellectuals.

According to influential commentators in the postwar period, many of the problems facing America at that time were the result of the recent prosperity that brought large numbers of poor people into the middle class.[120] No longer beset by economic difficulties, members of the new middle class were nevertheless filled with "status anxiety," which had deleterious political consequences. Constantly striving to prove that they belonged in the middle class, they attacked those around them whom they perceived as threatening: intellectuals, "communists," minorities, and immigrants. (The Intellectuals distinguished their own liberal anticommunism from the anti-intellectual, right-wing populist version.) Thus the newly empowered lower classes turned against America's established intellectual and cultural elites, and in criticizing minorities and immigrants, threatened elite values: tolerance, rationality, and tradition.[121] Critics feared that the masses would reject the "traditional cultural and educational leadership of the enlightened upper and middle classes."[122] Without regard for civil liberties and the rights of minority groups, the "lonely crowd" threatened to become a lynch mob. Born of the extreme democracy of American life, this mob wished to drag down to their level all who might be above them.[123]

One of the most dangerous features of this new mass society, in the view of New York Intellectuals Dwight Macdonald and Robert Warshow, was "mass culture." According to this point of view, the roots of mass culture began in the Industrial Revolution. Before the Industrial Revolution, there had been high culture for the elite and folk culture created by and for the common people. The Industrial Revolution created masses, dislocated crowds of atomized individuals. These individuals could read but had neither the time nor the background to enjoy high culture. Yet, having lost folk culture, they needed something to replace it. Thus a new kind of culture arose, neither high nor folk, which unlike previous forms was manufactured and sold in a large-scale market. Recalling the writings of the Agrarians, Macdonald argued that increased leisure time in the postwar period had led to the proliferation of cheap novels, Hollywood movies, popular songs, and comic books.

Although a few commentators saw positive aspects to this development, most believed such culture threatens democracy.[124] William Phillips argued that "political democracy," characterized by civil rights, free speech, acknowledgment of the value of the individual, and toleration of differences, does not require, and perhaps is even endangered by, "cultural pluralism." Many argued that by placing novelty and commercial worth before aesthetic value, mass culture threatens traditions and standards of excellence. Although the immediate effect is a de-emphasis on aesthetic values, in the long run mass culture instills in consumers an aversion to moral and political standards as well. In the words of Macdonald,

> Masscult is a revolutionary force, breaking down the old barriers of class, tradition, and taste, dissolving all cultural distinctions . . . producing . . . homogenized culture. . . . It thus

> destroys all values, since value judgments require discrimination.[125]

At the same time mass culture threatens respect for values and standards, it subtly diminishes citizens' capacity for independent experience and critical thinking. Mass culture, that is, turns citizens into mindless consumers. Whereas high culture because of its complexity requires an active interpretation by the spectator, mass culture builds the audience's reaction into the work of art itself. According to Robert Warshow, in Arthur Miller's *The Crucible* we are supposed to feel outrage toward the "bad" Puritans, and that is what we feel.[126] Ultimately, all emotions in mass culture boil down to approval or disapproval; a situation is presented, and we should either approve or disapprove. "Signals" replace ideas.[127]

To make matters worse, we then begin to experience life itself in the way that we experience works of mass culture: automatically. We react to friends and political leaders the same way we respond to the latest Hollywood movie, and slowly lose the capacity for authentic experience and critical thinking. Since a particular experience and emotion are built into the work itself, we are unable to find a detached place from which to criticize life.[128]

According to this argument, then, mass culture threatened to divest citizens of the capacity for independent thought they needed to resist communist ideology. In its destruction of the ability to think critically and feel authentically, mass culture paralleled and reinforced the communist political program. Communism sought to consolidate support over the masses by harnessing their energies to "ideas" that were actually empty symbols designed only to elicit approval.[129] Like mass culture, it robbed people of their capacity for authentic experience and critical thinking.

Warshow presents a case study of the connection between communism and mass culture in an essay entitled "The 'Idealism' of Julius and Ethel Rosenberg," a review of a published collection of letters written between the accused spies while in prison. The Rosenbergs, Warshow insists, spoke and thought in clichés of mass culture, as he shows by quoting from their letters:

> Did you ever notice the comfortable feeling one gets reading and listening to rain? I thought, what a wonderful world we live in, and how much man could do with the full utilization of his creative ability.[130]

Even in their letters to their children, expressions of love take the form of platitudes.[131]

Warshow blames the Rosenbergs' lack of authenticity, their clichéd experience, on their taste for mass or "middlebrow" culture, which he documents by quoting passage after passage. ("Middlebrow" artworks are mass cultural objects with the trappings of high art.)[132] Warshow quotes excerpts showing their "middlebrow" tastes:

> I walk and sing songs, mostly folk music, workers' songs, peoples' songs, popular tunes and excerpts from operas and symphonies. I sing Peat Bog Soldiers, Kevin Barry, United Nations, Tennessee Waltz, Irene, Down in the Valley, Beethoven's Ninth Choral Symphony.[133]

They mix high, middle, and low culture indiscriminately; Beethoven is on par with folk songs and pop songs, and they describe "Old Man Tosc" conducting the NBC orchestra as "positively incredible," as if speaking about a movie star. Even when they do partake of high culture it is only a status symbol to show how cultured they are or for immediate gratification. This clichéd approach to art shows that "almost nothing really belonged to them, not even their own experience; they filled their lives with the second-hand, never so much as suspecting that anything else was possible."[134]

Warshow argues that the Rosenbergs' communism paralleled and reinforced the deleterious effects of mass culture. In his view, the Rosenbergs were the perfect product of communism: they had lost the ability to distinguish good from bad, moral from immoral, and true from false, because they had given up their judgment, even their inner emotional life, to the Party. They had no ability to independently experience or evaluate, and thus nothing was really true or false for them; they simply "thought and felt whatever their political commitment required them to think and feel."[135] Yet for ordinary citizens mass culture creates a lack of critical thought in the same manner that the Party did for the Rosenbergs.[136]

If mass culture is the problem, high culture is the solution. In the New York Intellectuals' view, modernist novels, poems, plays, musical compositions, and paintings by their complexity are the very opposite of mass culture: the works are each unique, they demand thought by the spectator, they are high quality, and they are separated from the consumer market. Though this is especially obvious in the case of modernism, great works of realism have the same qualities. For the Intellectuals, standards of aesthetic excellence combat the relativism and destruction of quality inherent in mass culture. The permanence of great art stands in opposition to the market's annihilation of tradition. Presumably the spread of high culture would encourage critical, independent thought rather than ideology.

Yet it was precisely the kind of formulaic, uncritical thought they saw in communism and mass culture that plagued the cultural analyses of the New York Intellectuals themselves. Basic terms are rarely if ever subject to analysis; it is simply assumed that there are well-defined sets of objects called "mass culture" or "high culture." (Macdonald enjoyed listing examples of each.) Yet Levine has shown that in America the distinction between high and low (or even "folk") culture was a social construct that only arose in the last half of the nineteenth century, largely as a response to fears of democratization. Before this time, Shakespeare was popular entertainment, and at a concert in 1796, a Haydn overture was followed by the song "And All for My Pretty Brunette," and a Bach overture by "Oh, None Can Love Like an Irish Man." Folk songs, popular songs, and "classical" compositions rubbed shoulders, appealing to a heterogeneous audience.[137] Theaters, symphonies, and operas drew audiences from all classes of society, even if they sat in different sections of the auditoriums during performances.[138] Heterogeneity of audience and materials, then, far from representing a postwar fall from the natural division between high and low culture, represented the norm for substantial periods of American history.

Macdonald and Warshow also simply assume that citizens all receive works of mass culture in the same way: passively. Recent theorists have shown how individuals can actively use works of culture, even mass-produced ones, for a variety of purposes, including social criticism.[139] In short, there is certainly much of interest in the political role of popular culture, but the Intellectuals too often avoid the complex and difficult issues.[140]

More importantly, their analyses of communism evince the simplistic, ideological thinking they purport to be criticizing. While claiming that communists substitute "idealist" symbols for an accurate understanding of reality in its concrete particulars, Warshow constructs the Rosenbergs as examples of the "ideal Communist."[141] Out of their letters he creates a kind of comic book figure of the communist who has an absolute commitment to the proposition that "the truth was not to be spoken." For this communist, espionage is "the very crown of the 'decent, constructive' life of 'a progressive individual.'"[142] Ultimately Warshow concludes that it does not matter whether the Rosenbergs actually wrote the letters at all, for they "adequately express the Communism of 1953."[143] As he accuses communists of doing, Warshow analyzes politics according to a Manichaean narrative, leaving aside facts and particulars.

Such an unreflective view of communism had political consequences. The Intellectuals rarely spoke out against abuses of power perpetrated in the name of communism, worrying instead about "anti-anti-communism," defined as an "intense fear of McCarthyism . . . nurtured by the Communist . . . [that] directly serves the Communist purpose."[144] While they sought to distinguish their liberal anticommunism from McCarthy and the "radical right," they supported restraints on traditional legal rights in the name of anticommunism.[145] Arguing that when individuals join the Communist Party they forfeit their full rights as citizens, many New York Intellectuals contended that due process, the prohibition of guilt by association, and the right to obtain passports might not fully apply in the face of the totalitarian threat. Some suggested that taking the Fifth Amendment was an admission of guilt and should be treated as such. Many New York Intellectuals also argued that communists were unfit to teach, since they were subject to

Party control.[146] Finally, some, like Leslie Fiedler, cast doubt on the patriotism of those who questioned the verdicts in the Rosenberg and Hiss cases.[147]

With their growing concern about mass culture, the Intellectuals' emphasis on the arts' ability to aid democracy all but disappeared. The Intellectuals' increasing renunciation of the notion that the arts can or should encourage democracy can be seen by taking a closer look at the work of Dwight Macdonald. His writings are perfectly suited to such an illustration because, in the manner of a jazz musician recording a series of improvisations on the same composition over the course of a lifetime, he published different versions of the same article on mass culture in 1944, 1953, and 1960.[148] Although his central analysis of mass culture's effect on consumers remains constant, differences between the 1944 and 1960 versions reveal the New York Intellectuals' growing distrust of democracy and political action in general.

The first version appeared in the inaugural issue of Macdonald's own journal *Politics*.[149] Appealing to both Aristotle and Marx, Macdonald makes the case for political action as the only means for the citizenry to better its lot. *Politics* vows to "consider art, music, literature as social and historical phenomena; to pay attention to that vast 'popular culture' so strangely neglected hitherto by American intellectuals."[150]

Within this framework, Macdonald in the first version of the article explicitly rejects the antidemocratic response to mass culture of Eliot and Ortega: the reaffirmation of class lines in politics (aristocracy) and culture (strict separation of "high" and "low").[151] Rather, appealing to Trotsky, Macdonald wants to rescue popular culture through democratic socialism:

> Since my own convictions are democratic, I believe that the trouble with the revolt of the masses is that it has not been rebellious enough, just as the trouble with Popular Culture is that it has not been popular enough. The standard by which to measure Popular Culture is not the old aristocratic High Culture but rather a potential new *human* culture, in Trotsky's

> phrase, which for the first time in history has a chance of superseding the *class* cultures of the present and past.[152]

Here Macdonald argues that the problem with "popular culture" is that while appearing to express the sentiments of the majority it actually exploits them, impeding democracy. Macdonald sees popular culture as manufactured from above rather than truly coming from below. The solution, admittedly undeveloped, consists of a more democratic culture, which can only come out of a more democratic society.

By the late fifties, Macdonald's analysis of mass culture, while maintaining some key arguments (directly lifted from previous versions of the article), takes on a different cast, consistent with his description of himself as "leery of revolution even if it were possible" and "incline[d] to endure familiar evils rather than risk unknown and possibly greater ones."[153] After recounting his earlier analysis of mass culture, Macdonald admits that it could have antidemocratic implications. However, such an objection is no longer relevant, because the problem in America is not too little democracy, but "too much."[154] Now, assuming the perspective of democracy's critics, he seems to define it as a lack of standards or values: "Mass culture is very, very democratic; it refuses to discriminate."[155] He goes on to join Eliot in asserting that one can have democracy and one can have culture, but not both. In Macdonald's words, "The great cultures of the past have all been elite affairs, centering in small upper-class communities which had certain standards in common."[156] The Marxist (and sometimes Arnoldian) vision of an enlightened citizenry with a common high culture will never be realized.[157]

Macdonald admits that a return to political aristocracy is impossible; however, a revival of cultural aristocracy is not.[158] The only solution, then, is to create an avant-garde, a "cultural . . . elite" to ward off mass and middlebrow art and make sure political merit is not given priority over aesthetic value.[159] Thus does the work of a New York Intellectual who began with faith in the power of culture to aid democracy end by advocating the separation of politics from art and disparaging democracy itself.

It is true, of course, that the Intellectuals did not entirely reject democracy—they still believed in elections and individual rights. But what is striking is how quickly they retreat from the notion that literature can help ordinary citizens to have a greater role in shaping society. Instead they embrace a minimalist vision of liberal democracy, in which the majority is best left on the sidelines, lest their populist passions lead America into totalitarianism.

In the end, the New York Intellectuals envision a cultural elite that has no hope of either becoming a political elite or transforming society. Instead, artworks that teach democratic values are guarded from the corrupting influence of the *demos*. Certain artworks are still thought to politically educate; however, this education is confined to an elite group, not reaching the majority or encouraging the broad-based liberal democracy that the Intellectuals had sometimes called for.

By embracing literature as a symbolic world that is an alternative to politics, the Intellectuals ended up in the stance of their supposed opponents, the New Critics. It is true that their visions of the good society were quite different: elite-led liberal democracy on the one hand, religion-based hierarchy on the other. It is also true that the Intellectuals were more attentive to content than the New Critics. For the most part, they did not agree with Allen Tate's assessment that it was right for Ezra Pound to have received the Bollingen Prize for poetry in 1948, despite his anti-Semitism and radio broadcasts for Mussolini, because Pound's *Cantos* are "about nothing at all"; even if Pound were a "convicted traitor," Tate said, he would still have "performed one of his duties to society."[160] However, in their focus on writing not as an aid to action but as an alternative, and in their distrust of mass action and praise for the rule of intellectuals, their differences from the New Critics were fewer than has been supposed.

The story of the New York Intellectuals is finally a frustrating one. Perhaps it is unfair to ask short essayists to do more than stimulate and suggest; yet both their earlier and later work leave one with a sense of incompleteness. In their prewar phase, they hovered on the edge of a humanistic Marxist theory of the arts' political role, only to quickly retreat from it. The Intellectuals' subsequent call for literature that would strengthen liberal democracy was undercut both by their ironic failure to overcome in their own work the kind of cliché-ridden thinking that they saw as symptomatic of communism and mass culture, and by the lack of a clear theoretical underpinning in the face of their rejection of Marxism.[161] More importantly, their distrust of democracy and political action robbed their work of its potential for opposition to McCarthy.

What was needed was an account of the arts' political role in postwar America that theorized the arts' educative function in liberal democracy in a thoughtful and sophisticated way, avoiding the shorthand phrases about communism and mass society that had marred much of the Intellectuals' writing. Fortunately, such an account was produced by the most renowned New York Intellectual, Lionel Trilling, the subject of the next chapter. Yet, as we shall see, he too inherited the Arnoldian distrust of democracy.

# 2
# LIBERALISM, THE NOVEL, AND THE SELF
## Lionel Trilling and the Dilemmas of Political Action

Perhaps no figure better personifies the New York Intellectual than Lionel Trilling, whom Irving Howe called "[t]he most subtle and perhaps influential mind in the culture of the Fifties." According to Howe, Trilling "kept apart from the disputes agitating the surface of our intellectual life but at sensitive points he spoke for the *Zeitgeist.*"[1]

Trilling's contribution consists of his subtle analysis of how the novel politically educates readers for liberal democracy. Trilling argues that certain novels help create a morally mature individual, a strong self, and that (by implication) such morally mature individuals constitute a healthy liberal society. With his penetrating insights into the relationships among liberalism, the novel, and the self, he avoided the formulaic thinking that sometimes plagued his fellow New York Intellectuals. At the same time, as we shall see, he displayed an ambivalence about political action that weakened the force of his insights even as it illuminated art's ability both to connect citizens with politics and to draw them away from it. The tension in the Intellectuals' work between art as an aid to responsible action and art as an escape from the dangers of action is heightened and clarified in the work of their finest thinker.

### I

Liberalism is the most protean of doctrines. It constantly borrows ideas from other theories in order to strengthen itself. In particular, liberalism has survived by periodically subjecting itself to what Michael Walzer has called a "communitarian correction."[2] That is, in order to avoid the rationalism and atomistic individualism to which it is inclined, liberalism incorporates values from communitarianism or conservatism.

One of the vehicles for this periodic "correction" has been the arts. By reading Wordsworth, John Stuart Mill recovered from the "mental crisis" that had resulted from his living according to the rationalistic precepts of his father and Bentham, and Mill's experience led him to emphasize the role of the arts in his liberal theory. According to Mill, liberalism in its pure form gives rise to three problems: individuals have a tendency to be preoccupied with their own affairs and neglect relations with others; people pursue outer, material goals at the expense of inner, spiritual ones; and citizens face strong pressures to conform to majority beliefs and lifestyles. Art, for Mill, helps remedy these problems. Great works of art unite individuals in a shared appreciation of and feeling for beauty. At the same time, the arts promote individuality by urging people to pay attention to their inner selves and by exposing them to diverse points of view.[3]

Like Mill, Trilling sees the arts as a corrective to liberalism's problems, arguing that the novel can encourage attitudes and sentiments supportive of democracy. Yet as part of a *liberal* society, such literature should affect individuals in a different manner than did the propagandistic "proletarian literature" of the thirties. To persuade a reader in a rhetorical, dogmatic way to adopt liberal values would be self-contradictory. That is, literature that supports liberalism must help transform individuals in a way that preserves liberal values—openness, critical thought, and individuality. Trilling's account of how novels might carry out such a transformation is the subject of this chapter.

## II

In a career spanning more than four decades, Trilling took as his central theme the "inevitable intimate . . . connection between literature and politics."[4] No one would deny that some novels discuss political events and ideas, although one might question whether all novels do this. Going beyond this obvious fact, Trilling argues that literature has, and should have, a "practical, political and social use."[5] If pushed to define its use more precisely, Trilling would acknowledge that different kinds of literature have served a variety of functions in different cultures, but he focuses on the way in which the novel supports liberal politics. The novel has performed this function since its inception, he argues, but with the rise of modernism, it has abandoned this task. The best modern writers—in Trilling's view, Proust, Joyce, Lawrence, Pound, and Eliot—are either hostile or indifferent to liberalism, while liberal writers produce works of "social and political protest" devoid of imagination or thought.[6] The most prominent postwar literary theorists, the New Critics, try to divorce texts from their social and political context altogether. In the face of what he sees as modernist political conservatism and the New Critics' attempt to separate literature and politics, Trilling argues that the novel can help revive and support liberalism, and he dedicates his writings to showing how it can do this and how, if it fails, "we shall have reason to be sad not only over a waning form of art but also over our waning freedom."[7]

Trilling's fullest analysis of liberalism and the novel's role in promoting it is contained in his era-defining work, *The Liberal Imagination* (1950).[8] Trilling never precisely defines his central term. He insists that "[a]ttempts to define liberalism are not likely to meet with success," because liberalism is "a large tendency rather than a concise body of doctrine," yet the outlines are readily apparent.[9] Rather than a set of institutional or political arrangements, liberalism for Trilling represents a set of values: tolerance, diversity, rationality, critical thought, and a concern for individual happiness and development. Although liberalism is often associated with Enlightenment rationalism, Trilling argues that the "primal imagination of liberalism" combines the Enlightenment belief in the ability of human beings to transform the world through reason with the romantic knowledge of the tragic limits of rationality and human efficacy.[10] Liberalism at its best takes into account irrational, unpredictable forces within the individual and society; a liberal of this variety would recognize limits on change and act accordingly. This might seem a conservative liberalism, but Trilling sees it as true to the essence of liberalism. In an argument reminiscent of Hannah Arendt (whom he admired), Trilling claims that effective change, either social or individual, can only occur in the context of the acknowledgment of limits.[11]

Trilling distinguishes this mature liberalism from "weak or wrong expressions of itself."[12] The debased liberalism that Trilling sees as prevalent in his own time represents Enlightenment rationality untempered by a recognition of its own limits; the temptation that communism holds for liberals in his time shows this dangerous tendency of liberalism. This overreliance on rationality then threatens liberalism's core values of tolerance and freedom: government tries to mold society and its members according to transcendent, absolute ideas, and its attempts to eliminate imperfections and limitations inherent in human life lead to greater harm. In short, liberalism itself has become an ideology, closing off avenues of thought instead of opening them.

Literature, according to Trilling, helps transform debased liberalism by bringing to the fore its neglected sense of limits, "recall[ing] liberalism to its first essential imagination of variousness and possibility, which implies the awareness of complexity and difficulty."[13] Literature encourages readers to think critically and question their assumptions, especially their belief in moral absolutes. The best works of fiction embody "moral realism," stressing "the dangers of the moral life itself," reminding us that "to act against social injustice is right and noble but that to choose to act does not settle all moral problems but on the contrary generates new ones of an especially difficult sort."[14] The morally complex situations presented in novels make us think; the best literature "is involved with ideas" and its power "surely derives from its commerce . . . with systematic ideas."[15]

In praising the novel of ideas, particularly political ideas, Trilling had to contend with the New Critics' attack on such literature. In an essay entitled "The Meaning of a Literary Idea" Trilling argues that the New Critics have an overly narrow understanding of ideas. He acknowledges that certain kinds of "ideas"—abstract, system-based notions divorced from experience—do have a stifling effect on creativity, thought, and feeling.[16] But the New Critics tend to see all ideas as intellectualization, the "product of formal systems of philosophy."[17]

For Trilling, ideas can encompass feelings and thus play a role in art without turning the work into ideology. The New Critics, in their "anxiety lest the work of art be other than totally self-contained," neglect the emotional power of ideas, their ability to move people to action.[18] Ideas are not just "pellets of intellection or crystallization of thought, precise and completed," but "living things, inescapably connected with our wills and desires."[19] Rather than a reflection of an impersonal tradition, literary ideas express the individuality of the writer and his or her "strong, decisive, self-limiting voice."[20]

It is true, according to Trilling, that ideas detached from emotions are not likely to change people's actions. If they were, political tracts and essays would make novels unnecessary as vehicles for political education. Rather, in order for novels to help people become more tolerant and self-critical, they must connect our attitudes with our feelings; it is literature's capacity to do so that makes it such an effective means of political education. By creating compelling characters with whom readers identify and rich situations that draw them into the story, the novel "involv[es] . . . the reader himself in the moral life," allowing him to experience rather than simply observe.[21] Trilling is not rejecting thought in favor of feeling; rather, he stresses their interconnection. He cites with approval Goethe's notion that "there is no such thing as a liberal idea . . . [but] only liberal sentiments," but then argues that those sentiments influence our thoughts, for "the life of reason . . . begins in the emotions."[22] The best literature moves us, but this emotional reaction makes us rethink our attitudes and ideas, and this rethinking creates new emotional responses: "[J]ust as sentiments become ideas, ideas eventually establish themselves as sentiments."[23]

It is this connection between ideas and emotions that differentiates good novels from propagandistic, ideological ones. Recalling Eliot's "objective correlative," Trilling argues that while ideological literature presents abstract ideas without integrating them into the fictional action itself, good novels present ideas in the form of concrete human situations that reach our emotions.[24] When propagandistic works do provoke an emotional response, it is only the pleasure of approval or the displeasure of disapproval; Trilling makes a distinction between "the flattery of agreement" and "the real emotions of literature."[25]

Though Trilling does not precisely say so, he seems to believe that good literature creates emotional conflict, and this conflict creates reflection, for "[w]hat comes into being when two contradictory emotions are made to confront each other and are required to have a relationship with each other is . . . quite properly called an idea."[26] The longing for virtue in a world containing evil, or Faulkner's affection for the Old South despite his sense of its "inadequacy"—these oppositions presented in literature engender emotional conflict in readers, conflict that leads to a rethinking of attitudes and assumptions and ultimately to new modes of behavior. Like psychoanalysis, literature strengthens the ego by producing controlled mental conflict, conflict that neurotics and ideologues avoid with elaborate defenses and rationalizations. Ideological literature arouses the emotions but fails to produce the inner struggle that results in genuine thinking. Indeed, it is precisely the concern for "emotional safety," the wish to avoid mental conflict and the discomfort it produces, that leads to ideological thinking (or pseudothinking). Ideological novels produce rigid positions and automatic, simplistic emotional responses. Good novels demand reflective thinking, thinking that is likely to support a liberal society. For example, in his travels with Jim, Huckleberry Finn, after much internal struggle, learns to question the wisdom of slavery, "the moral code he has always taken for granted," and Twain's portrayal of Huck's transformation encourages the reader to examine his or her own convictions:[27]

> *Huckleberry Finn* is indeed a subversive book—no one who reads thoughtfully the dialectic of Huck's great moral crisis will ever again be wholly able to accept without some question and some irony the assumptions of the respectable morality by which he lives, nor will ever again be certain that what he considers the clear dictates of moral reason are not merely the engrained customary beliefs of his time and place.[28]

Even a novel by a conservative or reactionary like Faulkner or Dostoevsky can promote dialogue and thus advance liberalism.

Of course, Trilling's analysis of literature's political function assumes that readers will read a novel in a particular way. What prevents readers from missing the conflict altogether, or choosing the side they are predisposed to favor? Why will literature produce self-questioning when other influences (friends, newspapers, political speeches) fail to do so? If people avoid internal conflict so much, why will a novel break down their defenses?

Trilling's writings suggest some answers, although he does not directly address these questions. First, he assumes that novel readers are educated and open-minded. He would not claim to be able to affect those so influenced by "mass culture" that they cannot think independently or those so dogmatic as to refuse to consider opposing views.[29] Second, Trilling would argue, influenced by Freud, that because of its connection with the imagination, literature has a particular power over us. Images, feelings, fantasies—these are at our core, and literature has a power to touch that core in a way that rational arguments do not. Literature brings to the surface unconscious wishes, impulses, and images in order that we can consciously and rationally inspect them. The best novels affect our emotions in a way that produces critical thinking and responsible action.

## III

Alongside *The Liberal Imagination*'s insightful argument for the political benefits of literature, a very different view of politics and of the arts' role can be found in Trilling. This second Trilling fears political action and even action itself, reminding himself in an early journal entry, "Do not be afraid of action. . . ."[30] In this entry Trilling speaks of his work on an apparently aborted novel—that is, he tells himself not to fear putting action in the book's plot. But it can also be read as evidence of a more personal struggle, as a much later journal entry suggests:

> I saw as never before the assumption in which I was reared—the assumption that life lay with my mother (and father), that something not life, better than life, was for me. That pain, disaster, frustration might touch them, but not me. . . .[31]

As we shall see, this personal anxiety is part of a larger worldview that is present in Trilling's ideas about political action as well. This worldview undercuts Trilling's ostensible support for literature as an aid to political action and leads him to see art as an escape.

Trilling's ambivalence about action is most apparent in his only novel, *The Middle of the Journey*, published in 1947.[32] Although on the surface the book praises responsible political action, it ultimately fails to passionately defend liberalism and to bring political ideas to life through plot and character development.

*The Middle of the Journey* is a *Bildungsroman* about John Laskell, "a sincere liberal," sympathetic to the Left but not a Communist Party member (a "fellow traveler").[33] There is very little action in the book; the "story" consists of Laskell's intellectual development through his encounter with characters representing very different approaches to life. The novel takes place during a vacation in New England, where Laskell is recovering from a near-fatal illness. His illness has caused him to reflect on death and its relationship to life. He has found, to his surprise, that being ill gave him intense pleasure, the joy of a deathlike freedom from willing and acting. He becomes uncomfortable with this embrace of illness and goes to visit some close friends who are unusually "committed to life," hoping to shed this attitude.[34]

The friends are Arthur and Nancy Croom, idealistic young fellow travelers. The three are joined by Gifford Maxim, a character explicitly based on Whittaker Chambers. Maxim has left the Party, renouncing it and vowing to expose the murderousness of its ideals; he adopts in its place a Manichaean religious faith emphasizing the sinfulness of all.

Laskell is sometimes drawn to the Crooms and at other times to Maxim—to the Crooms because they affirm life, and to Maxim because he acknowledges death, validating his pleasure during his illness. But he comes to reject both views, seeing them as opposites that are complementary, both "hopeless extremes."[35] The Crooms embody liberal idealism at its most naive. With their belief in the ultimate triumph of good, they refuse to acknowledge the existence of evil in the world. Laskell's encounter with fatal illness bothers them greatly, and they want to avoid talking or thinking about it, because by holding onto their view that anything can be accomplished with enough commitment they think they can deny the ultimate limitation on human freedom—death.[36] Later in the novel, Trilling shows how such a belief in the primacy of the will, with its blind affirmation of life that cannot tolerate imperfection, ultimately leads to murder.

If the Crooms see human beings as totally free, Maxim's ethic is one of absolute submission to God. Just as the Crooms picture a shining, humanly made utopian future, Maxim blindly believes in an "apocalyptic" judgment day when God will mete out justice once and for all.[37] Though in acknowledging evil Maxim's view of life is more realistic than the Crooms', Trilling suggests that his thinking is as ideological as theirs; it is mired in "abstractions" and absolutes, favoring inflexible "maxims" over individuality and diversity.[38] Through Laskell's brush with death and his encounter with these extreme points of view, he ultimately arrives at a middle ground based on acceptance of the conditioned, limited nature of life. Rejecting both "absolute freedom" and "absolute responsibility," Laskell favors "the human being in maturity, at once responsible and conditioned."[39] He thus rejects as escapist his earlier embrace of illness and death but realizes that they must be acknowledged if one is to act responsibly.

The book ends with an apparent confirmation of liberal politics: political action tempered by a mature, realistic awareness of both the limitations of action and the existence of evil. For Trilling, this philosophy represents an affirmation of politics. Communism, in his view, was trying to eliminate politics by replacing compromise, contingency, and conflict with the certainties of an ideal realized in an absolute State.[40] Trilling is trying to rescue "real" politics, politics based on an awareness of "the conditioned."

In the end, however, *The Middle of the Journey* is a surprisingly weak defense of liberal politics. In part this is because Trilling could not create in his own novel what as a critic he demanded of others: fully developed characters whose meaning is revealed through actions as well as words. Instead, Laskell, Maxim, and the Crooms are mere mouthpieces for ideas unconnected to their personalities. Trilling thus commits the sin of which he accuses the New Critics—divorcing ideas from emotions and lived experience.[41]

But this disjunction between idea and emotion is only part of the problem, because the passages arguing for liberalism are the most devoid of feeling. Indeed, Laskell is the least memorable character in the book; his words and actions convey little passion, violating Trilling's own principle that to politically educate, ideas must be animated by sentiments.[42] Even in the midst of a heated argument, Laskell speaks in pale, measured prose that resembles nothing so much as a passage from one of Trilling's less-successful essays:

> I cannot absolve the world or society or God or my parents or nature from all blame from what I am or do. I didn't make myself and I don't dare cut my connection with all the things in the world that made me. I cannot hold myself free of these things. I will blame them when they injure and reduce me, as they do every moment of the day. And for that matter, I cannot avoid my gratitude to them.[43]

Yet the book comes to life when warning of the dangers of action. Maxim's speeches contain real passion and focus as he describes the sinfulness of human beings and our inability to act without engaging in evil:

> And so you and I stand opposed. For you—no responsibility for the individual, but no forgiveness. For me—ultimate, absolute responsibility for the individual, but mercy. . . . [S]ocial causes, environment, education—do you think they really make a difference between one human soul and another? In the eyes of God are such differences of any meaning at all? Can you suppose that *they* condition His mercy? Does He hold a Doctor of Philosophy more responsible than a Master of Arts, or a high school graduate more responsible than a man who has not finished the eighth grade? Or is His mercy less to one than another?[44]

Maxim's most passionate orations eloquently describe how those who try hardest to do good often perpetrate the vilest evil. In the end, Trilling's novel is political in a primarily negative way, revealing the dangers of a certain kind of politics; in its weak support for an alternative vision it implicitly warns against politics in general.

Even intellectual assertion poses danger, according to the novel. This danger can be seen in an incident in which a child, Susan Caldwell, is to recite a poem for a local fair. While she is rehearsing, the intellectual Laskell corrects her emphasis in a passage. When the recitation takes place, she reads it as she originally had and then stumbles, remembering Laskell's correction. Afterwards (rather implausibly) her father strikes her in punishment and, because of her weak heart, she dies. Laskell feels responsible for her death.[45] Thus even the intellect, so central to Trilling's vision of liberalism, only finds safety in a renunciation of action.

This renunciation is confirmed by the passion with which Trilling describes Laskell's embrace of illness, even though on the surface he ultimately rejects it as an approach to life. The reason for Laskell's contentment with his infirmity becomes apparent when he describes the hours he spent staring at a single rose. He describes his "contemplation" of the rose in aesthetic terms:

> He would become lost in its perfection, watching the strange energy which the rose seemed to have, for it was not static in its beauty, it seemed to be always at work organizing its petals into their perfect relation with each other. Laskell, gazing at it, had known something like desire; but it was a strange desire which *wanted* nothing, which was its own satisfaction. He had been so very much involved, was so quick to ask for it every morning of the three days it continued to bloom, that his nurse Paine had teased him about it. She had said dryly, "Well, you're having quite a love affair with that flower." . . . Yet what a strange love it was that was satisfied by its own desire and wanted nothing. It puzzled him, but even the puzzle was a happiness—for it was a puzzle that did not need solution and he did not try for one. He rested content with the contentment that this harmless activity gave him, a kind of fulness of being, without any of the nagging interruptions of personality.[46]

His puzzlement is short-lived, however, for he soon realizes the real meaning of his infatuation with the flower:

> That involvement with the rose, that desire that wanted nothing . . . what was it if not the image of death? . . . Quite a love affair with that flower, quite a love affair with death![47]

These passages vividly illustrate the way aesthetic engagement, which Trilling argued in *The Liberal Imagination* could empower liberal citizens, can become an end in itself, an escape from life, let alone action. Against the dangerous will of the Crooms, the book offers egoless, death-affirming aesthetic contemplation, though it claims to reject it.[48] In contrast to the Crooms' erotic love that produces children, Laskell offers his chaste, aesthetic love, which evokes in him the image of a fetus that does not want to be born.[49] It is true that he then speaks of the moment when the womb becomes a prison and the fetus must escape and be born, suggesting that one cannot remain in aesthetic contemplation. However, this sentiment is overpowered by the passionate description of such contemplation. The power with which the novel describes both the dangers of politics and the retreat into the aesthetic undercuts Trilling's wish to explore political questions and further healthy, liberal politics.

## IV

The weakness of Trilling's novel as a vehicle for liberal political education becomes more apparent by contrasting it to another political novel published the previous year: *All the King's Men* by the New Critic Robert Penn Warren. Such a comparison is useful for three reasons. First, despite strong differences between the New York Intellectuals and the New Critics, Trilling's and Warren's novels focus on a remarkably similar set of political themes. Second, there is a profound irony present. Warren as a New Critic presumably rejected political uses for the arts, yet he far more fully than Trilling himself realizes Trilling's ideal of a novel that brings political ideas to life through its characters and their actions. Finally, while Trilling's fears about action manifest themselves in his protagonist's retreat into the aesthetic, Warren's novel confronts the dangers of action but affirms its value and superiority to withdrawal.

*All the King's Men* and *The Middle of the Journey* share two central themes: responsibility and the dangers of idealism. Both books present the idea that we are neither absolutely free nor absolutely determined, yet must take responsibility for our actions; both books also show that good motives do not necessarily lead to good actions. However, Trilling can only communicate those ideas in impersonal speeches that could have been delivered by anyone. Warren uses action and personality, not just dialogue, to bring ideas to life, so that the ideas are inseparable from his characters and their experiences. As Bakhtin said of Dostoevsky, "We *see* the hero in the idea and through the idea, and we *see* the idea in him and through him."[50] Like Trilling, Warren advocates a middle ground between extremes, but this middle ground is achieved through the interaction between opposing personalities rather than through a merely conceptual resolution between two intellectual positions.

Like *The Middle of the Journey*, *All the King's Men* traces the education of its main character. In this case, the protagonist is Jack Burden, an aide to Willie Stark, a corrupt Southern governor. The story follows Burden from his days as a journalist to his work with Governor Stark until Stark is assassinated. But this story is interwoven with the tale of Burden's personal and family history; the two stories, personal and political, interact with each other and explore common themes.

*All the King's Men* also resembles Trilling's novel in that it centers around the protagonist's confrontation with two central characters representing opposing philosophies: in this case, Governor Stark and Adam Stanton, a childhood friend of Jack's who has become a highly respected physician. Stark believes in action and has little interest in ideas or ideals. In his view, the world consists entirely of "dirt," though he thinks one can use it for good, just as a diamond ultimately comes from dirt.[51] He runs his administration with this philosophy, "[p]ouring swill" to his constituents as he did to hogs on his farm.[52] In his view, "there ain't anything worth doing a man can do and keep his dignity."[53]

Goodness to him is what promotes an individual's or society's interest at any given time.[54] Employing corrupt means he builds a large children's hospital and various public works projects.

Adam Stanton represents the other extreme. He is a man of ideas, detached from life. He is also an idealist, with a clear vision of how things should be; when the world does not measure up, he rejects it altogether.[55] Despite (or because of) his idealism Stanton ends up committing murder, killing Stark.

Thus the corrupt politician does some good while the idealistic physician commits a heinous crime. With this paradox Warren illustrates the moral complexity of action—good is inevitably mixed with evil, evil with good. The moral intricacy of action is heightened by its inherent unpredictability; each action sets off a chain of events whose end cannot be known. As Hannah Arendt puts it,

> The perplexity is that in any series of events that together form a story . . . we can at best isolate the agent who set the whole process into motion; and although this agent frequently remains the subject, the "hero" of the story, we never can point unequivocally to him as the author of its eventual outcome.[56]

This insight is illustrated by a sequence of events that begins when Stanton tells Jack to silence Judge Irwin, Jack's friend who has become a critic of the governor, by digging up indiscretions from his past. Jack discovers that Irwin as state attorney general once took a financially rewarding position with a corporation in exchange for favorably setting a lawsuit against one of its subsidiaries. When Jack tells Irwin he has this information, the judge commits suicide, leading Jack's mother's to reveal that Irwin was actually his father; thus in Jack's mind the search for truth has led him to kill his own father.

However, Warren's novel suggests it is not that simple, because any event is only part of a chain, and thus responsibility cannot be precisely located. Jack discovered Irwin's misdeed by means of an old letter written by Mortimer L. Littlepaugh, who had been squeezed out of the job that went to Irwin in exchange for settling the lawsuit. One could then say that Littlepaugh rather than Jack "killed" Irwin. On the other hand, the judge's acceptance of the job began the chain of events, making his death a "suicide": "Mortimer killed Judge Irwin because Judge Irwin had killed him, and I had killed Judge Irwin because Judge Irwin created me, and looking at matters in that light one could say that Mortimer and I were merely the twin instruments of Judge Irwin's protracted and ineluctable self-destruction."[57]

Jack's discovery of the complexity, even absurdity, of action at first leads him to embrace determinism and deny the possibility of responsibility. He calls this the idea of the "Great Twitch": everything that we do is ineluctably caused by another action, so that our actions are like the twitch of a frog's leg stimulated by an electric current in a science laboratory.[58] But by the end of the book Jack rejects this view. Jack accepts that any action may result in evil, but unlike Laskell with his love affair with death, he realizes that to repudiate action is to will one's own demise. As Burden puts it, "Politics is action and all action is but a flaw in the perfection of inaction, which is peace, just as all being is but a flaw in the perfection of nonbeing."[59] The price of the pursuit of perfection is "nonbeing," nothingness. While Laskell rhapsodizes over the joy of such nonbeing, Burden comes to see inaction as an avoidance of responsibility and an action that has its own consequences. Though one cannot predict the consequences of one's action, one must take responsibility for them anyway, for acting in the world gives one "the awful responsibility of Time."[60] As Jack's surname suggests, taking action creates the "burden" of responsibility, but one worth bearing because the alternative is self-annihilation.

Why was Warren, the New Critic whose theory rejected political art, better able to realize Trilling's ideas of the political novel than the New York Intellectual himself? Warren is a better novelist, but I do not think that is the complete answer. The larger explanation is that while Trilling praises action and experience, he is really more comfortable with ideas; the world is such a dangerous place that he cannot even evoke it in his novel.[61] Ironically, such a view grew out of the very cold-war "realism" that was meant to facilitate responsible action. In a world of extreme ideologies and ruthless communists, Trilling seems to say, the best action is inaction—or at best a kind of holding action to preserve the status quo. Trilling's doubts about action, especially collective action by ordinary citizens, would grow by the mid-fifties in response to what he saw as the rise of "mass society."

## V

In the years following the publication of *The Middle of the Journey* and *The Liberal Imagination*, Trilling held out hope for a truly liberal society and believed that literature could help bring about that society. He took concrete steps to help give literature a larger audience by editing anthologies of literary works and serving as editor and judge of two book clubs.[62] By 1952 Trilling saw signs that his vision was beginning to be realized; he believed that due to the influence of writers and intellectuals, liberal ideas and sentiments were beginning to penetrate into the American consciousness.

> [A]t the present time the needs of our society have brought close to the top of the social hierarchy a large class of people of considerable force and complexity of mind. . . . Intellect has associated itself with power, perhaps as never before in history, and now is conceded to be itself a kind of power. . . . [We have seen] the entry into our political and social life of an ever-growing class which we must call intellectual, although it is not necessarily a class of "intellectuals."[63]

Trilling saw Stevenson's candidacy and the growing number of "men of ideas" in government, finance, industry, and journalism as evidence of this trend. In hindsight, the evidence that such a change was taking place is rather slim. Be that as it may, Trilling believed that the influence of reflective, critical thinkers was beginning to make American society more open and tolerant. He thus sang the virtues of accepting society as it was, praising the acknowledgment of the "conditioned" nature of our lives—the fact that "[material] things, habits [and] . . . customs" limit and shape us. Such acceptance avoids the dangerous commitment to remake the world according to abstract ideals, no matter what the cost.[64]

As the decade continued, however, Trilling saw signs that literature's salutary influence on society might be temporary. Like many other New York Intellectuals he believed that the rise of "mass culture" overshadowed and threatened thoughtful literature and the liberal politics associated with it. Trilling soon came to believe that despite great novels' influence on a few, mass society and its conformism made the critical thinking necessary for liberal society even more difficult. By the mid-fifties the words and phrases he used to describe American society reveal his menacing image of it: "all too efficient," "seductive," "grow[ing] in homogeneity and demandingness, even in those respects we think of as most free and benign." Meanwhile, in Trilling's view at this time, "the individual's old defenses against the domination of the culture become weaker and weaker."[65]

These changes in society caused Trilling to rethink his earlier views (as expressed in *The Liberal Imagination*) on the political functions of literature. A liberal society supports individuality; literature both encourages and draws support from this individuality. In the face of a conformist mass culture, however, literature can no longer produce individuals fit for, or constitutive of, liberal society; rather, literature can only free individuals *from* society, preserving the self in a hostile environment. In such a culture, literature presents minority views that are likely to be scorned by the majority. Consistent with Trilling's views in *The Liberal Imagination*, the critical thinking produced by literature allows the individual to retain and develop his or her individuality, but now individuality is in opposition to society. While he had earlier praised *Huckleberry Finn*'s "subversion" of traditional social values, he now believed that what was most necessary was to preserve those values from a society increasingly hostile to them. This new view of the relationships among literature, the self, and society is illustrated in a 1955 essay entitled "Freud: Within and Beyond Culture."

In his meditation on Freud, Trilling suggests that literature preserves the self by making the reader aware of death, or even by urging his or her symbolic death: "[L]iterature has always recorded an impulse of the self to find affirmation in its own extinction, even by its own extinction. . . ."[66] He goes on to add that Freud

> needed to believe that there was some point at which it was possible to stand beyond the reach of culture. Perhaps his formulation of the death instinct is to be interpreted as an expression of that need. "Death destroys a man," says E. M. Forster, "but the idea of death saves him." Saves him from what? From the entire submission of himself—of his self—to life in culture.[67]

But what, according to Trilling, is the precise relationship among literature, death, and the strong self? Literature, of course, cannot literally bring about death, and Trilling is not praising the literal ending of life. One's actual death may liberate one from the world, but not in a way that affirms the self. Yet literature can bring us knowledge of death, and such knowledge shows us that there are limits to what a government can force us to do or think, because we may choose to resist even at the cost of our own death. Literature can also remind us that individuals have inherited traits (or ones acquired very early or very strongly) that cannot be altered by a hostile society except by physically destroying those individuals. In opposition to what Trilling sees as communism's belief in the infinite malleability of human beings, novels can portray the inalterability of individual character traits, that "hard, irreducible, stubborn core" of biology "that culture cannot reach and that reserves the right . . . to judge the culture and resist and revise it."[68] Trilling also uses "death" symbolically to point to the desirability of accepting limitations, human mortality constituting the ultimate limitation.

This view that literature teaches us about limitation and death could be seen as consistent with Trilling's advocacy in *The Liberal Imagination* of liberal political action. In this reading, accepting that our control over life is limited liberates one for effective and responsible action. In psychoanalytic terms, acknowledging the reality principle, and even the death instinct, liberates one from narcissistic, grandiose fantasies of unlimited freedom and leads to more conscious, rational action. Paradoxically, accepting one's lack of control leads to greater control. Rather than presenting a utopian vision of the future or a critique of existing reality, great novels present the social and political world in its complexity. The best literature, with its "moral realism," points out the limits that enclose our selves and our political lives, and this awareness of finitude liberates the individual for a mature engagement with life. In addition, struggling *against* limitations is precisely what gives mortal lives meaning; a life without death would be neither human nor meaningful.[69]

Despite the plausibility of this reading, on balance "Freud: Within and Beyond Culture" evokes the self-abnegation of *The Middle of the Journey* rather than the politics of *The Liberal Imagination.* This return to quietism suggests that by the late fifties, the tension in Trilling's work between art as an educator for responsible action and art as an escape from the dangers of action was largely resolved in favor of the latter.

In speaking of Freud, Trilling asks what allowed him to move beyond the ideas of his time and culture. He gives several answers: his family, both a transmitter of culture and a "bulwark against cultural influences"; and his Jewishness, which made him an outsider.[70] But the most important factor was his ability, by means of his intellect, to inhabit the pure world of ideas:

> [W]ho can say what part in his self-respect, in his ability to move to a point beyond the reach of the surrounding dominant culture, was played by the old classical education, with its image of the other culture, the ideal culture, that wonderful imagined culture of the ancient world which no one but schoolboys, schoolmasters, scholars, and poets believed in? The schoolboy who kept his diary in Greek, as Freud did, was not submitting his ego or his superego to the debilitating influences of a restrictive society.[71]

Art no longer liberates individuals to act, prompting them to think about political ideas in order to become good citizens; instead, they use culture to escape from society and politics. (Ironically, this flight from social reality is what the New York Intellectuals criticized consumers of mass culture for.) Yet in doing so, those individuals submit themselves to a symbolic death. In a later essay Trilling speaks of Professor Cornelius, a character in a Thomas Mann story:

> For Professor Cornelius, who is a historian, the past is dead, is death itself, but for that very reason is the source of order, value, piety, and even love. . . . [W]e wonder if perhaps there is not to be found in the past that quiet place at which a young man might stand for a few years, at least a little beyond the competing attitudes and generalizations of the present, at least a little beyond the contemporary problems which he is told he can master only by means of attitudes and generalizations, that quiet place in which he can *know* something—in what year the Parthenon was begun, the order of battle at Trafalgar. . . .[72]

That quiet place "beyond culture" is a sepulchre. Although Trilling believes that by fleeing into art one saves the self, the self that acts in the world must die. Trilling calls this process "the self affirmed in self-denial."[73] The self is preserved because it refuses to be absorbed into the beliefs of the dominant culture, but at a heavy price: the renunciation of action in the world. As Michael Rogin put it, "You have to kill the self to save it."[74] Trilling's belief at this time that such a renunciation was the only way to preserve critical thought is a testament to his profound pessimism about political action and art's capacity to aid it.

One can see Trilling's increasing shift towards escapism as a failure, but his vacillations illuminate the double-edged nature of art's relationship to action. Although he might have discussed the problem more consciously, he insightfully illustrates art's capacity both to facilitate political action and to draw citizens away from action into the aesthetic realm.

## VI

Even if we emphasize Trilling's less quietistic side, reading his discussions of death and limitation as a call for more responsible and effective action, the place of actual politics in his work is problematic. How the critical thinking produced by literature creates political change is not entirely clear. While Trilling tells us that "everything begins in sentiment and assumption and finds its issue in political action and institutions," he never explains how this process occurs.[75] One might simply argue that Trilling is not interested in "real" politics or political action at all. He describes politics as "the politics of culture, the organization of human life toward some end or other, toward the modification of sentiments, which is to say the quality of human life."[76] One could say that Trilling is using the word "politics" incorrectly or so broadly as to be useless, but perhaps it is more fruitful to ask why he uses the word "politics" in the fashion that he does.[77] Trilling wants to stress the role of human agency in politics; he wants to reconnect politics and daily life in a way that anticipates (though with very different assumptions) the insights of the New Left and the feminist movement. He implicitly argues that many of one's attitudes and actions that are not connected with politics narrowly defined nevertheless contribute to one's stance toward others, a stance of domination or of toleration. For Trilling, great novels are "political" because they help create individuals who treat other individuals with respect.

One can surmise that for Trilling a society of tolerant, critically thinking individuals would constitute a healthy, liberal society. Aware of the dangers of moral passions, individuals in such a society would respect diversity and show a reluctance to impose a moral vision on others. Though the awareness that attempts to improve society often produce new evils ("moral realism") could lead to resignation or conservatism, Trilling means for such knowledge to lead to prudent and responsible politics. Literature strengthens the self; strong selfhood helps produce liberal society, although, as we have seen, such a society is not always attainable.

While Trilling focuses on literature's effect on the individual's capacity for moral complexity and critical thought, however, he neglects the social and political context within which reading occurs. Trilling looks at literature's production of ideas and at the effects of those ideas on individuals, but he does not locate this process within the context of political institutions, practices, or customs. Trilling is right to place a high political value on thinking, self-criticism, debate, and deeply experienced ideas and to see literature as a possible means to those ends, but he runs into problems when he implies that literature can perform this function in isolation from political practice. What Trilling needs is a sense of the historical conditions and institutions that are likely to produce individuals receptive to good literature; he also needs a more developed notion of what kind of society and politics would emerge from the triumph of liberal thinking. In short, he needs a fuller vision of liberal politics to augment his vision of liberal psychology. The individual struggle within the self is part of healthy politics, but the criticism and debate Trilling values require institutions and a social structure that support such discussion.

What kind of society and political system would be necessary to support Trilling's liberal novel-readers? Trilling later suggested like Tocqueville that societies with firm class boundaries support individuality and diversity, citing with approval the understanding of English novelists that "class . . . [is] a chief condition of personal authenticity."[78] From this point of view, being part of a class offers an individual an identity and a sense of security that allows him or her to think and speak without fear of offending the majority. Despite this favorable evocation of firm class boundaries, however, it is unlikely he wished to see them reestablished in modern America. At other times, Trilling seems to believe that if intellectuals were in power, a more liberal society would result. He sometimes speaks fondly of the nineteenth century, when (in his view) ideas had more power, when influential people in many professions were well versed in literature and spoke to an educated public.[79]

Beyond these nostalgic evocations of the past, Trilling insists that for novels to produce tolerant, self-critical thinking and action, they must be read in a society that values ideas. Yet it is the truth of this insight that limits the application of Trilling's argument to contemporary America. To the extent that our public life seems more devoid of ideas than ever, it is unlikely that even the best literature, no matter how widely read, could transform us into a nation of thoughtful, independent citizens.

Despite Trilling's neglect of reading's political context and his warnings against action, he and his fellow New York Intellectuals raised fundamental issues concerning literature's role in a liberal society. By the approach of the sixties, however, it became apparent that their time had passed. The Intellectuals had called for the arts to engage with experience, in order to get citizens to rethink rigidly held political beliefs. A new generation came along that connected experience, the arts, and politics as well, but in a new way. The civil rights movement, the New Left, and later the counterculture called for *politics* that derived from and touched the everyday experience of citizens, and the art of the sixties drew from that new vision. Whereas literature suited the quiet moral reflection imagined by Trilling and the New York Intellectuals, another art form was more appropriate to a close engagement with political action and everyday life: music. Would the political jazz and rock musicians of the sixties and their activist followers be able to resist the temptation, apparent in the work of the New York Intellectuals, to use art as an end in itself, as an escape from political action rather than an aid to it?

# 3
# THE SIXTIES
## Politics, Aesthetics, and Everyday Life

The New York Intellectuals, though giving us a rich model of art's role in liberal democracy, rejected the notion that the arts should be directly involved in political action. For them, art needed to be kept separate from practical politics in order not to lose the humanistic values that it embodied. Were art to become more directly politically engaged, it would forfeit its value as something apart from life, able to criticize and revise it. In the Intellectuals' view, it was mass culture's blurring of the two realms that posed such a danger to art and to politics. Similarly, aesthetic politics, politics that relied heavily on the arts to influence large numbers of people, conjured up the meticulously costumed, choreographed, and photographed Nazi rallies portrayed in the film *Triumph of the Will.* Politics at its best was the arena of compromise, moderation, and realism; art was the realm of creativity and self-expression. Were politics to become modeled on art, a dangerous idealism, or substitution of idea for reality, might prevail; one might forget that in politics people's lives are at stake and events have real consequences.

Theorists and artists in the sixties directly attacked these propositions, seeing art as a component of political action and politics as a means of self-expression and self-fulfillment.[1] Part of what was new about the sixties was the decade's blurring of the boundary between politics and art. Art became political in a manner not seen in this country since the 1930s, and on an unprecedented scale, while politics incorporated elements and goals of the arts. This coming together of the two realms led to a redefinition of each, fueled by the politicization of everyday life. As the definition of politics expanded to encompass choices made in everyday life, matters formerly seen as purely aesthetic (matters of "taste" like dress, hairstyle, interior design) acquired political meaning.

Herbert Marcuse announced this intertwining of politics and art in *Eros and Civilization.* Citing Kant, Schiller, and the surrealists, Marcuse argued that not only can art provide ideals for society; it can act as an important agent of liberation. Interpreting Schiller as an advocate of the emancipation of aesthetic sensuousness from the shackles of "higher" reason, Marcuse saw in Schiller's "play impulse" a counterforce to the repressive work ethic.[2] Reflecting the beginnings of the sixties sensibility, Marcuse ignored Schiller's statements connecting art with form and order and emphasized the liberating aspects of art and creativity.[3]

In *An Essay on Liberation*, published in the late sixties, Marcuse took these views even further. Art no longer merely represents an alternative to the work ethic; now he urges art to become part of life. With the "end of the segregation of the aesthetic from the real," art helps create a society based on creativity rather than repression; society itself becomes a "work of art."[4] Marcuse saw black music as a particularly promising tool for bringing about such a transformation.[5] Ultimately, for Marcuse, art and politics are both part of a common project, the liberation of the capacity for creativity, expression, and joy from internal and external repression.[6]

Politically, the decade can be divided in half, into an early sixties emphasizing community and authentic personal relations, and a late sixties stressing style, existential commitment, and the pursuit of experience.[7] While the early New Left used politics to bring about goals associated with art (self-realization, for example), the counterculture of the late sixties employed aesthetic means to bring about political goals.

Two central tensions dominated the sixties. The first concerns its politicization of the personal. A focus on personal life as a site of politics can function as part of the larger political project of developing a good community, a community that makes an unoppressive personal life possible and allows individuals to develop to their full capacity. However, two other results are possible. The emphasis on the personal might pull individuals away from action with others, leading them to see self-cultivation as the primary goal. Conversely, an emphasis on personal expression can lead to a community in which individuals gain emotional satisfaction by merging into a whole, stifling individuality. This merging took various forms: on the one hand, erotically bonded hippies at a rock concert, on the other, black Muslims under the strict subordination of Elijah Muhammed. All three of these relationships between the individual and the community—reciprocity, individualism, and merging—emerged in sixties politics.

The second tension concerns the decade's blurring of politics and art. On the one hand, the sixties' turn toward the aesthetic brought political ideals into the realm of experience, even into the body. Through political art and aesthetically influenced politics, political issues, questions, and concepts entered the realm of the senses. The danger, however, was that sensation and style would become ends in themselves—why go out and organize when one can turn on the stereo and be passively swept into a kind of political consciousness? We shall see that this danger loomed large in the late sixties, within both art and politics.

## II

### *The Early Sixties: The Ideals of Art Transform Politics*

"The sixties" has taken on mythic proportions in our national consciousness. Rarely has a ten-year period come to stand for so much, for both its supporters and detractors.[8] The sit-ins of 1960 that began in Greensboro, North Carolina and eventually spread to fifty-four cities galvanized the civil rights movement.[9] The year 1960 also saw the founding of the Student Nonviolent Coordinating Committee (SNCC), whose influence would be crucial, not only in civil rights but as a training ground for some important figures in the budding New Left. The civil rights movement, the New Left, and the counterculture: though active participants in these movements did not comprise a majority of Americans or even youth, they had a profound impact on the country's politics, aesthetics, morals, and agenda for debate. Young people could sense that a new era was dawning, creating a renewed sense of possibility.[10]

The political movements of the early sixties grew out of, yet went beyond, the liberalism celebrated by Trilling, Adlai Stevenson, and others.[11] *Brown v. the Board of Education* and, six years later, the election of John Kennedy created hope that the federal government could help eliminate race discrimination and other problems. The civil rights movement of this early period aimed at a liberal political goal: African American participation as equals in politics, society, and the economy.

However, the movement also created, partially through the methods used to try to achieve its liberal goals, a new conception of politics itself, and democratic politics in particular.[12] Although this notion of politics had roots in political theory, it developed less in theoretical treatises than in action: church meetings, sit-ins, organizing drives, and demonstrations. Notwithstanding its various forms and designations ("the beloved community," "group-centered leadership," "participatory democracy"), certain common features were present. This is not to minimize the differences between the political ideals of Martin Luther King, SNCC, and SDS; the conflicting positions each individual or organization took at different times; or the differing backgrounds of black and white activists. However, at least until about 1965, there was much cross-fertilization among the various movements. For just one example, New Left activists admired and emulated SNCC, and figures as various as Tom Hayden, Mario Savio, and Abbie Hoffman spent time in the South working with the civil rights organization.[13]

This new vision of politics had three aspects. First, activists argued that democracy required large-scale citizen participation beyond voting. They did not reject representative democracy altogether; one of the ways SNCC activists sought to empower citizens was to register them to vote, and SDS at first sought to supplement rather than replace representative democracy with elements of direct democracy.[14]

However, both black and white activists in the first part of the decade sought to bring aspects of direct democracy—consensus and widespread participation beyond voting—into their own organizations, their political practice, and their vision of a transformed society. For example, SNCC founder Ella Baker urged members to avoid authoritarian, hierarchical organizing principles and keep the movement democratic by "group-centered leadership."[15] She argued that decisions should be arrived at by conversation and consensus rather than the prerogatives of leaders or even impersonal methods like voting.[16] In SDS, this principle was called "participatory democracy."[17] Despite the many ambiguities of that term, it clearly drew on the tradition of direct democracy. As Todd Gitlin puts it,

> The New Left style of politics was an extension of a much older small-d democratic tradition. It wanted decisions made *by* publics, *in* public, not just announced there.[18]

Second, this new model widened the site of politics to encompass everyday life. Pluralist political scientists in the fifties saw politics as a means of processing competing demands of interest groups; in Lasswell's often-cited definition, politics meant "who gets what, when, and how."[19] In the sixties "personal" choices in daily life—how one dresses, where one eats, what music one listens to, which water fountain one is able to drink from—came to be seen as political. This is partly because everyday life was seen as oppressive in various ways; an analysis of that oppression, therefore, required a critique of larger social forces and arrangements. However, everyday life was the focus of the solution as well, through the idea of prefiguration.

Prefigurative politics called for people to begin living a better society immediately, acting in daily life as if the desired political changes had already taken place.[20] Through political action, those in the civil rights movement hoped to change society and government policy, but they also tried to create in their personal and political lives a "beloved community" that would prefigure the society they were hoping to bring about. One did not simply write one's congressperson to desegregate lunch counters; one sat at those lunch counters, even at the risk of arrest or assault. The New Left, and later the counterculture, tried to live its ideals in prefigurative fashion as well. The danger here, of course, was that living as if the good society had been achieved might take precedence over acting to create that society.

Finally, politics became a means to express and affirm individuality and personhood. In the civil rights movement, the language of self-respect was prominent.[21] Diane Nash of SNCC argued that for an African American student, activism would result in "a new awareness of himself as an individual." She hoped that the movement would "bring about a climate in which there is appreciation of the dignity of man and in which each individual is free to grow and produce to his fullest capacity."[22] In the New Left, the language of "authenticity"—the need to find and act upon one's "true self" in the face of pressures to conform—was more common.[23] As Tom Hayden put it in *The Port Huron Statement*,

> Men have unrealized potential for self-cultivation, self-direction, self-understanding, and creativity. It is this potential that we regard as crucial and to which we appeal—not to the human potentiality for violence, unreason, and submission to authority. The goal of man and society should be human independence: a concern not with image or popularity but with finding a meaning in life that is personally authentic; a quality of mind not compulsively driven by a sense of powerlessness, nor one which unthinkingly adopts status values; nor one which represses all threats to its habits, but one which has full, spontaneous access to present and past experiences, one which easily unites the fragmented parts of personal history. . . . [24]

There are important differences between the ideals of self-respect and authenticity: the first sees individuality emerging from a supportive community characterized by "mutual regard," the second in opposition to the larger society.[25] Yet for both of them self-development is a primary political goal.

What is striking is that in this new conception politics is called upon to perform many functions that the New York Intellectuals and their predecessors assigned to art. Realizing one's potential, nurturing a whole and autonomous sense of self and independence of mind, enhancing creativity, and developing tolerance toward others came about not through reading or writing a novel but by walking into a segregated bus terminal or attending a demonstration.[26] As Lionel Trilling said in 1968, although it was equally true of the early sixties, "For young people now, being political serves much the same purpose as being literary has long done—it expresses and validates the personality."[27] New Left activists used politics to try to bring about a freer, more humanistic society, but at the same time they strove to make politics itself more expressive, creative, and fulfilling, challenging the Weberian connection of politics with violence and coercion.[28]

This vision of politics was not completely new. Its roots go back to Aristotle, with connections to the Puritans, Thoreau, abolitionism, Randolph Bourne, and populism, as well as African American culture.[29] CORE had organized nonviolent direct actions in the 1940s.[30] Yet if none of this was absolutely new, it took on a new urgency and swept up large numbers of people and the nation's consciousness in a way that had not happened before.

The late sixties saw the various movements—African American and white, nonviolent resistance and black power, New Left and counterculture—split apart. Yet here too there was a common theme: the pursuit of experience and style, the desire to live now as if the ideal society had come to pass. Despite obvious differences, this ethic tied together hippies, Black Panthers, and Weathermen.

This new model of politics developed out of tensions within the movement. Until about 1965, self-realization and self-expression took place through political action: meetings, sit-ins, and demonstrations. However, a tension existed between activists emphasizing political action and those more concerned with cultural or aesthetic expressiveness. In African American politics, this conflict can be seen between the nonviolent, morally centered politics of the early SNCC and King, and the growing cultural nationalism, sometimes allied with "black power." In the New Left, the tension was between (in James Miller's words) "civic republicanism" and what R. D. Laing called the "politics of experience," the latter emerging most fully in the counterculture.[31]

In about 1965, black power and the politics of experience came to the fore, leaving the earlier ideals to dwindling groups of followers. In the terms described at the beginning of this chapter, this meant a turn away from a community integrating individual and group and toward the extremes of individualism and merging—and at times the pursuit of experience at the expense of politics.

## III

### *Late Sixties Politics as Style (i): Black Power and Cultural Nationalism*

The second half of the decade saw a decided shift in the nature of African American politics, summed up by the phrase "black power." While the phrase carried multiple and conflicting meanings, the core idea encompassed black autonomy and self-definition. Advocates stressed the need for African Americans to control their own politics and economics rather than being dependent on white assistance. While the "beloved community" sought to incorporate a variety of groups, black power encompassed solidarity and love primarily among African Americans. In the words of Carmichael and Hamilton,

> [Black power] is a call for black people in this country to unite, to recognize their heritage, to build a sense of community. It is a call for black people to begin to define their own goals, to lead their own organizations and to support those organizations. . . . *Before a group can enter the open society, it must first close ranks.*[32]

This might encompass electing African American leaders in black majority communities as well as building and supporting economic institutions that kept money within the community.[33]

In addition to its call for economic and political power, "black power" had psychological and cultural components. Theorists argued that African Americans have values, styles, and modes of thinking ("black consciousness") that are different from the prevailing (white) ones. Thus part of the movement consisted of bringing "blackness" into everyday life through the "soul" style of dressing, talking, cooking, and moving through the world. As one historian of the era puts it,

> In this sometimes crazy quilt world of the cool, the hip, and the hustle, stylized forms of personal expression were developed which not only conveyed necessary social information, but also could be utilized to promote a revitalized sense of self. At its most fundamental, soul style was a type of in-group cultural cachet whose creators utilized clothing design, popular hair treatments, and even body language (stance, gait, method of greeting) as preferred mechanisms of authentication.[34]

In essence, "soul" style was the realization of the idea of a "black aesthetic" in everyday life.[35]

The popular embrace of "soul" both aestheticized and politicized everyday life. Pierre Bourdieu has argued that power is transmitted through "the most apparently insignificant aspects of the things, situations, and practices of everyday life"; "the ways of looking, sitting, standing, keeping silent, or even of speaking . . . are full of injunctions that are powerful and hard to resist precisely because they are silent and insidious, insistent and insinuating."[36] In the black power era, African Americans sought to resist domination through the reappropriation of such quotidian practices. The soul handshake ("giving and getting skin") became both a form of self-expression and a ritual of black solidarity. Wearing a "natural" hairstyle or African-influenced clothing set one apart from white society and affirmed racial identity. Cooking and eating "soul food," sometimes presented as derived from African cuisine, performed similar functions.[37]

Language itself became a form of political art. Theorists have long recognized that "relations of communication . . . are also relations of symbolic power"; language is a medium "in which one's whole relation to the social world, and one's whole socially informed relation to the world, are expressed."[38] More specifically, Bourdieu and Bakhtin have shown how officially approved, "standard" language functions to maintain ideological unity by opposing and foreclosing other kinds of language and the diversity of thought they represent.[39] "Black talk" of the late sixties represented a questioning of official, "correct" English and its racial hegemony. Black English set African Americans off from whites, created a sense of solidarity, and overturned grammatical and valuative conventions so that, for example, "bad" becomes good. The terms "Afro-American" or "black" allowed for self-definition, self-naming rather than being defined by the dominant society.[40]

Some advocates of black power criticized cultural nationalism as inconsequential. Huey Newton disparaged the movement as "pork chop nationalism," arguing that culture itself is not a force for change and that cultural nationalism is consistent with political reaction.[41] Others, however, defended culture's political role as integral to black solidarity. In the words of Black Arts movement leader Larry Neal,

> A revolution without culture would destroy the very thing that now unites us, the very things we are trying to save along with our lives. That is the feeling and love-sense of the blues and other forms of Black music. The feeling of a James Brown or an Aretha Franklin. That is the feeling that unites us and makes it more possible for us to move and groove together, to do what is necessary to liberate ourselves. John Coltrane's music must unquestionably be part of any future revolutionary society.[42]

While Neal may have overstated the case for culture's efficacy, we will see that such overstatement accompanied other attempts to unite the aesthetic and the political, including the counterculture.[43]

### *Late Sixties Politics as Style (ii): The Counterculture, the Politics of Experience, and Aesthetic Politics*

White activists did not need to reclaim their culture in the same way black cultural nationalists did: after all, European culture was dominant in America. However, culture—both the arts and in the broader sense of lifestyle, values, and customs—became swept up in the white political movements of the late sixties. First, extending the early-sixties expansion of politics to everyday life, the counterculture tried to enact a nonrepressive society by living aesthetic ideals of creativity and sensory pleasure. Second, extending artists' merging of their art with everyday life into the political realm, groups like the Yippies brought aesthetic elements into politics. Of course, many New Left activists continued into the second half of the decade without absorbing elements of the counterculture, but the turn toward aesthetics had an influence on much of the movement.

Once again, Marcuse is a key figure here.[44] In the late thirties New York Intellectuals drew on the early Marx and the German romantic thinkers who influenced him to envision a society with a new sensibility, captured in modernist art. Marcuse drew on the same sources, as well as the surrealists, to more explicitly call for a society liberated from constraints on the imagination and play, in which unbound creativity, expression, and sensory enjoyment would not be focused on a realm of art but be an integral part of everyday life.[45]

This political vision was influenced by a resurgence of interest in psychoanalysis. Ironically, many of the New York Intellectuals of the previous decade had embraced psychoanalysis as well. Like the New Left, they saw the need to free the individual from mass society and realized that mass society's political oppression had a psychological correlate. However, the New York Intellectuals' view of what a psychologically liberated individual looked like differed greatly from the generation that followed, and this difference reveals much about the political thrust of the counterculture.

Trilling saw psychoanalysis as a method to make people more effective and independent by freeing them from illusions. According to Trilling, Freud believes there are two ways of relating to the outside world: the regulation of libidinal gratification by the realistic ego, which is "the right way," and the "fictional" approach, imagining in fantasy that our desires are fulfilled instead of satisfying them within the limitations of what is possible. For Freud, claims Trilling, "Reality is an honorific word, and it means what is *there*; illusion is a pejorative word, and it means a response to what is *not there*."[46] Trilling criticizes those romantics in whose thought we see "the effective, utilitarian ego being relegated to an inferior position and a plea being made on behalf of the anarchic and self-indulgent id."[47] The true artist is not necessarily a neurotic but rather is one who takes his inner demons and "subjugates" them; he "shapes his fantasies, he gives them social form and reference."[48]

The New York Intellectuals' interpretation of Freud as an advocate of reality over fantasy in personal life went hand in hand with their project to help rid the nation of what they saw as the utopian political illusions (i.e., socialism) that had dominated the nation since the adolescent thirties. Whereas Trilling's Freud warns of the dangers of the unregulated id and stresses the reality principle, Marcuse uses the surrealists' understanding of Freud to criticize the other "harsh master," the superego, and urge a collective rebirth of the pleasure principle. Marcuse sees much of the repression that Freud believed was an inevitable cost of civilization as "surplus repression," the result of a capitalist social organization and therefore dispensable. According to Marcuse, fantasy reveals the potential for pleasure and freedom denied by modern capitalist society: "[T]he forbidden images and impulses of childhood begin to tell the truth that reason denies. Regression assumes a progressive function."[49] Unlike Freud, Marcuse believes that a nonrepressive society, or at least one that is nearly so, is possible.[50] When Eros is truly free, it will not take the destructive form that Freud had predicted, because a liberated imagination does not give itself over to an unrestrained id but rather views "reality" more expansively than the Freudian reality principle.

> In its refusal to accept as final the limitations imposed upon freedom and happiness by the reality principle, in its refusal to forget what *can be*, lies the critical function of phantasy. . . . The surrealists recognized the revolutionary implications of Freud's discoveries. . . . Art allied itself with the revolution. Uncompromising adherence to the strict truth value of imagination comprehends reality more fully.[51]

In the last half of the decade, Marcuse's philosophy was taken up by the growing counterculture.

The counterculture has its roots in the youth culture of the fifties. A growing number of young Americans in the late 1950s were attracted to the Beats, despite (or perhaps because of) excoriation by the leading critics of their time, including many of the New York Intellectuals.[52] Though full-fledged disciples of Ginsberg and Kerouac constituted a tiny group, their style and ethos became part of a rebellious youth culture. Not necessarily artists themselves, members of this culture were united by aesthetics and style: mannerisms, argot, a way of dressing, and music.

In addition to the Beats, other disaffected whites adopted the "hip" attitudes and mannerisms of black "bebop" jazz musicians. These "white Negroes," as Norman Mailer called them in an influential essay, paid tribute to their black forebears by calling themselves "hipsters."[53] Hipsters appeared everywhere in the fifties: Marlon Brando (in *The Wild One*) and James Dean (in *Rebel Without a Cause*) played characters who refused to conform to social conventions, flaunting their status as outsiders.

With the rise of this youth culture came a growing fear of its social effects, particularly juvenile delinquency. For intellectuals, the threat was larger, and related to the communist menace: relying on the purported connection between mass society and totalitarianism, critics feared both that youth would reject all order, rules, and morality, and that they would lose all their individuality and become part of a gang (and, eventually, the Communist Party). Some of the concerns also mirrored the fears of adult "mass culture" outlined in chapter 1: mass culture would make people unthinking, uncritical, and therefore easily manipulated. Thus Vance Packard thought teenage music was foisted upon adolescents by disc jockeys.[54]

In the next decade youth culture, in the form of the counterculture, attained an even larger political significance. The counterculture stood for cooperation rather than competition, a rejection of leadership and organization, liberation of the body, and freedom of thought from the barriers of conformity.[55] People were urged to immediately live these ideals rather than take political action to transform society; in Michael Rogin's words, "the counterculture brought New Left ideals down to earth and into the body."[56] Wearing colorful clothes and long hair, experimenting with drugs, listening to rock music, or living in communes incorporated play, creativity, and bodily pleasure into everyday life. Although such activity at times seemed primarily private and individual, much of it took place in collective settings. Sometimes countercultural activities were more overtly political: the Diggers, a group taking their name from seventeenth-century English revolutionaries opposed to private property, gave away free food and opened a "free store."[57]

Part of the counterculture's attempt to liberate the capacity for creativity entailed the transformation of life into art, constructing a society in which (as one manifesto puts it) "every man would be an artist."[58] Public events became collective aesthetic rituals; in the words of Charles Perry, "The early hippie rock dances with their multimedia aspects—music, dance, light shows, costume, body painting—were widely understood as pop art happenings."[59] Some such events had an overtly political message, like a "Death of Money" march organized by the Diggers that featured dollar signs carried on sticks, a coffin, and pallbearers in various costumes.[60]

Yet aesthetic activities did not always take such an organized form. Everyday life itself became a form of theater, with its own costumes and playacting. As Perry puts it,

> Daily life in the Haight had the usual theatrical quality of making the scene, and beyond that, people consciously organized moments of theater for their friends, even for unsuspecting strangers. This was called "blowing someone's mind," arranging some experience so completely unexpected—say, pulling from your pocket a tiny bell with a sweet, pure tone but decorated with a death's head, and ringing it within an inch or two of the mind-blowee's eyes—that the person's mind would be "blown," destroyed.[61]

The aestheticization of life was meant to accomplish a number of objectives: shake up conventional ways of thinking, in the manner of the surrealists; incorporate creativity into everyday life; and make life a sensation-filled experience. Writers in an underground paper thus urged readers to experience "ecstatic living" by decorating their houses with undulating strips of cloth blown by fans, rotating "stages" covered with pieces of mirror, and revolving light displays.[62] Implicit in such endeavors was an attack on the hierarchies by which we prioritize our activities: life becomes a series of discrete sensations, each of equal value to the next, suggesting a kind of temporal democracy.[63]

Not all of the counterculture's activities were "aesthetic"; living in communes was not particularly so. But music, psychedelic design, and style of dress were as important for the counterculture as its attack on traditional morality. In addition, it took many of its ideals from the aesthetic realm: creativity, self-expression, and the pursuit of sensation. As we have seen, this was true of the early-sixties' vision of politics as well. But SNCC and the early New Left assumed an authentic, core self that needed nurturing and expression. For the counterculture, the quest was not for an authentic self—perhaps there was no such thing—but for varieties of experience, a donning of different masks in turn rather than searching for the true face beneath the mask.

To what extent was such activity political? In theory the aestheticization of everyday life can support social change: breaking free of established patterns of thought and action might prepare people for larger transformation. In addition, the counterculture created the kind of shared experience that is a necessary precondition for social transformation. But there is always the danger that concern with consciousness and experience can become an end in itself, a kind of consumeristic hedonism, and therefore a means of avoiding shared political concerns.

While some were trying to use aesthetics to live the ideals of a liberated society, others in the counterculture took politics itself as their medium, turning political action into performance art. The most prominent example was the Yippies, founded in 1967 by Abbie Hoffman, Jerry Rubin, Ed Sanders of the rock group the Fugs, and Paul Krassner, the editor of the underground newspaper *The Realist*. In his range of influences, Hoffman was typical: he had worked with SNCC in Mississippi in 1964 and 1965, and later cited Marcuse as "with the exception of [Abraham] Maslow, the teacher who had the greatest impact upon me."[64] The Yippies revitalized the political side of surrealism, confronting the establishment with pranks, hoping to disrupt the flow of society with laughter, pointing out the ridiculousness of society by making absurd juxtapositions, striving in the process to liberate the human capacity for play and creativity. Rubin, when subpoenaed before the House Unamerican Activities Committee, showed up in a Revolutionary War uniform. Two years later he appeared before the same committee wearing Viet Cong black pajamas, bandoliers stretched across his body, and a toy M-16 machine gun, his body covered with red war paint.[65] In another famous stunt in 1967, Hoffman and some friends poured money onto the floor of the New York Stock Exchange from the visitors' gallery, hoping to reveal the greed of American society by creating the sight of brokers in business suits groveling on the floor snatching up bills.

Perhaps the best-known Yippie events centered around the Democratic convention of 1968. At the convention they held demonstrations, running their own "candidate" for president, a pig named Mr. Pigasus. They turned the Chicago Seven trial into a circus, putting pictures of Che Guevara on the defense table, displaying a National Liberation Front flag, and introducing songs into evidence.

Influenced by "W. C. Fields, Ernie Kovacs, Che Guevara, Lenny Bruce, the Marx Brothers . . . [and] the Beatles," Hoffman envisioned "a society in which every man would be an artist."[66] Citing Artaud's *The Theatre and Its Double*, he called the Yippies' actions "protest as theater," performed in the "museum of the streets."[67] Recalling Schiller's play principle, Hoffman believed that "there ought to be fun in a revolution." He quoted Cohn-Bendit, one of the theorists of the May '68 French student movement: the "revolution will come through joy and not through sacrifice."[68] Acting out Marcuse's theories in a way that the German theorist himself sometimes disapproved of, Hoffman by employing "fun" in politics repudiated the work ethic and the repressive delay of gratification imposed by modern society.[69] Democracy for the Yippies meant the absence of political authority and the end of the rule of reason over emotion, reality over fantasy, conscious over unconscious, and ego over id. Whether the Yippies in practice stood for democracy, or rather for leader-based media politics, is still open to question. However, they captured an influential mode of politics in the latter half of the sixties.

While sixties political activists pursued notions of democracy influenced by art, and made aesthetic style political and politics aesthetic, artists themselves produced works embodying those political visions and educating citizens in them. In the next two chapters, I analyze musical performances from the sixties for their educative possibilities, using "free jazz" (chapter 4) to think about music's political role in the context of the changing civil rights movement, and Bob Dylan (chapter 5) to explore how folk and rock taught the shifting ideals of the New Left and the counterculture.

In each case study I ask, How exactly did musical performances express the thoughts and feelings of political activists in the sixties? What possibilities for political education were contained in them? What vision of democracy did such performances express, assume, or support? What were some of the limits of this music as a source of democratic political education in the sixties?

# 4
# "LET FREEDOM RING!" Jazz and African American Politics, 1950–1970

Ever since Africans arrived in America, mostly in chains on slave ships, the two words of the compound "African American" have sat together uneasily. DuBois's well-known formulation still says it best:

> One ever feels his two-ness—an American, a Negro; two souls, two thoughts, two unreconciled strivings; two warring ideals in one dark body, whose dogged strength alone keeps it from being torn asunder.[1]

One "solution" to the anxiety of doubleness is assimilation; Langston Hughes described the "urge within the race toward whiteness, the desire to pour racial individuality into the mold of American standardization, and to be as little Negro and as much American as possible."[2] Yet such a path represents self-annihilation, and there have always been movements for the celebration of blackness instead. In David Walker's *Appeal to the Colored People of the World* (1829), he expressed pride in being black, the color that God made him.[3] In 1858 John S. Rock extolled black physical features, comparing them favorably to those of whites:

> When I contrast the fine tough muscular system, the beautiful, rich color, the full broad features, and the gracefully frizzled

> hair of the Negro, with the delicate physical organization, wan color, sharp features, and lank hair of the Caucasian, I am inclined to believe that when the white man was created, nature was pretty well exhausted—but determined to keep up appearances, she pinched up his features, and did the best she could under the circumstances.[4]

This celebration of blackness sometimes took the form of separatism, as in Marcus Garvey's teaching of the "pride and purity of race," rejecting "mongrel types."[5] Other thinkers simply wanted, like DuBois, to "merge" their "double self into a better and truer self," while "wish[ing] . . . neither of the older selves to be lost."[6]

Artists played an important role in articulating and transcending this dilemma. African American artists were often urged by white critics to submerge the role of race in their work, on the grounds that a racial emphasis would bar the work from entrance into the hall of "universal" art. As the white critic Waldo Frank once claimed,

> The gifted Negro has been too often thwarted from becoming a poet because the world was forever forcing him to recollect that he was a Negro. The artist must lose such lesser identities in the great well of life. . . . [The Negro is] forced every moment of his life into a specific and superficial plane of consciousness.[7]

Black artists in America have often rejected this formulation, striving instead to convey their experiences as African Americans through their art. Artists in the period of the civil rights movement were no exception, and this chapter interprets 1960s jazz as an expression of the concerns that animated that struggle. Beginning in the late fifties and early sixties, when black protest entered America's streets, lunch counters, and bus terminals, jazz musicians politically educated Americans using music.[8] Works like Max Roach's "Freedom Now Suite," Charles Mingus's *Charles Mingus Presents Charles Mingus*, and Ornette Coleman's "Free Jazz," all recorded in 1960, explored the idea of freedom.[9] This exploration was sometimes explicit and conscious, as the title of Roach's piece suggests. In other cases, works that on the surface seemed concerned with only aesthetic freedom communicated a message about political freedom when composed and performed in a context saturated with African American political aspirations.

These works express political ideas in a number of different ways. Roach's suite comments on the African American experience using words accompanied by music, creating a narrative of black history from slave days to the present. Mingus and Coleman, on the other hand, use instrumental music to explore what freedom itself means, in both negative and positive senses. Negatively, they reject musical conventions that restrict individual expression and discard traditional hierarchical roles within the small group. At the same time they create positive representations of a better society. These performances aesthetically enact Martin Luther King's conception of the beloved community, maximizing individual expression in the context of a cohesive group of equals and calling into question liberal democracy's dichotomization of group and individual.

The musical principle that underlies this reconciliation of individual and group is polyphony, the simultaneous presence of independent melodies.[10] Through polyphony, musicians created egalitarian conversations, with voices taking the lead only to recede to the background and respond to the lead of others; through empathy the result was not anarchy but a democratic community represented in music. These prefigurative works allowed musicians and listeners to learn about and experience freedom, even if it did not yet exist in society as a whole.

## I

Music has traditionally played a larger role for African Americans than it has for most whites.[11] Singer and activist Bernice Johnson Reagon argues that "music has always been integral to the Black American tradition." She sees the "freedom songs" of the late fifties and early sixties as "not luxury, not leisure, not entertainment, but the lifeblood of the community."[12] As her then husband, a SNCC activist organizing in

Mississippi, put it, "Without these songs, you know we wouldn't be anywhere. We'd still be down on Mister Charley's plantation, chopping cotton for 30 cents a day."[13]

Why has music been so important for African Americans? Part of the reason is that more overt forms of political expression were often prohibited; music was a way of speaking about things that could not be said more directly. In contrast to the white youth subculture of the sixties, "Black culture . . . has always been a 'counter-culture.'"[14] Another reason stems from the West African roots of African American culture.[15] In West Africa music has an importance far beyond its traditional European role.[16] As opposed to the modern European view of music (with the exception of "lesser," popular forms) as belonging to a distinct sphere of life called "art," West African music has always been functional. Such music includes "songs used by young men to influence young women (courtship, challenge, scorn); songs used by workers to make their tasks easier; songs used by older men to prepare the adolescent boys for manhood, and so on."[17] A collective, rather than individualist, base is built into the structure of the music, through the use of polyphony and "call and response," where a leader's exhortation is "answered" by the group in a kind of musical dialogue. West African music also differs from European music in its emphasis on the vocal. While there is obviously a vocal tradition in Western "classical" music, in West African and African American music from B. B. King to Ornette Coleman instrumental music often has a "vocalized" quality. Thus, in this tradition, music remains tied to speech, while European music has moved away from it. After all, drums in West Africa are literally a means of "speaking." Finally, improvisation is central to African music, whereas it has been rare in Western classical music since Beethoven.[18]

Many of these features of African music were carried over into America, although they were necessarily changed because of the severe restrictions on the slaves' music.[19] "Work songs" mirrored the rhythm of labor, utilizing "call and response" and improvised lyrics. Adapting white hymns to African musical conventions, slaves also created spirituals that kept alive the dream of freedom by evoking the Israelites in bondage to the Egyptians and sometimes transmitted covert instructions to listeners.[20]

Most would agree with jazz master McCoy Tyner's statement that jazz is "an amalgamation of the two cultures—the African and the European culture," and much jazz has retained the functional quality of West African music.[21] New Orleans jazz was both collective and functional. There were no real "soloists"; instead the emphasis was on a polyphonic group sound. It was also collective in the sense that the audience became part of the music, dancing and shouting encouragement like a congregation to a preacher.[22] The music was functional in that it accompanied every important community event, the most prominent of which was the funeral. Typically the band would play spirituals at a funeral, affirming life in the face of death, uniting the community, and providing the means to celebrate.[23] Musicians were connected with the innumerable secret societies and brotherhoods in the city that afforded a social place for its members (slowly replacing the church in this regard), offering sick benefits and providing music for funerals.

Improvisation itself has political overtones for African Americans because it consists of an assertion of individual and group identity in the midst of a society that has sought to ignore or destroy it. However, the more explicit representation of political themes in jazz developed only gradually. Duke Ellington in the 1930s and 1940s saw his music as a celebration of African American culture, and gave his pieces titles such as "Harlem Air Shaft," "Take the 'A' Train," and "Black and Tan Fantasy."[24] In his words,

> My men and my race are the inspiration of my work. I try to catch the character and mood and feeling of my people. The music of my race is something more than the American idiom. It is the result of our transplantation to the American soil, and it was our reaction to plantation days, to the life we lived. What we could not say openly we expressed in music. The characteristic, melancholic music of my race has been forged from the very white heat of our sorrow and from our gropings.[25]

However, despite Ellington's claim that "social protest and pride in the Negro have been the most significant themes in what we've done" and that "[i]n . . . music we have been talking for a long time about what it is to be a Negro in this country," jazz pieces were rarely explicitly political.[26] Jazz's status as "entertainment," particularly in the popular white "swing" bands, hampered the development of political aspects of the music. Performances like Billie Holiday's 1939 recording of "Strange Fruit," a poem about lynching, represent important exceptions.

In the forties, however, many jazz musicians reacted against the co-optation of their music by mainstream white society by creating new styles that could not be so easily assimilated. The first such style became known as "bebop" (or "bop"). Beboppers created jazz so difficult that it could not easily be copied and so intense that one was unlikely to dance to it or even listen casually.[27] In this sense, jazz separated from dance and social life, becoming more like "art" in the European sense, and indeed Charlie Parker at times wanted acceptance from the white musical establishment, recording music with strings.[28] In the difficulty of the music, with its vertical harmonies and blinding tempos, beboppers tried to better whites at their own game.[29]

But bebop opposed mainstream culture at the same time it accepted some of its standards. The technical dexterity of the music and its dissonant quality can also represent group and individual assertion.[30] Beboppers rebelled through lifestyle as well, with unconventional dress and mannerisms (goatee, horn-rimmed glasses, beret), the use of drugs (especially heroin), and slang. Words like "crazy" as a term of approbation called into question mainstream norms and standards of rationality, while a term like "dig" proclaimed the value of looking underneath the surface of society.[31]

Bebop was not the only culturally assertive style of African American music to come out of the postwar period, however. The forties saw a style called "rhythm and blues" that more explicitly expressed black cultural pride both in its lyrics and its "funky," "bluesy," and "soulful" music.[32] Coinciding with a new phase of African American political activism, in the fifties jazz itself joined this trend with a style known as "hard bop," featuring musicians like Horace Silver and Art Blakey. In addition to the gospel and "rhythm and blues" influence, hard bop's expression of black pride is apparent in song titles of the time, from the use of African American argot ("Dis Hyeah," "Cookin'") to references to Southern black church experiences ("Wednesday Night Prayer Meeting," "The Sermon," "The Preacher") to evocations of

Africa ("Africa," "Bantu," "African Violets").[33] Although some saw this music as an attempt at commercialization, Manning Marable argues that "jazz played a powerful role in the cultural education of millions of young blacks and whites during this time."

> For blacks, jazz represented on the "cultural front" what the Montgomery boycott, demonstrations and the new militant mood were in politics. It shattered established conventions; it mocked traditions; in form and grace, it transcended old boundaries of life and thought. It became the appropriate cultural background for their activities to destroy Jim Crow.[34]

The sixties brought the political potential of earlier jazz to fruition. Most jazz musicians were not political activists; however, some expressed political ideas and sentiments through their music. This was not done in the service of a particular platform or party, but as an expression of the experience of the musician as an African American in the sixties. As the influential saxophonist John Coltrane put it, when asked whether "political issues and social issues that Malcolm talked about" were important,

> Oh, they're definitely important; and as I said, the issues are a part of what *is* at this time. So naturally, as musicians we express whatever is.[35]

Yet the music did more than represent what existed; it contained an alternative vision as well. Coltrane said that "in music I make or I have tried to make a conscious attempt to change what I've found" and that "music is an instrument . . . [that] can create the initial thought patterns that can change the thinking of the people." He also called music an expression of "higher ideals."[36]

The most important such ideal for activists and musicians in the early sixties was "freedom." As Coltrane put it in 1962, "[W]e all know that this word which so many seem to fear today, 'Freedom'[,] has a hell of a lot to do with this music."[37] Sometimes the struggle for freedom was expressed through lyrics, song titles, and album titles; jazz musicians celebrated freedom in albums and songs like "Freedom,"

*The Freedom Rider*, *Free for All*, "Freedom Now Suite," and "The Freedom Suite."[38] "Let Freedom Ring!" was both an exhortation in Martin Luther King's "I Have a Dream" speech and the title of a jazz album in the early sixties.[39]

Other musicians made the political meaning implicit in such titles clearer through the use of lyrics. Max Roach's "Freedom Now Suite" illustrates how music and lyrics worked together in the service of political education.

## II

The "Freedom Now Suite" was recorded in 1960 under the leadership of drummer Max Roach and featured the vocals of Abbey Lincoln and instrumental contributions by several prominent American jazz musicians.[40] The work, with music by Roach and lyrics by Oscar Brown Jr., was originally commissioned by the NAACP to be performed at the centennial of the Emancipation Proclamation.[41] The suite contains five parts commenting on the black experience from America to Africa, following a roughly chronological sequence. The suite begins with "Driva' Man," a blues-based evocation of slave life.[42] This track, and thus the album, begins with the crack of a whip, represented by the slap of Roach's tambourine. The "whipping" continues as Lincoln sings of the brutality and sexual exploitation of the overseer:

Driva' Man he made a life
But the mammy ain't his wife
Pull that cotton don't be slow
Betta finish out ya row
There's just one thing on my mind
Driva' Man and quittin' time

Driva' Man da kinda boss
To ride a man and lead a hoss'
When that cat-o'-nine-tails fly
You'd be happy just to die

There's just one thing on my mind
Driva' man and quittin' time . . .

Each "crack" of the "whip" lands on the last beat of the song's unusual five beat measures, giving it an unexpected quality, reflective of the fact that a slave could be beaten at any time for no reason whatsoever.[43]

After a brief interlude, a saxophone solo follows, accompanied only by the bass. The saxophonist is Coleman Hawkins, a patriarch of jazz known as the "father of the saxophone" for his rescuing of that instrument from humorous vaudeville music so that it could be used for serious jazz in the 1930s. He fashions a brooding, intense solo that builds as he ascends into the upper register's cries and squeals with a mixture of sadness, anger, and determination. The track ends with Lincoln's intoning, "There's just one thing on my mind / Driva' Man . . . [long pause] and quittin' time." The pause suggests that what needs to be quit is the current racial oppression as well.

The second track is a celebration of the freeing of the slaves, "Freedom Day," amid a triumphant fanfare of horns. The song chronicles the passing of the word of the emancipation among the incredulous slaves:

Whisper, listen
Whisper, listen
Whisper, say we're free
Rumors flyin', must be lyin'
Can it really be?

Can't believe it
Can't conceive it
But that's what they say
Slave no longer, slave no longer
This is freedom day.

But of course the current quest for freedom is being evoked as well. Although the air of celebration of "Freedom Day" might contradict the other songs' emphasis on the incompleteness of the victory, the line "Can it really be?" injects a note of doubt, leading the listener to wonder if freedom really has been realized.[44]

The third piece, called "Triptych: Prayer/Protest/Peace," is a duet between Roach's drums and Lincoln's wordless vocals. "Prayer" represents, in Roach's words, "preparation" rather than "supplication," preparation for the fight against oppression.[45] It is a meditative call and response between drum and vocal, each echoing and supporting the other, like a prayer meeting before a sit-in to gather strength and concentration and create mutual support. "Protest" is an angry exorcism in which Lincoln literally screams at full force while Roach pummels the drums with a barrage of rhythms and counterrhythms. Here, pure catharsis has replaced any interaction between the musicians. The force of the piece expresses and illustrates the depth and intensity of the pain and anger that oppression causes, and the way such emotions obliterate dialogue. "Peace" is, in Roach's words, "the feeling of relaxed exhaustion after you've done everything you can to assert yourself. You can rest now because you've worked to be free."[46] Yet, in Roach's view, one rested only so one could get up the next day and do the same thing again.[47]

"Triptych" reveals, in microcosm, the educative nature of the suite. It recapitulates a process of political education beginning with the longing for release from pain, moving through anger, and then coming to terms with that anger while continuing to fight for freedom.

While the first side of the album deals with America, the second side evokes Africa with "All Africa" and "Tears for Johannesburg." Both are predominated by African percussion instruments, with some horns and vocals, mostly wordless. In the first piece, Lincoln intones the names of African tribes over a groundswell of polyrhythmic drums, while Nigerian drummer Michael Olatunji "relates a saying of each tribe concerning freedom."[48] Evoking the movements in West Africa for independence from colonial rule, both compositions extend the struggle for freedom beyond the borders of the United States.[49]

The "Freedom Now Suite" politically educates in two ways. First, it indicts America's current and past treatment of African Americans and expresses rage at oppression. Second, the album attempts to unite blacks temporally and geographically. Temporally, the album attempts nothing less than an integration of African American experience from slave days to 1960, in the manner of a national epic. In Roach's words, the Suite is a "document" of the past that also "points to the future" as it urges the listener to think about ways that the work of the past is unfinished and needs to be continued.[50] The connection of past and present is mirrored in the choice of musicians and in the music itself. Coleman Hawkins, who ruled the jazz world in the 1930s and early 1940s with his classic renditions of romantic ballads like "Body and Soul," plays alongside members of the budding avant-garde like trumpeter Booker Little. Musically, the drum-vocal duets are in one sense avant-garde and in another sense hark back to African musical forms. Finally, there is a geographical integration, connecting the civil rights movement with the efforts of African nations to be free from colonial rule. Utilizing the Nigerian drummer Olatunji, the Afro-Cuban percussionists Raymond Mantilla and Tomas du Vall, and African American jazz musicians, the suite attempts to encompass black freedom struggles from Africa to the diaspora.

In a sense, such an attempt at unity was artificial—blacks in America are separated by class and geography, among other things. When the suite attempts to extend unity among blacks worldwide, the task becomes even more difficult, given differences between ethnic groups even within a single African country. Yet perhaps the suite was trying to convey something narrower: the notion that blacks need to put aside their differences, in order to struggle against the oppression that all experience, if not all to the same degree. In the words of Martin Luther King,

> [G]roup unity can do infinitely more than any action of *individuals*. We have been oppressed as a group and we must overcome that oppression as a group.[51]

The vast majority of African Americans, the music seems to say, are descendants of slaves; all feel rage at oppression and need to be aware of these commonalities to fight together. And as *African* Americans, American blacks drew support from and supported African independence movements. Yet these ideas, abstract on the printed page, were communicated in a form central to black life: music.

## III

Although the "Freedom Now Suite" called for freedom and created a narrative of the movement from slavery to liberation, it did not explore what freedom itself was or what a free society might look like. However, other musicians performed precisely this task, musically creating a free society in performances they called "free jazz." Although the musicians did not necessarily consciously see their work as part of a political program, the notion of freedom explored in these works mirrored and sometimes anticipated that of important civil rights leaders and activists. For those in the forefront of the civil rights movement from the mid-fifties until about 1963—primarily Martin Luther King and SNCC organizers—the immediate goal was the dismantling of the system of racial inequality in America.[52] They called for liberal or negative freedom, liberation from constraints. Yet such a liberation, while a necessary first step, was not enough; the final goal was positive freedom only attainable in a particular kind of community.[53]

According to King, the "ultimate aim" of the movement was the beloved community.[54] In a broad sense, this simply meant the kinship of all humanity. Yet beyond this, the term refers to a particular type of community, one in which there is "mutual regard" or "empathy."[55] Love, says King, while necessary for the beloved community, is not sufficient; there must be empathy, the ability to see things from the point of view of another. Empathy, as opposed to pity, puts one on a level of equality with others.[56]

With the concept of the beloved community, civil rights activists imagined a community that emphasized solidarity without threatening individuality, that created unity but not uniformity.[57] Rather than crushing its members' autonomy or subsuming them under a race, the beloved community enhances individuality by giving the individual the support necessary for a stronger sense of identity and efficacy than he or she could achieve in isolation. In the words of one SNCC representative, "We seek a community in which man can realize the full meaning of the self which demands open relationship with others."[58] Or as King puts it, evoking Martin Buber, "'I' cannot reach fulfillment without 'thou.' The self cannot be self without other selves."[59]

Although activists preferred the term "freedom," as used in this context it encompassed a democratic vision: one was not free unless one had a chance to influence collective decisions. As John Lewis said,

> Being involved tended to free you. . . . [Y]ou saw yourself as the free man, as the free agent, able to act.[60]

Taken by itself, this statement could be extolling individualistic, liberal freedom; but Lewis is clearly talking about collective action in the civil rights movement. Or as King put it, quoting Cicero, "Freedom is the participation in power."[61] Though certainly not rejecting representative government, the early civil rights notion of freedom clearly drew upon the tradition of direct democracy and its notions of participation, consensus, and community.

In incomplete form, presixties jazz enacted this notion of freedom, supporting both individuality and group solidarity. Jazz has served as a forum for individual expression, one of the few public forums for African Americans for much of United States history. Saxophonist Archie Shepp made this point and alluded to its political implications when asked what the base of the jazz tradition was:

> Self expression. And a certain quality of human dignity despite all obstacles, despite the enslavement of the black man and then his oppression. And each of the great players has had so distinctive, so individual a voice. There is only one Bird [Charlie Parker], one Ben Webster, one Cootie Williams. That's jazz—the uniqueness of the individual. If he believes in himself, every person is not only different but valuably different.[62]

Although jazz musicians begin by imitating the style of admired players, only by assimilating and transcending those influences can they attain excellence.

The main vehicle for individual expression in jazz has been the improvised solo. In modern (post–1940) small group jazz, a series of solos follows the playing (and embellishing) of the written melody of the song. The individual soloist is free to musically express ideas and emotions, referring to the melody of the song but often abandoning it completely, developing his or her own themes. Improvisers base their melodies on the harmonic structure of the song—either a progression of chords, or, in "modal" jazz, a single scale.

Self-expression through improvisation is not confined to the soloist, however. As the soloist improvises, the "rhythm section" (usually consisting of piano, bass, and drums) supports him or her by playing complementary chords, bass lines, and drum rhythms. Even accompanying musicians, in their empathic roles, have considerable freedom. The pianist can use different voicings of chords, substitute appropriate chords, and vary their frequency and rhythm. The bass player also has many choices about how to approach a given chord progression. Finally, while it is crucial that the drummer keep accurate time, he or she has many options concerning tone, rhythmic patterns, accents, and intensity. Thus one improvises even as one accompanies.

At the same time that it encourages individual expression, presixties jazz partially embodies positive freedom, freedom as empathic interaction among equals in a strong group. Good musicians strive to express their individuality in tone and style, but a successful performance, one that "swings," results from empathy within the group. It is essential that musicians listen to one another, each striving to complement the other harmonically, rhythmically, and melodically. As the legendary New Orleans drummer Baby Dodds put it in describing his role in musical performance,

> I feel them out. I work with all of them because they all belong to me. I feel I'm the key man in that band. In drumming you have got to pay attention to each, everyone. You must *hear* that person distinctly, and what he wants. You got to give it to him. . . . You must study a guy's human nature, study about what he will take, or see about what he will go for. . . . Without a drummer that knows how to *help*, there's no band.[63]

The more sympathetic the rest of the group, the better the soloist is able to develop his or her individual statement *and* the more solidarity there is. Thus jazz calls into question the classical liberal assumption that the stronger the group the more individuality must be curtailed.

Presixties jazz, then, allowed the soloist considerable individual expression within a group context. However, this freedom was limited in three ways. First, when someone soloed or played the melody, the others either "accompanied" him or her or remained silent. The musicians who were not soloing were not free to speak as forcefully as the soloist; rarely did all the instruments play equally prominent melodies simultaneously. Second, bass and drums took a clearly subsidiary role, often not "soloing" at all, but remaining in the background. Finally, all instruments were bound by a chordal structure, meter, and tempo.

In the 1960s members of the "free jazz" movement dramatically expanded the freedom inherent in earlier jazz, rejecting many previous rules of harmony, meter, and song form, giving the individual musician many more choices. In addition, they experimented with polyphony to create a more egalitarian group process. The growing musical freedom created by the budding avant-garde came to be used by Charles Mingus and Ornette Coleman to express rebellion against an unjust society by breaking musical conventions and to create new forms that posited an egalitarian alternative to the American racial hierarchy.[64]

## IV

One does not have to probe beneath the surface to see Charles Mingus's music as political commentary. The most obvious starting place is his song titles: "Work Song" (1955), "Haitian Fight Song" (1957) (which he said could be titled "Afro-American Fight Song"), "Fables of Faubus" (referring to the segregationist governor of Arkansas) (1959), "Prayer for Passive Resistance" (1960), and "Meditations on Integration" (1964).[65]

Sometimes these politically titled songs had lyrics, as in "Fables of Faubus":

Oh Lord, don't let them shoot us
Oh Lord, don't let them stab us
Oh Lord, don't let them tar and feather us
Oh Lord, no more swastikas!

Oh Lord, no more Ku Klux Klan!

Name me someone ridiculous
[answer:] Governor Faubus!
Why is he so sick and ridiculous?
[answer:] He won't permit integrated schools
Then he's a fool! . . .[66]

Although these lyrics make their message clear, Mingus's purely instrumental works convey a more subtle and complex political meaning. Sometimes the music expresses an emotional response to injustice. For example, about "Haitian Fight Song," which features a long, bluesy solo by Mingus himself, he said:

> I can't play it right unless I'm thinking about prejudice and hate and persecution, and how unfair it is. There's sadness and cries in it, but also determination. And it usually ends with my feeling: 'I told them! I hope somebody heard me.'[67]

And, indeed, much of the dissonance and emotion in his music mirrors the anger over racism that he often expressed verbally.

It is significant that the blues plays such an important role in Mingus's music, for it has always communicated a complex mixture of pain and determination. As Richard Wright put it,

> The most astonishing aspect of the blues is that, though replete with a sense of defeat and down-heartedness, they are not intrinsically pessimistic; their burden of woe and melancholy is dialectically redeemed through sheer force of sensuality, into an almost exultant affirmation of life, of love, of sex, of movement, of hope.[68]

Although Wright is speaking of blues songs with lyrics, the same feeling pervades many instrumental blues, or even music with blues elements.

In addition to its cathartic element, Mingus's music moved toward the representation of a positive alternative by creating a group that supported and encouraged strong individuality. Though he never considered himself part of the "free jazz" movement, in many of his pieces he tried to break down the hierarchy of instruments as well as the strictures on time, note choice, and rhythm that had existed in earlier jazz. As titles like "Percussion Discussion" and "Conversation" suggest, Mingus tried to reproduce in musical form the dynamics of a good conversation or meeting.[69] Bringing about such conversations required the lifting of restrictions on some instruments and the creation of structures in which all musicians in the group could speak freely together, rather than being confined to a series of solo statements. "Percussion Discussion" illustrates the liberation of the rhythm instruments and "Conversation" portrays collective improvisation.

"Percussion Discussion," as the title suggests, is a dialogue, a musical interchange between Mingus on bass and Max Roach on drums. To add to the original "conversation," recorded live in a nightclub in 1955, Mingus overdubbed a "three-quarter bass," an instrument pitched between a bass and a cello. The piece consists of various interactions between the instruments—sometimes they all play together, sometimes in pairs, and sometimes alone. Near the end Mingus and Roach have a back-and-forth section in which they trade ideas, Roach often rhythmically and melodically echoing (or contrasting) Mingus's ideas.

By the unprecedented act of banishing all instruments except bass and drums, Mingus liberates those two instruments from their subordinate roles, allowing each to express itself in ways not previously possible. In the process, the distinction between rhythm and melody breaks down—Roach plays melodies and Mingus achieves percussive effects by striking the bass with the bow and snapping the strings against the neck.[70] This expansion of expression on the part of these two instruments represents a large step toward true polyphony—bass and drums, instruments that had been primarily supportive, part of the "rhythm section," step into the forefront as lead voices. One can see in this group without musical second-class citizens an anticipation of the movement forward of African Americans, a group in the "background," to be heard as equals.

"Conversation" illustrates the beginnings of the breakdown of solo form and the rise of polyphonic group improvisation. Here collective improvisation grows out of traditional form. After the horns have each soloed for a chorus, they trade two-measure phrases, which is not unusual; however, what follows is: a chorus of trading one-measure phrases and then half-measure (two-beat) ideas.[71] Finally, the dialogue having been taken as far as it will go, the musicians engage in a chorus of collective improvisation. By taking the practice of trading phrases to its limit, where it turns into a collective improvisation, Mingus shows how the polyphony of the budding avant-garde grew out of, yet transformed, the polyphony within earlier jazz. Early New Orleans musicians employed collective improvisation within traditional harmony, meter, and song form; in the sixties, jazz musicians revived polyphony in the context of an attack on previous conventions and the exploration of musical freedom, giving it a new meaning.

Mingus's first full-scale attempt at polyphony, if not entirely successful, took place in January 1956 with "Pithecanthropus Erectus." According to Mingus, this instrumental piece is about domination and conflict:

> [I]t depicts musically my conception of the modern counterpart of the first man to stand erect—how proud he was, considering himself the "first" to ascend from all fours, pounding his chest and preaching his superiority over the mammals still in a prone position. Overcome with self-esteem, he goes out to rule the world, if not the universe; but both his own failure to realize the inevitable emancipation of those he sought to enslave, and his greed in attempting to stand on a false security, deny him not only the right of ever being a man, but finally destroy him completely.[72]

The applications of this anthropological tale to American race relations are obvious.[73]

How does the music reflect this theme? The final section of the piece seems to represent the anarchy of unorganized rebellion—saxophones scream into the extreme high register, the pianist pounds out tone clusters, and the bassist and drummer flail away on their instruments. It is as if in the state of war, discourse has been replaced by shouting; individual voices cannot be heard in the melee. Yet within the piece lies an alternative to the state of war, for another section features interactive group improvisation—individual members can be heard "conversing" in a polyphonic manner, playing simultaneous melodies that fit together because of the musicians' responsive listening. Here we can see echoes, in musical form, of the kind of empathic collective process, balancing individual and group, that King and others were beginning to speak about.

Although the piece represents an important step on the road to the musical representation of the beloved community, the polyphony is limited. During the interactive group section one can hear each voice, but no one makes a strong statement, even for a moment; in the rest of the piece, the musicians "solo" in the standard manner. It is as if the group, musically and politically, does not yet have a strong enough sense of itself to trust individuals to "speak out" without endangering the whole. Four years later, Mingus would break through these limitations on expression.

## V

The album *Charles Mingus Presents Charles Mingus*, recorded in 1960, represents the full flowering of the polyphonic improvisation begun during the previous decade. The album contains one of his most explicitly political compositions with lyrics, "Fables of Faubus." It also contains his most radical extension of the conversational technique in a piece called "What Love," in which Mingus on bass and Eric Dolphy on bass clarinet engage in a literal dialogue on their instruments, mimicking human voices in a "discussion" free of tempo or bar lines. However, "Folk Forms #1" best embodies the fully realized total group improvisation toward which Mingus had been striving.

What strikes one first about "Folk Forms #1," a twelve-minute performance, is the expressiveness on the part of the individual players. The musicians use their instruments in every conceivable way; the horn players, for instance, employ growls, honks, and smears, taking conventional harmony to its limits. Yet the piece's real achievement is its polyphony. Each section of the piece begins by featuring one of the musicians, whose solo consists of three sections: at first he plays alone or with a fairly traditional accompaniment; then he engages in duets with the other instruments; and finally the entire group joins in a collective improvisation featuring much New Orleans-style counterpoint and call-and-response. Despite this preset structure, the effect is one of great collective spontaneity and improvisation: the piece juggles bass, drums, saxophone, and trumpet in every combination while constantly shifting meters, rhythms, moods, and dynamics.

Whitney Balliet's account captures the spirit of the performance:

> It begins with Mingus playing a simple blueslike figure. He is joined by [Dannie] Richmond [drums], in ad-lib time. [Eric] Dolphy enters (on alto saxophone), and is almost immediately followed by [Ted] Curson [trumpet], who is muted. The horns converse, the rhythm slips into four-four time and is interrupted by breaks and out-of-tempo passages. Dolphy and Richmond drop out, and Mingus backs Curson. Richmond and Dolphy return, and all four men swim around and come to a stop. Mingus solos without backing, and Richmond reappears, pulling the horns after him. There is another stop, and Dolphy solos against broken rhythms, and the four take up their ruminations again. After a third stop, Richmond solos and he and Mingus go into a kicking, jumping, unbelievably swinging duet. Mingus falls silent, allowing Richmond to finish his solo, and there is a stop. Mingus solos briefly, and all converse intently until the rhythm slows, Dolphy moans, and they go out.[74]

More than any other Mingus piece up to this time, "Folk Forms" is a truly polyphonic work. Prefigured by "Percussion Discussion," bass and drums transcend their supporting roles and become lead melodic voices. Each instrument is an equal participant; one voice in the conversation momentarily takes the lead, only to be "answered" by another. A near-perfect example of polyphonic group improvisation, "Folk Forms" balances group and individual in a remarkable way. Based upon, yet transcending, the confines of the twelve-measure blues form, the piece has a sense of risk, as if the musicians are stretching their individual freedom and expressiveness to the limit, yet this individual risk-taking is only made possible by an empathic, cohesive group.

Mingus achieved this musical realization of positive freedom, maximizing individual expression and group solidarity, by simultaneously insisting on two apparently contradictory things. First, he demanded that his musicians develop an individual, personal style, that their improvisations come from "who they were"; he was most harsh on those who played standardized phrases ("licks"), especially those derived from Charlie Parker.[75] Another technique that Mingus used for bringing out individuality was to stop the band during a performance and have someone play an unaccompanied solo. According to drummer Dannie Richmond, "He had a theory that if you couldn't play alone first, [then] . . . you couldn't play with anyone else."[76] Yet he simultaneously insisted that the ideas his musicians improvised fit into the style, mood, and structure of his often elaborate compositions. Thus, despite the unity of the music, many musicians attested to the fact that they developed their own personal style by working with Mingus. As saxophonist Jackie McLean put it,

> After I left the Mingus band, I really began to be Jackie McLean. I had a more open mind to improvisation and a more individual sound. Prior to that time, I was still very much into Bird. My experience with Mingus really helped me grow.[77]

This development of individuality in the context of a cohesive group calls into question liberalism's dichotomization of group and individual.

Despite the fact that, like any good leader, Mingus had a strong vision that brought order and coherence, his best performances employed a collective process. Instead of Mingus conducting the rather complicated pieces, the group moved together by careful listening. There were cues, but anyone could give the cue if he sensed the group was ready. Like citizens in a classical democracy, people took turns leading, with all the risk and excitement such leadership brings.[78] Each had equal responsibility and freedom as long as he paid attention to the group process. Many of the compositions themselves were written collectively; as with Ellington, improvisations that worked were incorporated into the composition.

Thus Mingus's mature polyphonic work allows for both great individual expression and group solidarity, representing the free democratic society that reconciles them. What Mingus began, others continued. Ornette Coleman's "Free Jazz," which gave a movement its name, carried "conversational" improvisation to new heights, lifting even more restrictions on individual expression while hoping to preserve group solidarity.

## VI

Although Ornette Coleman, unlike Mingus, did not express political sentiments through song titles and lyrics, his music represents a radical musical freedom that in the context of its time embodied the positive and negative freedom civil rights activists were fighting for.[79] Indeed, from interviews it is apparent that he had experienced a lot of racism and was passionately concerned with its elimination.[80] One of the themes running through his interviews and his work is his quest to be recognized as a full human being: "I would rather think human first than think of being defeated because I'm black."[81] His music, as we shall see, presents a vision of freedom consonant with this quest for recognition.[82]

Like Mingus, Coleman draws heavily upon the blues. True to his roots playing rhythm and blues in Texas, Coleman's saxophone playing is replete with bent notes and nearly literal "cries." One hears in his playing the mixture of sadness and determination alluded to in Wright's discussion of the blues. Yet his music also points beyond this level to a representation of a better society.

"Free Jazz" was recorded in 1960 with an unusual ensemble: two drummers, two bass players, two trumpeters, Eric Dolphy on bass clarinet, and the leader Ornette Coleman on a plastic alto saxophone.[83] The work consists of one "take" (uninterrupted recording) of thirty-eight minutes. There are brief, partially written, partially improvised ensemble themes that introduce five- to ten-minute sections of free improvisation, but for the most part the music is collectively created through improvisation.

What strikes one most immediately about the piece is its range of expression: the work encompasses styles from the avant-garde (Don Cherry) to the "straight ahead" (Freddie Hubbard). As with Mingus's "Folk Forms," a chord-playing instrument such as piano or guitar is absent, giving the soloist more freedom in note choice. In fact, as Coleman himself once emphasized, the lack of predetermined chords encouraged the player to create his own melodies rather than play licks:

> Usually, when you play a melody, you have a set pattern [i.e., chords] to know just what you can do while the other person's doing a certain thing. But in this case, when we played the melody, no one knew where to go or what to do to show that he knew where he was going. . . . I finally got them to where they could see how to express themselves without linking up to a definite maze [i.e., chord progression]. . . . I think it was a case of teaching them how to feel more confident in being expressive like that for themselves.[84]

The soloists used this freedom for expressive purposes: in this and later efforts, Coleman and others extended the tonal possibilities of their instruments by such devices as playing extensively in the extreme lower register, playing in the very high register, using squeaks and squawks, playing below the bridge on the bass, and rattling the keys on a saxophone for a percussive effect. Coleman and Dolphy in particular seemed to be striving with their tones to "speak" through their horns, evoking individuality and the metaphor of speech.

But alongside the great diversity and individual expression, the performance maintains a remarkable group cohesiveness. After the theme of each section is played, one instrumentalist begins his solo, accompanied by the bassists and the drummers. Unlike standard jazz playing, here the soloist improvises without reference to a set of chords or to a song with a particular meter or number of measures. Obviously, however, in order to work there must be some relationship between what the soloist plays and what the bassists and drummers are doing, but this is arrived at in an intuitive and aural manner rather than being decided beforehand. The improvisation becomes even more "collective" when the other horn players join in. They may

- "answer" the soloist;
- "talk to" each other;
- play counterpoint (New Orleans style);
- play background figures ("riffs") or held notes, sometimes in unison or in harmony with others;
- attempt to play in unison with the soloist;
- deliberately play against the others;
- put forward an idea of their own.

Very quickly, the soloist no longer stands out, and the group conversation takes precedence. The soloist is then briefly allowed to play alone again with the "rhythm section," until the members of the group come in. This back-and-forth process continues until, presumably cued by Coleman, the ensemble plays a written passage again. It is as if the soloist makes a statement that is then bandied about in a group discussion.

The only change in the format comes during the bass solo section, where the bassists have a conversation among themselves without horns, and the drum solo section, where the drums play together without accompaniment. This is a necessity, a recognition of the fact that because of the bass's timbre and volume and the drums' relative inability to play pitched notes they will not be heard as prominent solo voices if the horns are playing as well. As in any good discussion, the structure is altered to accommodate those who are not so easily heard, like a meeting that quiets for an elderly person.

This collective improvisation, combining unprecedented individual freedom and expression with group coherence, carries to new heights the polyphony present in traditional jazz performances. Without preset chords or meter, musical empathy is even more necessary for a successful performance. In the words of the leader Coleman:

> The most important thing was for us to play together, all at the same time, without getting in each other's way, and also to have enough room for each player to *ad lib* alone—and to follow this idea for the duration of the album. When the soloist played something that suggested a musical idea or direction, I played that behind him in my style. He continued his own way in his solo, of course.[85]

Not that the individual disappears into the whole; Coleman says that he played behind the soloist in his "own style" and the soloist continued "in his own way." He insisted that his musicians not "accompany" anyone but express themselves in a manner that contributed to the music as a whole. As he put it,

> What I have always wanted my bands to do is have every man express *anything*, but yet at the same time show the thing that is allowing us to make music together, which has something to do with the person seeing in his mind the difference between making music total together or trying to make someone sound good. . . . I don't like to do something just to make someone sound good because it's giving a false image of you. . . . As long as they [the other musicians] don't do anything to make me sound good but they get with the music, then that's beautiful. . . . [Y]ou've got to blend your instrument with other instruments to make music, not to give support to some other instrument simply because it needs your support to sound good.[86]

The distinction between "making someone sound good" and contributing to the music seems to contrast self-abnegation with an equal, or polyphonic, group process. That is, Coleman suggests that the way to support another person is not to conform to them, giving up one's own identity for theirs, for that would represent a kind of inauthentic role-playing ("giving a false image of you"). Rather, what supports and frees one's fellow individual is to contribute to the whole of which both are a part ("get[ting] with the music").

In what he calls "free group improvisation," Coleman tries to go beyond jazz's previous dichotomization of group and individual, where, he says, "the individual is either swallowed up in a group situation, or else he is out front soloing, with none of the other horns doing anything but calmly awaiting their turn for *their* solos."[87] "Free Jazz" strives for a polyphonic relationship between soloist and ensemble, with a willingness to interact freely, even allowing the soloist to be submerged temporarily. The soloist becomes less of a star or a virtuoso striving to outdo the other musicians and more of a first among equals.

As in any group conversation, some voices are more compelling than others. In "Free Jazz" this is the result of characteristics of the instruments as well as differences in the strength and individuality of the musicians. Perhaps acknowledging his role as a leader, Coleman's solo section is longer than the others. But all in all, it is a very balanced conversation.[88]

## VII

We can thus see the jazz performances of Mingus and Coleman as musical enactments of the ideas of freedom put forward in the growing civil rights movement. Sixties jazz broke musical conventions to increase individual expression, mirroring the efforts of civil rights leaders to lift rules and conventions constricting the lives of African Americans. Musicians developed modes of individual expression previously unavailable in jazz, sometimes expressing a relatively unsublimated anger and sadness reflective of the situation of many African Americans at that time. This is negative, liberal freedom, or liberation; each member of the group could conceivably use this freedom for purely individual ends, creating anarchy.

However, the vision of positive freedom contained in the idea of the beloved community was also represented in jazz performances through the process of polyphonic group improvisation. Much of presixties jazz was polyphonic in the sense that all instruments improvised simultaneously to some degree. However, "free jazz" took the polyphony inherent in jazz to unprecedented completeness. Musically, as never before in jazz, all the members of the group became equals. Yet such equality did not lead to anarchy; rather, the resulting musical product was remarkably coherent. Musicians achieved coherence not by subordinating individuality to the group but by the kind of empathy and "mutual regard" found in democratic group discussions. While King spoke of the need to "transform the jangling discords of our nation into a beautiful symphony of brotherhood," jazz musicians created performances that both reflect the dissonance of a society torn by racial strife and offer a model of harmonious brotherhood.[89] At the same time that civil rights marchers called for the smashing of racial hierarchy and the formation of the "beloved community," jazz musicians like Mingus and Coleman sought to overthrow established musical strictures and create musical democracy. Perhaps due to jazz's dual insistence on individuality and group cohesiveness, these musicians created models of democratic community without merging their voices into one.

Despite its momentary achievement in music, the beloved community was not to become a reality in America. The year 1960, when "Free Jazz" was made, was a year of relative optimism for African Americans. The hope was that white society could be moved by the force of morality, that love could bring about a beloved community, not only liberating blacks but transforming America in the process.

The translation into social action of what had been achieved musically by Coleman and Mingus came up against severe obstacles, however. As the decade wore on, the tremendous white resistance to change became apparent; ideals came up against intransigence, repression, and brutality. And many began to realize that the elimination of discrimination was not enough; much of the problem was the entrenched poverty that demanded economic solutions.

In response to the perceived limitations of the civil rights approaches of the early sixties, the black power movement emphasized group solidarity rather than the beloved community. The beloved community's vision of a group that retained individuality ran counter to modern interest-group politics. Black power called for African Americans to unite on the basis of interest, which implicitly accepted mainstream group politics in which individuals within a group are more or less interchangeable. It was as if the political vision captured in the music of Mingus, Roach, and Coleman had been premature. Though it provided a model of freedom that could be applied to African Americans, America was not ready. The African American community first had to strengthen itself.

Black power's rejection of the beloved community was also reflected in the development of jazz. The polyphonic balance between group and individual achieved in 1960 failed to hold. "Ascension," recorded by eleven musicians under the leadership of John Coltrane in 1965, typifies the jazz of the mid-sixties in the same way that "Free Jazz" represents the music of the first few years of the rapidly evolving decade.[90] Coltrane had earlier indicated his affinities with the civil rights movement and its cultural components with compositions like "Liberia"; "Dahomey Dance," whose melody was taken from an African drum performance; "Africa"; and "Alabama," based on the cadences of a King speech and dedicated to children killed in the bombing of a Southern church.[91] He also recorded a powerful version of "Song of the Underground Railroad" in 1961.[92] Coltrane was seen as the musician on the cutting edge musically, and by some, politically.[93] In "Ascension," Coltrane experimented with free jazz in a way he had not done before.

Like "Free Jazz," "Ascension" alternates structured ensemble passages with solos backed by a rhythm section (in this case, a standard one with another bass added). In "Ascension," as in "Free Jazz," there is no preset meter or harmony for the solo sections. Here the similarities end, however. First, while during the solo sections of "Free Jazz" the soloist alternates between foreground playing and collective interaction with the others, during the solo sections of "Ascension," the other horns stay silent. It is true that there is a "dialogue between soloists and the rhythm section," and more so than in most jazz performances since there is no preset harmony, yet there is nothing like the collective interaction in "Free Jazz."[94] Whereas in "Free Jazz" the partially written ensemble passages that introduced the solo/interactive sections are quite brief, in "Ascension" these introductory passages are equal to or longer than the solo sections.

Second, although the introductory ensemble sections of "Ascension" feature some free-sounding collective improvisation, this group improvisation is much different in character from that in "Free Jazz." In the collective passages of "Ascension," one has to strain to hear a particular instrumentalist. During the free-improvisation sections, the players tend to repeat one phrase, or simply to "scream" through their instruments (or pound away, in the drummer's case).[95] Rather than a conversation, it is a collective religious ritual, an act of transcendence ("Ascension") rather than of liberation ("Free Jazz").[96] One might call it "textural" group improvisation rather than real polyphony.[97]

The communal textures created in "Ascension" have undeniable power. By nearly merging, the individual musicians produce tremendous energy; something transcendent does seem to emerge from the combination of the individuals' forces, as in a large political demonstration. But politically, the textural group improvisation of "Ascension" reflects the rejection of the early civil rights movement's unique vision of democratic politics in favor of politics as a matter of group power. Prefiguring both the interest-oriented group called for by the emerging black power movement and the subsequent militaristic cadres like the Black Panthers, the individuals are not integrated into the group as individuals but are subservient to the group sound.[98] Whereas "Free Jazz" as the beloved community overcomes the dichotomy between group and individual, "Ascension" is unable to do so, alternating collective catharsis with individual soloing.[99]

As the decade wore on, the breakdown of the democratic community balancing group and individual, freedom and structure, became more evident, musically and politically. Some chose order over individuality, pursuing an emotionless formalism, heavily influenced by modern European "classical" music. Saxophonist Anthony Braxton, for example, titled his pieces with mathematical formulas and explicitly stated that he wished to remove all feeling from music.[100]

Other developments reflected the opposite, though complementary, trend in African American politics. For these musicians, democracy became anarchy; "free jazz" became Dionysian "energy music." Political passions had given life to the technical liberation of the early fifties and led to the collective creation of new forms to embody those sentiments. Now passion exploded all form; dialogue gave way to the chaos prefigured in the "apocalypse" of Mingus's "Pithecanthropus Erectus." There is an incident in a Coltrane concert recorded in Seattle in 1965 in which after several minutes of intense, free-form squealing by Coltrane and saxophonist Pharoah Sanders, the musicians lay down their instruments and begin to wail, as if in agony.[101] While the failure of jazz to give form to feeling led to Coltrane's scream in a Seattle nightclub, America's failure to give form to black political aspirations brought forth shouting in the streets of Watts the very same year.

## VIII

It is difficult to pinpoint any direct influence of sixties jazz upon American race relations, partly because such influence by works of art is quite rare and partly because it had so few listeners. As Andrew Ross has argued, "[I]t may be fair to say that the public controversy generated by James Brown singing 'Say it Loud, I'm Black and Proud' *mattered* in a way which the controversy over Max Roach's 'We Insist—The Freedom Now Suite' did not."[102] However, jazz did justice to the complexity of the civil rights movement's ideas in a way the James Brown song did not. Because of its direct connection to the senses and the emotions, free jazz allowed its few listeners to experience and understand the kind of freedom SNCC and King talked about in a way that words alone could not convey.

Yet the music was no mere reflection of preexisting ideas and actions. Some of the early experiments in free jazz preceded the political developments of the movement, prefiguring the activism of the sixties. In the words of SDS activist Carl Oglesby, "[In the sixties] politics itself . . . continued the march formerly begun in art, in the consciousness which the black and white jazz and the white and black poetry of the '50s began to instill and focus."[103] It is as if jazz musicians and black political activists, in different forms, were groping toward similar understandings of their experience, understandings that gave birth to the activism of the civil rights movement and the New Left.

Why did free jazz fail to maintain its vision of democratic community in the face of the late-sixties attack on that vision by those opposed to civil rights and by many in the movement itself? Perhaps there was a sense that a limit had been reached: How does one continue to develop a model of freedom, dimly grasped but present, when society turns its back and refuses to create egalitarian social and political structures? In addition, free jazz made extraordinary, perhaps impossible, demands on the listener. In a polyphonic, free performance, there are no fixed key centers, melodies, or lead instruments to hold on to; it is up to the listener to weave out of the various threads a tapestry of his or her own, perhaps a different one upon each listening.[104] Even many jazz musicians disliked free jazz; they argued that freedom requires structure and (incorrectly) saw none in free jazz.[105] They also felt that the music, since it sounded like it required no training, threatened their sense of professional standing.

Despite the political and musical rejection of free jazz and its values, its performances show that the beloved community is possible, even if only in a small group, and teach us something about its conditions. Most of all, the successful free, polyphonic works of Mingus and Coleman suggest that empathy is crucial to freedom, for without it individual expression easily becomes anarchy (or the war of each against all), and group solidarity threatens individuality.

Among those who listened to jazz in the late fifties and early sixties was a group of white college students who became active in the civil rights movement and then the New Left. They formed a subculture centered around coffeehouses, Beat poetry, jazz, and folk music. One of its members was a young singer who would change the face of popular culture in the sixties: Bob Dylan.[106] Drawing many more listeners than free jazz, Dylan's music would become a part of the political education of the New Left and the counterculture.

# 5
# AUTHENTICITY AND SURREALITY
## Bob Dylan, the New Left, and the Counterculture

Bob Dylan stood at the center of the intersection of politics and rock music in the sixties. Although as a purely musical influence Dylan shared the limelight with several other artists, for white political activists he stood alone. The Beatles and the Rolling Stones sold more albums, but for both the New Left of the early sixties and the later counterculture, Dylan had heroic status. In the words of Todd Gitlin, former president of SDS, "Whether he liked it or not, Dylan *sang for us*. . . . We followed his career as if he were singing our song; we got in the habit of asking where he was taking us next."[1] Richard Flacks, another important SDS figure, "only half-joking," claimed that "to understand *The Port Huron Statement*, you have to understand Bob Dylan."[2] Journalist Andrew Kopkind compared him with Tom Hayden, describing how on some level he confused the singer and the political activist:

> When pondering a political or existential decision, I would flash on Hayden and guess what he'd say, or think or do. I'd sometimes confuse him with Dylan . . . : in their obviously different ways, they seemed to express the tones, shades, colors of a generational spirit that others could merely put into words.[3]

How exactly did Dylan's songs embody the thoughts and feelings of many political activists in the sixties? What vision of democracy did they express? What were some of the limits of Dylan's music as a source of democratic political education in the sixties?

I focus on the music of Bob Dylan, not because he was the sum total of rock music in that era, but because his songs have much to teach us about rock's various resources for political education in the context of the changing politics of the 1960s. Dylan's "folk" music embodies the early New Left's civic republicanism, with its faith in truth and reason and its vision of a virtuous community of authentic souls. These early songs seek to unmask evil by portraying it truthfully and teach authenticity, the rejection of social roles in favor of the honest presentation of a core self. His later, electric songs reject the ideas of a core self and truth, and indeed all ordering hierarchies, embracing the counterculture's devotion to unmediated experience, play, and spontaneity. Despite their political potential, both the ideal of authenticity and the counterculture's emphasis on experience could lead away from politics toward an emphasis on the self. Did Dylan's late-sixties work succumb to the temptation to turn inward, away from politics?

Both Dylan's folk and rock music grew out of the culture of the 1950s, and we must begin there to understand their role in political education.

## I

Rock and roll as a social phenomenon emerged out of the very changes in society that the New York Intellectuals grouped under the pejorative term "mass culture."[4] Work had become increasingly routinized for many Americans.[5] Yet while there seemed to be a prescribed life course consisting of school followed by a sometimes monotonous job and the renunciation and conformity it required, the increasing consumer economy urged people towards hedonism and impulsiveness.[6] In response, Americans increasingly turned to leisure for pleasure and self-fulfillment.[7] Leisure activities became important for defining oneself in a way that they had not before. Technology also helped create a youth culture built around music—the portable radio and the 45 rpm record allowed music to be part of people's daily lives in a way that was rarely possible before.[8]

While youth embraced rock and roll, it shocked adults in a manner hard to appreciate from our vantage point. The sound itself had the biggest impact. It was "noisy"—loud, raw, and disorderly—with distorted guitars and garbled vocals. The volume and tone quality of the electric guitar in rock-and-roll songs seemed to be an attack on order and tradition, an exhortation to "roll over, Beethoven," in the words of the Chuck Berry song. Seeing in rock and roll a physicality mostly absent from American popular music, adults feared that rock rhythms inflamed the libido, overwhelming teenagers' fragile superegos. This fear was exacerbated by the suggestive nature of some of the dances accompanying the new music.[9]

Part of rock and roll's rawness came from its blues heritage, and its association with African Americans created hostility among racist whites. Blacks had long been associated in the white mind with that which was desired but repressed: play, passion, and sexuality.[10] Campaigns to rid the nation of rock and roll focused on its "jungle rhythms."[11] Indeed, rock and roll not only brought white and black music together in its mixture of country and blues, blurring traditional (segregated) categories of music, but whites and African Americans sometimes listened together.[12] And whether or not physical integration occurred, many white musicians and audiences identified with African Americans in a way that threatened middle America. When Buddy Holly's mother asked him if he got along with blacks in the other bands he had toured with, he replied, "Oh, we're Negroes too, we get to feeling like that's what we are."[13] (Of course, not all white teenagers knew or approved of the black roots of rock and roll.) While the fifties saw movement away from the cities to the suburbs, with increasing racial segregation, urban working-class culture presented adolescents with an alternative vision.[14]

This alternative worldview can be seen in rock-and-roll lyrics. Before the mid-fifties, popular music consisted largely of romantic, sometimes saccharine love songs, with some cleverly turned phrases in the best ones. Rock-and-roll songs of the fifties, however, constructed a new world of "cars, streets, suede shoes, alleys, hotels, motels, freeways, juke boxes, stations, parties, and parents. . . ."[15] These songs helped to create and reinforce an iconography for a burgeoning counterculture. Some expressed rebellion directly, attacking the repressive nature of society and its institutions, particularly school. The stifling voice of the establishment was parodied in songs like "Get a Job" and "Yakety Yak (Don't Talk Back!)."[16] Chuck Berry's "School Days," a tale of students who lived for the three-o'clock bell, pitted the freedom of rock-and-roll music and its culture against school's oppressive conformity, asking the music to "Deliver me from the days of old."[17] These songs counterposed fun, dancing, and sex to school, work, and routine ("Rock around the Clock"). "Leader of the Pack," "He's a Rebel," "Jailhouse Rock," "Chain Gang," and "No Particular Place to Go" glorified society's alienated outsiders.[18] Other songs like "Blue Suede Shoes" celebrated nonconformist style and clothes.

The extent to which rock and roll actually engendered opposition to the dominant values of the fifties is a subject of debate. Some argue that its lyrics show an acceptance of mainstream American definitions of success (house, nuclear family, and economic abundance) as well as racist and sexist assumptions.[19] For these writers, rock and roll's emphasis on pleasure ("fun") rather than being liberating is just another form of consumerism.[20] Such critics tend to stress the music's limitations as a vehicle for changing consciousness, because of its seeming inability to seriously consider questions of economic and political power.[21] Others refuse to reduce fifties rock and roll's embrace of pleasure to consumerism.[22] These critics argue that rock and roll served as a means of publicly considering the meaning of past and present, creating dialogue, and making connections between private experience and public issues.[23]

Resolving this dispute is beyond the scope of this chapter, which is primarily concerned with sixties music. Clearly rock and roll did not single-handedly cause political activism or questioning of established values; however, one is hard-pressed to name an aesthetic movement that has ever done so. Rock and roll acted as part of a larger movement, encompassing the Beats and "youth culture," that opened up possibilities more fully realized in the sixties. In particular, identifying with African American culture gave white youth freedom to explore alternative ways of being.

Rock-and-roll listeners thought of themselves as a distinct group, set off by clothes and mannerisms but also by an ethos of adventurousness and action, embodied in the snarl of Elvis's voice. Buying the same records as their peers gave youth a sense of community with common values.[24] In an influential article in 1950, David Riesman argued that there were two groups of music listeners: the majority, who accepted the popular songs pushed by the music industry, and "minority" listeners, who rejected bland, commercial music for more pure, authentic music, often black-influenced. He noted that these listeners tended to form a coterie with a private language and certain countercultural attitudes—identification with African Americans, belief in the equality of the sexes, and a distrust of mass-media images.[25] By mid-decade the music's popularity escalated, and its listeners no longer constituted a coterie. Rock and roll became more commercial, but its followers nevertheless retained some of the "countercultural" characteristics described by Riesman. Thus rock and roll's claim to politically educate rests on a complex whole encompassing music, lyrics, and lifestyle.

Rock and roll was not the only countercultural music of the fifties, for "folk music" also created a rebellious subculture, at least for whites.[26] The American use of folk music for social protest goes back at least as far back as the 1930s; some trace its roots even further back, to the International Workers of the World ("Wobblies").[27] The Russian Revolution and the Soviets' championing of "folk culture," as well as the Depression, spurred the American Left to embrace folk music in the thirties, although its account of the "folk" and its music was largely mythical, rooted in a vision of a unified, harmonious, precapitalist life.[28] Mike Gold and other proponents of "proletarian literature" at times endorsed folk music, seeing popular and classical music as ruling-class art.[29] The Almanac Singers and the People's Songs movement of the forties, both involving Pete Seeger, also had some success among leftists, singing for civil rights and unions.

The fifties saw a growing audience for folk music, prefigured in

1950 when the Weavers, a group featuring Seeger, scored a number-one hit for thirteen weeks with their version of black "country blues" singer Leadbelly's "Goodnight Irene."[30] However, the overtly left-wing politics of the group came under fire, and they were abandoned by their record company and blacklisted.[31] Cold-war anticommunism and its explicit attack on folk music put a damper on popular folk music until the late fifties.[32] For a while, folk music was driven underground and flourished in small basement clubs along with progressive jazz and countercultural comedians like Lenny Bruce.[33]

A popular folk revival began in 1958 with the Kingston Trio's enormously successful version of "Tom Dooley." Although the group's records did not sound much like conventional folk music, others, like Joan Baez, presented more traditional performances. And while they were not enormously popular, records by the Carter Family, Mississippi John Hurt, Blind Lemon Jefferson, the Memphis Jug Band, and other folk pioneers were reissued in the fifties and influenced their young white disciples. In one form or another folk music found a widening audience. Coffeehouses featuring folk performers became popular at colleges, and sales of acoustic guitars "more than doubled in each of the three years following 'Tom Dooley.'"[34]

The center of the revitalized folk scene was Greenwich Village. Washington Square Park had been host to folk minstrels since the late 1940s, and by the 1950s the streets surrounding the park were filled with coffeehouses like The Gaslight, The Bitter End, and Gerdes' Folk City, which featured a variety of folk performers from the traditional to the commercial, the known to the unknown.[35] By the end of the fifties, folk music was more vibrant and oppositional than rock, which had been supplanted by syrupy crooners like Pat Boone, Tab Hunter, and Frankie Laine.[36] The early sixties saw the audience for folk grow even further while the music took on new political significance.

Folk music was rebellious in a rather different way from rock and roll. The lyrics of many of the folk songs in the late fifties and early sixties were overtly political, whether they were union-organizing songs from the thirties or parables of injustice that had been handed down for hundreds of years. Folk musicians emphasized the lyrics, in contrast to the sometimes inarticulate exclamations of rock and roll.[37]

Many of these songs fell into the "realist" category; their purpose was to unmask the lies disseminated by those in power and to reveal the truth about society. Folk music and the culture surrounding it also embodied the ideal of authenticity—a plea for individuals to build their lives around honesty and simplicity, and to remake society according to those goals. This ideal would become central to the politics and culture of the sixties.

In addition to rock and roll and folk music, fifties alternative culture had a nonmusical component: the Beats. Centering around New York City's East Village and San Francisco's North Beach district, writers like Jack Kerouac, Allen Ginsberg, Neal Cassady, and William Burroughs strove for authenticity and spontaneity, both in their lives and in their art.[38] They sought to free the unconscious from the repressive social superego, liberating the human potential for creativity. In a society that stressed material accumulation and conformity to accepted models of behavior, the Beats cultivated experience for its own sake, coming to see drugs as a way of exploring and expanding that experience. The Beats sought out the taboo, participating in the world of drugs, criminality, madness, and homosexuality.

In their pursuit of alternative values, the Beats (like rock-and-roll musicians) modeled themselves self-consciously on African Americans. In the opening lines of Ginsberg's *Howl,* "the best minds of my generation" are found "dragging themselves through the negro streets at dawn. . . ."[39] The improvisational feel of their writing represented a kind of freedom they associated with black bebop jazz musicians, and though they sometimes exaggerated the absence of planning in both jazz and their own work, they tried to imitate with their prose the jagged rhythms and long, improvised phrases of musicians like saxophonist Charlie "Yardbird" Parker.[40] They also sometimes read their poetry to improvised jazz music. Emancipatory as it was, however, the Beats' evocation of African Americans was often marred by stereotyped views of blacks as "primitive," in touch with a primal reality untouched by civilization.[41]

The Beats opposed reigning aesthetic constraints as well. Both the New York Intellectuals and the New Critics thought that while writing ultimately draws on an individual's experience, the best art represents experience reflected on from a distance. Wordsworth's "emotion reflected in tranquility" was their ideal. To attempt to render experience directly would result in, at best, a kind of naive prose; at worst, to an antinomian encouragement of unregulated desire that ultimately leads to totalitarianism. What is valuable in art, they argued, is the public, universal knowledge and experience that is gleaned from the merely private and personal in the process of contemplation and revision.[42]

Whereas Trilling valued reflection and distance, in their writing Ginsberg and Kerouac strove for spontaneity above all else. Influenced by the surrealists and their predecessors like Rimbaud and Apollinaire, they sought in their poems and novels to capture the unimpeded flow of thoughts, as in free association.[43] Using these methods, the Beats attempted to break down the barrier between art and life. Writing became an extension of late-night conversation in coffeehouses; writers strove to use everyday language. Their approach represented a denial of the artistic mask, an attempt to express one's experience as directly as possible. Ginsberg symbolically proclaimed this tenet when he disrobed at poetry readings.

Politically, the Beat movement was ambiguous. Beat writers did not have a specific political program. Yet Ginsberg bristled when an interviewer suggested that his concerns were not political, arguing that "[p]olitical activity without discovering your own identity or nonidentity is in vain because it's just mechanical. . . . The experiences through which you've gone, in conjunction with many others, is [*sic*] an indispensable state for reorganizing the system." Citing Dylan as someone who used music to transform consciousness, he claimed that the singer learned from him that one cannot "create new structures until you have transformed consciousness."[44]

In addition, the Beats took part in a social rebellion in an era of extreme conformity. Though their ethos had tendencies toward mysticism and individualism, at least it was an alternative in a time when few others existed. In their critique of American society they anticipated much of the rebellion of the sixties, which was transformed through the civil rights movement and the New Left into a political rebellion as well. More importantly, the Beats' attempts to use art as a vehicle for discovering, transforming, and expressing individual experience in a public way, breaking down the barrier between art and life, was prophetic of the next decade.

Budding activists at the time came under the influence of the fifties' intertwining subcultures. The important SDS figure Bob Ross revered the bebop saxophonist (and Beat idol) Charlie Parker and hosted a jazz radio show at the University of Michigan. Upon attending a lecture by attorney Leonard Boudin, he discovered that many of the jazz fans he had met through his radio show were also interested in progressive politics.[45] According to James Miller, the SDS activist Richard Flacks's "political awakening" came out of contact with the Beats, experimental theater, and folk music.[46] Tom Hayden hitchhiked to Berkeley in 1960 after reading *On The Road*. One teenager who fell under the spell of the Beats as well as folk music was an aspiring rock-and-roll musician named Bob Dylan.

In the liner notes to his retrospective album *Biograph*, Dylan discusses the excitement he felt upon first encountering the Beats:

> Jack Kerouac, Ginsberg, Corso and Ferlinghetti—*Gasoline, Coney Island of the Mind* . . . oh man, it was wild—*I saw the best minds of my generation destroyed by madness* that said more to me than any of the stuff I'd been raised on. *On the Road*, Dean Moriarty, this made perfect sense to me. . . . America was still very "straight"; "post-war" and sort of into a gray-flannel suit thing, McCarthy, Commies, puritanical, very claustrophobic. And whatever was happening of any real value was happening away from that and sort of hidden from view. . . . I got in at the tail end of that and it was magic. . . .[47]

Rock and roll, folk music, and the Beats: these formed the alternative culture of the fifties that influenced Bob Dylan and others. These three art movements shared a connection with African Americans, either through music, jazz prose rhythms, or a concern for civil rights. All three spawned small "countercultures," with rock and roll going beyond that to gain mass popularity.

Though oppositional in a limited way, what these three fifties movements lacked was a large-scale political youth movement with which to connect. It was only when the civil rights movement gained strength, eventually spawning the New Left and the counterculture, that the potential of these artistic movements for political education was realized. Bob Dylan was able to combine all three movements in a shifting musical style that managed to capture the decade's political twists and turns like no other.

## II

Bob Dylan (Robert Zimmerman) was born to Jewish parents in 1941 in Duluth, Minnesota and moved to the small mining town of Hibbing at the age of six. As a youth, Dylan rebelled against the small-town business world of his father, becoming a "greaser" and motorcyclist, identifying with Marlon Brando and James Dean. He also liked rock and roll as a teenager, listening to Bill Haley, Johnny Ray, Buddy Holly, and Hank Williams. As early as 1955 he performed with a band in a high school concert. His hair piled high like Little Richard's, playing rock and roll at a screeching volume, Dylan mystified many of his schoolmates that night. According to his 1959 high school yearbook, his ambition in life was to "join the band of Little Richard."[48]

A turning point in his life, however, came in the late fifties when he fell under the spell of Woody Guthrie. Visions of Guthrie wandering the country singing traditional folk songs, often adding verses of his own, gave Dylan a new role model. Like Guthrie, Dylan would come to use left-wing political themes and topical news in a repertory consisting of blues, white traditional ballads, hymns, country-western songs, circus tunes, and music-hall songs.[49]

Converted to folk music by Guthrie, Dylan began voraciously listening to records of traditional folk music and assimilating their styles. In December 1960, Dylan moved to Greenwich Village and became an active member of the folk scene there, befriending such musical stalwarts as Dave van Ronk and Ramblin' Jack Elliot and playing at local clubs. Although it is not clear that he disliked rock and roll with the intensity of many folk musicians, he now found it inferior to folk. According to Dylan, while songs like "Tutti Frutti" and "Blue Suede Shoes" "weren't as serious or didn't reflect life in a serious way," folk expressed "deeper feelings," containing more "real life" and complexity."[50]

His first album, entitled simply *Bob Dylan*, released in March 1962, serves up a smorgasbord of American folk styles. The selections range from a traditional white Kentucky mountain song ("A Man of Constant Sorrow") to black blues and songs influenced by spirituals ("Time of Dyin'," "See that my Grave is Kept Clean") to humorous versions of traditional Scottish folk tunes ("Pretty Peggy-O").[51] The album features only two original songs, one a tribute to Woody Guthrie, using a Guthrie-derived melody. The most striking feature of the album is the "unpretty" use of his voice: at various times he "whispers, chuckles, grunts, growls, and howls"; at one point he even yodels to imitate a train whistle.[52] Nothing could be further from either the slick pop arrangements that dominated the airwaves or the elevated clarity and precision of the classical "art song." For that matter, Dylan's "rough" style, even if a bit calculated, had little in common with smooth, commercial "folk music" either.

Dylan's mature folk style is represented by his next two albums, recorded within a year: *The Freewheelin' Bob Dylan* (May 1963) and *The Times They Are A-Changin'* (January 1964), both consisting almost entirely of original compositions accompanied only by his acoustic guitar and harmonica.[53] Of the twenty-three songs that comprise the two albums, ten are overtly political in nature, and those are the ones upon which I will focus; this approach may be unbalanced, but the political songs were the ones that became famous and influenced countless songwriters and listeners.[54]

These early works embody the civic republicanism of the New Left of the Port Huron period.[55] According to this strain of republican thought, if individuals act authentically, without masks, following the dictates of their natural reason, a virtuous community will result.[56] This tradition emphasizes the power of reason and truth to make people moral. It particularly values community and discussion and the simple, agrarian virtues.[57]

Dylan's work takes part in a civic republican search for truth in two respects. First, the truth of society is sought by unmasking and criticizing injustice and by creating realist narratives to help middle- and upper-class listeners see the poor and oppressed more clearly, bringing to life what for most of his audience were merely abstract categories. Second, these songs take part in a quest for the truth of oneself by presenting and encouraging the ideal of authenticity.

Dylan's early songs depict a world of simple truths masked by deception and evil. The world and the self are not obscure; they do not need deciphering. Rather, Dylan seems to say that if people only see what is right in front of them, the truth will be revealed: "How many times must a man look up / Before he can see the sky?"[58] Discovering the truth about politics, determining what the right or just course of action is, is no more difficult than looking up and seeing that the sky is blue.

Why, then, does injustice occur? Two kinds of deception stand in the way of goodness, according to these songs. First, leaders conceal their actions and motives, preventing the exposure of evil. Second, people refuse to see what there is to see—like drivers speeding past a stranded motorist, they turn their heads or rationalize problems away. That is, there are two kinds of masks: those used by evil people to prevent their injustices from being seen, and those good people willingly wear, deceiving themselves.

The purpose of art is both to rip the mask off the evil institutions, exposing their true nature, and to lift the self-imposed veil from people's eyes. Thus, Dylan tells the "masters of war,"

> You that hide behind walls
> You that hide behind desks
> I just want you to know
> I can see through your masks[59]

Here Dylan suggests that exposing the truth in American politics necessitates an assault on the bureaucratic mentality ("walls," "desks") that depoliticizes events like war by reducing them to technical jargon and interoffice memos. In reply to the question, "Why are we in the midst of a folk music boom?" Dylan replied, "because the times cry out for the truth . . . and people want to hear the truth and that's just what they're hearin' in good folk music today."[60] Although undoubtedly many people listened to his songs for other reasons, Dylan seeks to educate the listener by unmasking evil.

Other early Dylan songs present the truth about society in a different way. Realist narratives create images of the oppressed that promote empathy with them. "Ballad of Hollis Brown" tells the true story of a farmer who, distraught over poverty and failing crops, kills his family and himself. Eschewing symbols and broad generalities, "Hollis Brown" evokes the burdens of poverty through detail:

> Your children are so hungry
> That they don't know how to smile . . .
> Your baby's eyes look crazy
> They're a-tuggin at your sleeve . . .[61]

Similarly, details in "The Lonesome Death of Hattie Carroll" bring to life the (true) story of a rich tobacco farmer who killed a black maid and received only a six-month jail sentence. The murderer, William Zanzinger, kills Hattie Carroll:

> With a cane that he twirled around his diamond
> ring finger
> At a Baltimore hotel society gath'rin'[62]

Dylan contrasts Zanzinger who "at twenty-four years / owns a tobacco farm of six hundred acres" with Hattie, who "was fifty-one years old and gave birth to ten children / Who carried the dishes and took out the garbage." Such use of narrative detail takes social and political problems out of the realm of abstraction and makes it easier for listeners to think about or even feel them; it also helps listeners empathize with those different than themselves. Songs like "Hollis Brown" and "Hattie Carroll" helped middle- or upper-class college students see "the poor" as a group of real individuals. These songs appeal to a vision of a common humanity, operating on the assumption that each of us is capable of understanding the situation of another, no matter how different, and that such empathy is the key to political renewal.

Songs like "Masters of War" and "Ballad of Hollis Brown," then, provide tools for citizens in a participatory democracy. Dylan's unmasking songs teach individuals to look behind government and media accounts of reality and develop their own critical judgment. Realist narratives draw attention to politically important circumstances or events, sometimes little-known ones. They also make concepts like racism and poverty concrete through stories and promote empathy. Empathy is a particularly important political quality because without it, citizens remain stuck within their own private perspective and fail to think in terms of the larger public or take into account the views of others who differ.[63] This is not to say that information, the ability to think critically, or empathy eliminate the need for political action and theory, but without these resources and skills, participatory democracy stands little chance of success.

In addition to their search for political and social truth, these early Dylan songs present and encourage the notion of an authentic self. Dylan sings alone with an acoustic guitar—for members of the folk subculture this signified the "real" Dylan, without mask or artifice. This point is further emphasized by the rough, unpleasing nature of his voice. As he put it the liner notes to a Joan Baez album, "'The voice t' speak for me an' mine / Is the hard filthy gutter sound / For it's the only thing that I can touch / An' the only beauty I can feel."[64] The music itself is stark and unembellished, like the grainy black-and-white photograph of Dylan that graces the cover of *The Times They Are A-Changin'*. Although the ideal of authenticity is communicated through form, style, and stance rather than directly through lyrics, Dylan's writings at this time are replete with references to it: "But I learned t'choose my idols well / T'be my voice an' tell my tale"; "An' I'll sing my song like a rebel wild / For it's that I am an' can't deny"; "I 'expose' myself / every time I step out on stage."[65]

Indeed, the whole folk scene was built around the ideal of authenticity, however incompletely realized. Blue jeans, work shirts, and folk music all expressed a rejection of artifice and complexity, which to participants represented deception. As Pete Seeger said in praise of the documentary film *Union Maids*, "No, it's not wide screen, not color. Hell with all that. It's real."[66]

In a sense, folk music's ideal of authenticity embodies a critique of mass culture similar to that of the New York Intellectuals; indeed, Dwight Macdonald had seen folk culture as well as high culture as an alternative to mass culture.[67] Both the New York Intellectuals and folk musicians saw mass culture as deceptive and manipulative, threatening to destroy authentic thought and feeling. However, there is an important difference between the two critiques. The New York Intellectuals looked to an intellectual avant-garde, hoping it could help preserve liberal democracy; although the folk scene at times resembled a coterie, its political ideal was participatory democracy.

It is true that the notion of authenticity can lead to individualism, pulling people away from political action rather than toward republican community: each person pursues her or his own authentic muse without any thought of others. Woody Guthrie, Dylan's early hero, is the archetype here—a self-made man wandering the country.[68] Yet Dylan's evocation of authenticity had a collective function, encouraging others to "be themselves," although perhaps not everyone felt they could be as unique as Bob Dylan.[69]

Dylan's music invites us into a community of authentic citizens.[70] His songs' popularity suggests that they articulated ideas and feelings common to many. In addition, folk music, with its singable melodies, encourages group involvement. This, of course, was vitiated somewhat by folk "concerts," separating performer and audience. But in the early sixties, folk concerts took place at small coffeehouses, with many "regulars," creating a kind of community even within a concert setting. Furthermore, Dylan's music created a sense of solidarity among listeners.

A recording of "Who Killed Davey Moore?" reveals the feeling of community at a Dylan concert.[71] The song, the story of a boxer killed in the ring, builds dramatically as Dylan begins each verse with the question "Who killed Davey Moore?" only to receive a denial from the referee, the crowd, the boxer's manager, a gambler who bet on the fight, a sportswriter, and finally his opponent, the man who "laid him low." Dylan sings with a sense of urgency as he shouts the accusatory question in each verse. One can hear, and almost feel, the audience respond like a congregation to a preacher as he builds in intensity. They laugh when the song takes a humorous turn and applaud when Dylan expresses a strong sentiment with which they agree. Dylan's performance binds the audience together through shared emotional experience.

The emotional appeal of these songs is heightened by the music. The slow, triple meter strumming on songs like "Masters of War," "A Hard Rain's A-Gonna Fall," and "With God On Our Side," suggests a slow marching into battle, a gathering of forces for the confrontation. The music rises and falls in volume and in pitch, like an impassioned sermon. Dylan's singing itself is speechlike, passionate, and exhortational.

But does the emotional solidarity created by Dylan's music subsume individuality into a cult of celebrity, thus undercutting its democratic elements? To a degree perhaps, but such a tendency is countered by folk music's emphasis on individuality and by Dylan's emphatic refusal to present himself as a role model. In addition, the ideal of authenticity represented by Dylan's music at this time implies a kind of participatory democracy. In contrast to the elitism of high culture, nearly anyone could sing folk music; what mattered was not one's talent but the revelation of one's authentic self. Also, unlike high culture, folk music was tied up with life in a way that made it more accessible. Folksingers employed talking, chuckling, crying, and shouting as part of "singing" as well as (in traditional folk music) using household objects like washboards and jugs for instruments.[72] Admittedly, fighting aesthetic elitism is not the same as trying to eliminate its social and political counterpart. However, the ideal of authenticity supports political democracy, because it suggests that what is crucial is not expertise but rather that all perspectives be heard.

Despite its democratic tendencies, however, the concept of authenticity itself contains numerous problems. Most prominently, the notion of a core self upon which it is based has been called into question by Nietzsche and his postmodernist descendants, among others. Even granting the notion of a core self, it seems that Dylan violates the ideal of authenticity that his music conveys. After all, is it an expression of the authentic self for a middle-class Jewish singer from Minnesota to intone Appalachian folk melodies with a "hillbilly" accent ("The times they are *a-changin'*")?[73]

However, the judgment is less harsh if one sees artists as, in Henry Louis Gates's phrase, "cultural impersonators"; for Gates, *Famous All Over Town*, a novel of Chicano life written by a non-Hispanic under the pseudonym "Danny Santiago," perhaps "can usefully be considered a work of Chicano literature."[74] From this perspective, Dylan's use of the "folk" persona allowed him and his listeners access to parts of their identities otherwise inaccessible or discouraged by mainstream American culture. The folk self-presentation was partly a pose, but one that allowed musicians and listeners to experiment with incorporating values like honesty and skepticism toward dominant institutions into their everyday lives. Though based on a notion of true self that has been called into question by recent theory, the ideal of authenticity spurred artists and activists in the sixties to examine the ways social institutions shaped and disciplined them, and to explore alternate modes of being.

In sum, Dylan's early songs communicated the New Left's ideal of civic republicanism in concrete, experiential ways, educating for participatory democracy and creating community through images, music, and emotions. But how effectively did the songs politically educate? Several limitations are apparent.

First, Dylan's use of common, even hackneyed, symbols sometimes discourages the critical thinking that is a necessary part of democratic political education.

> Yes, 'n' how many seas must a white dove sail
> Before she sleeps in the sand?
> Yes, 'n' how many times must the cannon balls fly
> Before they're forever banned?[75]

On the one hand, this use of symbols in "Blowin' in the Wind" has a powerful impact upon many listeners. On the other, Dylan's use of stock symbols like the cannonball and the dove can provoke a standard response rather than producing real thought. Second, the dramatic opposition between good and evil, with no middle ground, in songs like "Masters of War" turns political actors into abstract symbols: "You that build all the guns / You that build the death planes / You that build the big bombs."[76] One could even argue that by dehumanizing his enemies this way, Dylan took on the very qualities he was criticizing, something he acknowledged later in 1964's "My Back Pages":

> Half-wracked prejudice leaped forth
> "Rip down all hate," I screamed
> Lies that life is black and white
> Spoke from my skull.[77]

Dylan seemed to be acknowledging that his protest songs displayed the simplistic, unthinking dogmatism of those he was trying to oppose.

Third, mystical and religious elements in Dylan's songs undercut his calls to political action. When Dylan uses natural events (rain, flood, thunder, waves) to symbolize political change, he seems to say: change will come, inevitably. Thus, when in "The Times They Are A-Changin'" he compares the political ferment of the sixties to a flood that cannot be stopped, politics no longer is something under the control of human beings but rather governed by natural or divine forces. The profusion of "sevens," signs, and portents in "Hollis Brown" (before the murders/suicide, "A cold coyote calls" as if a sign from God) suggests that poverty, and Brown and his family's death, is the result of such mystical forces rather than the distribution of wealth in America.[78]

This sense of inevitability is mirrored in the structure of the songs. Dylan's repetition of a phrase over and over like an incantation gives the songs a sense of moral urgency:

> Where the people are many and their hands are all empty,
> Where the pellets of poison are flooding their waters,
> Where the home of the valley meets the damp dirty prison,

> Where the executioner's face is always well hidden,
> Where hunger is ugly, where souls are forgotten
> Where black is the color, where none is the number. . . .[79]

At the same time, Dylan's incantations evoke a kind of religious or mystical romanticism reminiscent of Christopher Smart, Ginsberg, and Whitman.[80] This use of repetition suggests a sense of fatalism that undercuts Dylan's political message that we can change the world. Dylan also sometimes sees human events as circular, as in the end of "Ballad of Hollis Brown," when, after the death of the seven people on Brown's farm, "Somewhere in the distance / There's seven new people born."[81] This ending suggests that nothing really changes; the past just returns over and over. The modal, static harmony takes us out of the flow of history and creates a sense of timelessness that cuts against the contemporaneity and urgency of the song's message.

As time went on, the republican ideal of authenticity contained in Dylan's early songs waned in significance in sixties politics. Rather, a new vision of society arose corresponding to the politics of experience, emerging most fully in the counterculture, and Dylan's songs came to embody this vision. The counterculture rejected hierarchy, repudiating leadership and organization, and sought a nonrepressive society, calling for liberation of the body and freedom of thought from the barriers of conformity. In contrast to the early New Left notion of authenticity, here the emphasis was not on a core self but on expression, experimentation, and play, through which temporary selves are created and constantly recreated rather than discovered.[82] Central to all this is the surrealist belief, popularized by Marcuse, that a liberation of the unconscious—the realm of dreams, fantasies, childhood, and art—will lead to a better society.[83]

Surrealists saw art as the key to liberation from a society that restricted thought and action. Surrealism's vision of freedom grew out of psychoanalysis and its belief in the primacy of the unconscious and the damaging effects of repression on human freedom, energy, and creativity. However, while Freud stressed the tragic tension between society's need for repression and our boundless and potentially destructive instinctual energies, the surrealists saw in the unconscious an alternative world of creativity and joy that needed to be liberated from the shackles of civilization. They called such a liberation "total liberty," and saw the imagination as its catalyst.[84] Such liberty would not only free individuals but would remove artificial barriers that separate them from one another and from the world. The surrealists saw in dreams, play, the absurd, insanity, mad love *(l'amour fou),* and childhood a "higher reality" (sur-reality), the key to a lost unification between individuals and with the universe, which has been stifled by rigid logic and narrow, instrumental rationality.

Surrealism tried to create art that drew on the unconscious, but in the process it also called into question traditional European conceptions of art—art as a body of "works," separate from the rest of life. Artworks were merely vehicles; the ultimate goal was that everyday life take on some of the qualities of art. As Octavio Paz put it, "Surrealism proposes not so much the making of poems as the transformation of men into living poems."[85] Indeed, in 1939 André Breton called for the end of "durable" artworks in favor of planned or unplanned "events" or, as they came to be called in the late fifties and early sixties, "happenings."[86] The artist was not a creator but a passive recorder of "the marvelous" passing through his or her unconscious.[87]

Surrealists in the 1920s and 1930s used a number of means to gain access to the "surreality" that they called "the marvelous." One was "automatic writing," in which a person simply writes whatever is in his or her head without regard to logic and syntax, striving for "thought dictated in the absence of all control exerted by reason."[88] This was similar to Freud's technique of free association, but whereas Freud used free association as a path to rationality and control, the surrealists used it to loosen the hold of the ego and superego. They also devised ways to elicit the dream state in unwitting observers through the creation of absurd objects and situations. Fur teacups, useless machines, maps of impossible towns, paintings of melting watches, a loaf of bread fifteen yards long placed in a public square—these were meant to shock people out of their commonsense view of the world by literally creating an alternative reality.[89]

However, the surrealists' intention was not only to shock; rather, they juxtaposed apparently unrelated objects in order to reveal hidden connections between them. Thus a prototypical surrealist thinker once defined beauty as "the unexpected meeting, on a dissection table, of a sewing machine and an umbrella."[90] Such images were meant to jar the reader, breaking up established patterns of thought, but also to reveal the higher reality beneath the surface of everyday life. They were also designed to mirror and stimulate the kind of associative thinking that is characteristic of the unconscious.

Dylan's connections with surrealism are manifold. By the mid-sixties when Dylan took up rock, his frantic music and absurdist lyrics had a Beat-like spontaneity about them, suggesting the inspiration of intoxication, dreams, and free association.[91] Indeed, he has often cited the protosurrealists Rimbaud, Baudelaire, and Apollinaire as influences on his work, and his description of his method of composing at this time bears a striking resemblance to "automatic writing":

> [On my first three albums], I knew what I wanted to say, before I used to write the song. All the stuff which I had written before which wasn't song, was just on a piece of toilet paper. When it comes out like that it's the kind of stuff I would never sing because people would just not be ready for it. . . . [N]ow, I just write a song, like *I know* that it's just going to be all right and I don't really know exactly what it's all about, but I do know the minutes and the layers of what it's all about.[92]

Dylan here seems to say, if somewhat obscurely, that in his electric songs the free flow of imagination takes precedence over a predetermined content. Material which before might have been thrown away ("toilet paper") now remains in the song; even if the songs no longer have the logical coherence they once did ("I don't really know what it's all about"), they express the truth of Dylan's free psychic process, his "minutes and layers."

The new surrealist theme of freedom of imagination, play, and spontaneity in opposition to the isolation and confinement of individuals is anticipated in an early song, "Talkin' World War III Blues," on *The Freewheelin' Bob Dylan*, an album mostly made up of more overtly political songs like "Masters of War."

"Talkin' World War III Blues" begins, appropriately enough for a surrealistic song, with a dream:

> Some time ago a crazy dream came to me,
> I dreamt I was walkin' into World War Three.[93]

Disturbed by the dream, the narrator goes to a psychiatrist, who pronounces him "insane" but wants to hear about the dream anyway. Dylan then commences a rather disjointed, stream-of-consciousness style monologue in which he wanders around in a city devastated by nuclear war and tries to talk with various people. His attempts to communicate are constantly thwarted by the suspicions and hostilities of others: one fires a shotgun at him, the other runs away thinking he's a communist, and when he meets a woman and suggests they "play Adam and Eve," she cynically replies, "'Hey man, you crazy or sumpin' / You see what happened last time they started.'" Soon, however, the doctor interrupts him and tells him he's been having similar dreams, except that "I dreamt that the only person left after the war was me. / I didn't see you around." Then the narrator tells us that the doctor is not unique:

> Well, now time passed and now it seems
> Everybody's having them dreams.
> Everybody sees themselves walkin' around with no one else.

The song appears to end in despair—individuals are trapped in an atomistic society, with people too scared or cynical to communicate. Yet the final lines belie this despair and call forth a vision of community: "I'll let you be in my dreams if I can be in yours." Although apparently a retreat into the private consciousness of the dream world, then, the song ends by presenting the possibility of the overcoming of alienation by means of a shared vision. In his next albums, beginning with *Bringing it All Back Home*, Dylan brings the surrealist vision hinted at in "Talkin' World War III Blues" to fuller realization. Will these newer songs have the same faith in a shared vision? Will his songs encourage the exploration of consciousness for its own sake or in the service of a larger political liberation? Will these songs unite people in a shared consciousness or encourage them to retreat into their own private experience? Might this community of shared consciousness threaten individuality? How do these songs educate listeners in the politics of experience?

## III

*Life only seemed worth living where the threshold between waking and sleeping was worn away in everyone as by the steps of multitudinous images flooding back and forth, language only seemed itself where sound and image, image and sound interpenetrated with automatic precision and such felicity that no chink was left for the penny-in-the-slot called "meaning."*

—Walter Benjamin

From the first note of *Bringing It All Back Home* (March 1965) it is obvious that there is a new Dylan.[94] This album, along with *Highway 61 Revisited* (September 1965) and *Blonde on Blonde* (June 1966), burst through the folk paradigm and created a new sensibility.[95] In addition to electric instruments and rock music, which increased expressive possibilities but outraged the folk community, these works contain whimsical, sometimes baffling, wordplay reminiscent of the Beats and their surrealist predecessors rather than overtly political "protest" lyrics.[96]

Dylan's peers accused him of abandoning political and social concerns for a devotion to private, individual liberation, the freedom of each individual to pursue pleasure. Thus Joan Baez characterized Dylan's stance as "Let's all go home and smoke pot, because there's nothing else to do."[97] Dylan himself provided ample evidence for the notion that he was rejecting collective life in favor of escapist individualism. In an infamous, rambling speech accepting the Tom Paine award for his contribution to civil rights, he disavowed "anything trivial such as politics," although he did follow this with "I'm thinking about the general people and when they get hurt."[98] He often repudiated what he called "message type" or "finger-pointing" songs, even to the point of telling Phil Ochs that

> The stuff you're writing is bullshit. It's all unreal. The world is, well, it's just absurd. . . . What's wrong with the world goes much deeper than the bomb. What's wrong is how few people are free.[99]

Dylan saw politics, even protest politics, as a trap, another rigid ideology that limits and defines one's experiences.

Yet his statement to Ochs bears closer examination, because it suggests that while Dylan rejected traditional political methods he still cared about freedom. Even if few listeners hung on every word, as they had in Dylan's folk phase, the striking phrases that flowed into their ears helped create a kind of thought and experience consistent with the emancipatory ideals of the counterculture—most particularly, its rejection of hierarchy: "There are no kings inside the gates of Eden."[100] This rejection encompassed an attack on social authority, particularly as embodied in norms and expectations. However, it also represented a more general renunciation of any ordering systems of life, including the organization of time by the clock and the imperative toward economic production that it implied; aesthetic standards and the difference between art and non-art, "high" and "low" culture; and the rule of the rational ego over other parts of the self.[101] In the place of rational systems of valuation, Dylan's songs celebrate spontaneity, experience for its own sake, and play, and conjure up an image of radical democracy, or even anarchy. This meaning is partly communicated through lyrics, but Dylan's delivery of those lyrics, and the music that accompanied them, heightens their effect on the listener.

Dylan's songs of 1965 and 1966 portray people constrained by societal expectations and value systems.

> While one who sings with his tongue on fire
> Gargles in the rat race choir

Bent out of shape from society's pliers
Cares not to come up any higher
But rather get you down in the hole
That he's in.[102]

Here, consistent with the ideas of the counterculture (and the New Left), Dylan attacks a society that prescribes a life built around the pursuit of economic gain and rigid patterns of human relationship (marriage and employer-employee, among others). In response to pressures for conformity, Dylan says, "I got nothing, Ma, to live up to."

Dylan rejects not only rules and standards for success in life, but traditional cultural and aesthetic valuations as well. In "Ballad of a Thin Man," Dylan suggests that high culture is simply irrelevant, unable to prepare us for modern life. "Mister Jones" is well-versed in high culture, yet none of it has prepared him for living in a radically changing society; the old culture and values are no longer sufficient:

You've been with the professors
And they've all liked your looks
With great lawyers you have
Discussed lepers and crooks
You've been through all of
F. Scott Fitzgerald's books
You're very well read
It's well known

Yet, Mr. Jones is still uncomprehending:

Because something is happening here
But you don't know what it is
Do you, Mister Jones?[103]

In opposition to the New York Intellectuals' notion that high culture and traditional aesthetic values promote freedom, Dylan portrays them as a constraint.

In place of high art, Dylan celebrates popular culture. On the album cover of *Bringing it All Back Home* Dylan sits surrounded by various pop and folk cultural icons: a magazine with Jean Harlow on the cover; albums by African American bluesman Robert Johnson, Lotte Lenya, Eric Anderson, and the Impressions; and Dylan's own album *Another Side of Bob Dylan*. He is surrounded by a swirling light that distorts everything in its path, suggesting a halo that proclaims, like Ginsberg's "footnote" to "Howl," that all is holy.[104]

More generally, Dylan attacks the separation between high and low culture by mixing symbols from both realms in his songs, creating scenes in which, for example, not only does Beethoven roll over but literally lies down with the blues singer Ma Rainey.[105] (The confluence of black and white culture is also present in this image.) "Desolation Row" portrays cultural luminaries in absurd situations, calling into question traditional societal and aesthetic standards: Einstein, "disguised as Robin Hood," "bum[s] a cigarette" and goes off "sniffing drainpipes / And reciting the alphabet," while Ezra Pound and T. S. Eliot, are "[f]ighting in the captain's tower / While calypso singers laugh at them."[106] In other songs, particularly on *Highway 61 Revisited*, symbols of authority and fictional characters from high culture like Paul Revere, Einstein, Romeo, Ophelia, Galileo, Beethoven, the Good Samaritan, John the Baptist, "the Commander in Chief," Eliot, and Pound cavort with "freaks," "geeks," and low-culture icons like the "one-eyed midget," "the king of the Philistines," Cinderella, the Hunchback of Notre Dame, the Phantom of the Opera, mermaids, "Dr. Filth," and "the sword swallower," suggesting all are equally important. Even the title *Blonde on Blonde* is a merging of the avant-garde concept of "white on white" paintings, in which one shade of white is superimposed upon another, with the American popular cultural symbol of "the blonde."

Like the Beats whom he admired, Dylan ultimately calls into question the notion that art is separate from and more perfect than life itself. In response to the question, "Do you think of yourself primarily as a singer or a poet?," he replied, "Oh I think of myself more as a song and dance man, y'know."[107] Leaving on a botched beginning to "Bob Dylan's 115th Dream" makes the same point—this is no work of art; when Dylan bursts out laughing after the failed introduction, he is laughing at the listener's expectations of completeness and finitude.[108]

Art for Dylan is no longer a means of romantic self-expression; rejecting the idea of a true self, he seems to say that there is only the flux of experiences. When he says "i accept chaos," the use of the lower case suggests a dethroning of the rational ego, a call for what Susan Sontag, referring to Artaud, calls a "[d]emocracy of mental claims."[109] Although a poem or a song presents "a naked person," that person has no core self or essence but, in Whitman's words, "contains multitudes."[110]

Although as a folk musician he strove for naturalness and truth, in these later songs Dylan celebrates free expression, even invention, for its own sake. As his references in the liner notes of *Bringing It All Back Home* to "false eyelashes," "dark sunglasses," and "pierced ears" suggest, the focus is now on artifice, costume, pose, and design.[111] Whereas on the cover of *The Times They Are A-Changin'* he appears in a grainy "realist" black-and-white photograph wearing a work shirt, his later albums feature him in outrageous psychedelic clothes and accoutrements like purple cuff links. In the cover photograph of *Bringing It All Back Home* the bank of light surrounding Dylan, which I earlier interpreted as a halo, can also be viewed as a frame, painting's tribute to artifice. However, whereas in traditional paintings the frame contains the aesthetic and separates it from the world, here the swirling distortion suggests that the boundary between art and world is not so clear.

This attack on social organization, standards, and hierarchy is embodied in the form and structure of the songs as well as in their lyrics. Most popular and folk songs, including Dylan's early works, tell a story building to a climax and conveying a message. Such form embraces an orderly, progressive notion of time, and a sense of meaning to its passage. In contrast, songs like "Subterranean Homesick Blues" fail to tell a coherent story or convey a clear message, calling into question temporal progress and meaning. While most popular songs have a lead instrument or voice to create order, in Dylan's songs the instruments are nearly equal in volume with each other and with the vocal, each vying for attention, with few solos. The song creates in the listener the experience of time as a stream of moments without an ordering system and without significant events to structure it.[112]

Dylan evokes a similar experience by radically shortening the line:

Maggie comes fleet foot
Face full of black soot
Talkin' that the heat put
Plants in the bed but
The phone's tapped anyway . . .[113]

Here the song is reduced to a series of words and the words themselves to sounds and syllables. Dylan creates this effect both by the percussive, one-syllable words that punctuate the song ("Badge out, laid off") and by his flat, clipped delivery. While for Arnold and Trilling art imposes order on a chaotic universe or society, "Subterranean Homesick Blues" portrays life as a series of discrete, unconnected sensations, none of which take precedence over another and which together constitute no coherent, meaningful reality.

At other times, Dylan subverts stability and order by singing Beat-like long lines, in which he tries to squeeze the continuous flow of his thoughts into one breath, threatening to burst the boundaries of song structure: "But even the president of the United States / Sometimes must have / To stand naked."[114] In another instance Dylan plays a fairly traditional blues but makes the final line of each verse a practically unsingable string of words: "Your brand-new leopard-skin pill-box hat."[115] Here words are no longer used to fill a line whose length is set by songlike melodies. Instead, the sentence takes precedence over the line; it determines the length of the line rather than vice versa. Thus the sentence from everyday life threatens the boundaries of art.

These alterations in song structure make the songs less participatory. Although Dylan did produce tuneful songs like "Rainy Day Women #12 & 35" ("Everybody must get stoned"), it is hard to imagine singing along with "Subterranean Homesick Blues" or "It's Alright Ma (I'm Only Bleeding)."[116] In this sense, Dylan was moving away from the early New Left republican ideal and toward a more individualistic aesthetic.

Through lyrics, music, and structure, then, Dylan's electric songs call into question social and aesthetic hierarchies. Yet Dylan's work at this time does not simply tear down boundaries; it contains a positive vision as well. This surrealist vision encompasses the liberation of the unconscious, the celebration of play, and the unity of all individuals in "the marvelous."

These themes can be seen most fully in "Subterranean Homesick Blues." Although the song on first hearing seems like a collection of nonsense verses, perhaps out of a child's jump-rope song, upon closer inspection it contains an attack on the empty rituals of conventional society:

> Ah get born, keep warm
> Short pants, romance, learn to dance
> Get dressed, get blessed
> Try to be a success

The song begins by referring to someone who is "in the basement"—that is, "subterranean." On a literal level, "underground" refers to hiding from the police. There are many images of being trailed by agents in trench coats, hiding, having one's phone tapped, and so on.[117] "Underground" has a larger philosophical meaning, however. Like Dostoevsky's "Underground Man" or Ellison's "Invisible Man," who also lives in a basement, Dylan's subterranean rejects conventional values and lifestyles.[118] The refrain, "Look out kid / It's something you did/God knows when / But you're doin' it again" suggests that the subterranean man is not a criminal by virtue of a specific violation of the law; rather, the transgression is a fundamental opposition to society and its values. This reading suggests that withdrawal is the solution.

But a third understanding of the "subterranean" metaphor leads to a more positive, and potentially political, idea of freedom: going underground entails exploring buried realms of consciousness that are ignored or repressed in mainstream society. Here the underground is the unconscious, to be experienced through drugs ("Mixing up the medicine") or sexual liberation. As opposed to the sterile, utilitarian vision presented in the stanza quoted above ("get born, keep warm"), the song puts forward the idea of play, the nonutilitarian liberation of individual creativity: "Don't follow leaders / Watch the parkin' meters."[119] In a sense, then, Dylan's return to rock brought back the fifties music's theme of pleasure, though tied even more explicitly to the body and to a vision of social transformation.

Songs like "Subterranean Homesick Blues" also celebrate connection between people and between individuals and the world. The surrealist rhymes and opposing images that dominate Dylan's songs express a vision of psychic freedom, but they also suggest a unity of the world and people in "the marvelous." In some of Dylan's earlier works ("Masters of War," "Times They Are A-Changin'"), rhyming is a rhetorical device reinforcing an urgent moral message.

> And the Negro's name
> Is used it is plain
> For the politician's gain
> As he rises to fame
> And the poor white remains
> On the caboose of the train
> But it ain't him to blame
> He's only a pawn in their game.[120]

The rhyming in "Subterranean Homesick Blues," by contrast, uses sound to connect apparently unrelated ideas.

> Get sick, get well
> Hang around a[n] ink well
> Ring bell, hard to tell
> If anything is goin' to sell
> Try hard, get barred
> Get back, write braille
> Get jailed, jump bail

Connecting seemingly dissimilar ideas by rhyme questions our conception of a logical, orderly world and strives to create a dreamlike reality based on association, the principle of the unconscious. Such rhyming suggests that an unconscious logic connects the apparently separate objects in the world, striving to overcome fetishism and world-alienation.

Antitheses serve a similar purpose. In the earlier songs, oppositions are used to point out injustice: "Heard one person starve, I heard many people laughin.'"[121] In his later songs, like "Tombstone Blues," Dylan juxtaposes radically opposing images for a different reason:

> The ghost of Belle Starr she hands down her wits
> To Jezebel the nun she violently knits
> A bald wig for Jack the Ripper who sits
> At the head of the chamber of commerce[122]

Juxtapositions like these evoke the hallucinatory visions brought on by drugs or dreams. Like the surrealist "fur teacup" or Rimbaud's "arctic flowers," the image of a "bald wig" asks the listener to bring into play the imagination unhampered by conventional logic.[123] Jezebel the nun, "violently knits," and the vision of Jack the Ripper at the head of the Chamber of Commerce suggest an overturning of the established order and the return of repressed aggression and sexuality. Dylan also subverts our sense of order and meaning by reversing phrases within a sentence, as in "I ordered some suzette, I said / 'Could you please make that crepe,'" or "he just smoked my eyelids / An' punched my cigarette."[124] But these juxtapositions suggest connections between apparent opposites as well.

More generally, the "honky-tonk" piano and electric organ of "Ballad of a Thin Man" conjure up "the marvelous" by evoking dance halls, old movie theaters, and soap operas, nostalgic icons of popular culture. As Walter Benjamin said of Breton:

> He was the first to perceive the revolutionary energies that appear in the "outmoded," in the first iron constructions, the first factory buildings, the earliest photos, the objects that have begun to be extinct, grand pianos, the dresses of five years ago, fashionable restaurants when the vogue has begun to ebb from them.[125]

"Rainy Day Women #12 & 35," featuring a New Orleans-style march, complete with the "oompah" of a tuba, "tailgate" trombone, and "whoops" from the crowd, evokes a similar atmosphere.

Surrealism, then, helps us to understand how Dylan's mid-sixties work, though abandoning overtly political topics, is a vehicle for attacking social, aesthetic, and psychic hierarchy in the service of a politics of experience. These songs thus are part of the counterculture's attempt to widen the capacity for experience, particularly of the unconscious. Contrary to a move "back to nature" in some quarters of the counterculture, Dylan's music celebrates artificiality, urging individuals and groups to invent themselves and their worlds, using the imagination as a guide.

More concretely, Dylan's electric music seems to call for, and create experience preparatory for, a fundamentally altered society. It envisions a rejection of the work ethic, of fixed roles and expectations, and even of the ordering of the day by the clock and its call for productivity and delay of immediate gratification. In short, this music evokes the Marcusean vision, influenced by the surrealists, of the end of repression and the emancipation of the id. Consistent with Marcuse, art is one of the means for bringing about such a mode of existence.

Politically, this individual emancipation and rejection of authority is ambiguous. An attack on hierarchy might support democracy, where decisions are made by consensus among equal individuals, as in countercultural communes. A more extreme version could lead to anarchy. But could the vision contained in Dylan's electric music be translated into actual politics? The surrealists thought of themselves as social and political revolutionaries. They often used two phrases to state their goals: "To change life" (Rimbaud) and "To transform the world" (Marx).[126] For a while they allied themselves with the Communist Party, and then Trotsky.[127] Yet they never pursued politics systematically; the demands of organizations and the need for compromises never appealed to their spirit. On some level, they were not interested in politics. As Breton put it,

> For us revolutionaries it is of little importance which conception of society is preferable. . . . Our general attitude . . . must

be in the direction of a *revolutionary reality*, and must take us there by any means and at any price.[128]

On a more general level, their political vision is problematic. They seem to assume a unitary "surreality" that will unite everyone, but what if people's dreams and fantasies lead them in different directions? In reality, the surrealists were held together by Breton and his sometimes dictatorial stance rather than by a shared experience of "the marvelous." To what extent does the liberation of the unconscious and the imagination bring people together and to what extent does it tear them apart? This question, arising naturally in an analysis of the surrealists, came back to haunt their descendants in the counterculture of the 1960s.

Even if the surrealistic unity called for by the counterculture and evoked in Dylan's songs were achievable, it would be troublesome politically. First, politics, though seeking to create some kinds of harmony, takes place where there is conflict and limited resources. As such, politics demands choices, not the infinite reveling in equal possibilities. In democratic politics, those choices are made collectively and publicly, but without choices there is no politics. Second, democratic politics requires the recognition of differences, which the surrealist vision of unification threatens. The community envisioned by surrealism seems to exclude individuals whose inner life differs from that of the majority. Finally, although bringing politics down to the realm of the feelings through music helped make it less abstract and more connected with everyday life, the danger is that sensation becomes an end in itself, in contrast to more public goals. Dylan's retreat into the private imagination, away from politics and collective life, soon became even more apparent.

## IV

Despite their limitations, Dylan's songs in the mid-sixties imagined a kind of community. Yet as time went on, the songs offered less a shared vision than Dylan's private fantasies. Much of "Desolation Row," for example, while containing provocative images, is virtually incomprehensible:

Dr. Filth, he keeps his world
Inside of a leather cup
But all of his sexless patients
They're trying to blow it up
Now his nurse, some local loser
She's in charge of the cyanide hole
And she also keeps the cards that read
"Have mercy on His Soul"
They all play penny whistles
You can hear them blow
If you lean your head out far enough
From Desolation Row[129]

"Talkin' World War III Blues" and "Desolation Row" both explore dreams, but whereas the former offers the possibility of a shared vision ("I'll let you be in my dreams if I can be in yours"), the latter revels in its own solipsism. It is ironic that Dylan opposes the alienation and the lack of communication of mainstream society (the "wasted words" of "It's Alright Ma"; the incomprehension of "Mister Jones"), yet, like his surrealist forebears, sometimes ends up speaking a private language. Given a series of practically random images, listeners interpret and connect them according to their unconscious associations, constructing their own "reality." Meaning is no longer objective and public, but private.

Dylan's press interviews at the time reveal a similar rejection of meaning. These interviews are dadaist subterfuges, in which he answers questions about the meaning of his songs, his intentions, or his feelings with a joke, nonsense, another question, or whatever happens to come into his head at the time.

*Do you consider yourself a politician?*
Do I consider myself a politician? Oh, I guess so. I have my own party, though.
*Does it have a name?*
No. There's no presidents in the party—there's no presidents, or vice presidents, or secretaries or anything like that, so it makes it kinda hard to get in.

> *Is there any right wing or left wing in that party?*
> No. It's more or less in the center—kind of on the Uppity scale. . .
> *Is there anyone else in your party?*
> No. Most of us don't even know each other, y'know. It's hard to tell who's in it and who's not in it. . . .
> *What are your own personal hopes for the future and what do you hope to change in the world?*
> Oh, my hopes for the future: to be honest, you know, I don't have any hopes for the future and I just hope to have enough boots to be able to change them. That's all really, it doesn't boil down to anything more than that. If it did, I would certainly tell you.[130]

When called to task for such answers, Dylan argued for the impossibility of shared meanings for words and therefore of real communication:

> I just know in my own mind that we all have a different idea of all the words we're using. . . . I really can't take [this interview] too seriously because . . . if I say the word 'house' . . . we're both going to see a different house. . . . So we're all using these other words like "mass production" and "movie magazine" and we all have a different idea of these words, too, so I don't even know what we're saying.[131]

With its lack of faith in the ability of people to communicate about a common world, such an attitude seems quite distant from the New Left's vision of participatory democracy.

The surrealists thought that the liberation of the unconscious would lead to the transformation of society. "To win the energies of intoxication for the revolution" was how Benjamin described the surrealist project.[132] They believed that art, by evoking the dream world, would break down barriers between people, "loosen[ing] . . . individuality like a bad tooth."[133] Dylan's mid-sixties work encouraged an antihierarchical sensibility that might have contributed to movements for political democracy. Instead, it facilitated a retreat into the exploration of purely private consciousness. Dylan, perhaps like the surrealists themselves, ultimately retreated into hermetic individualism, although others found inspiration from him for their own quest for individual exploration.[134]

In the end, Dylan's songs captured, and helped listeners experience, important political ideas in each half of the sixties. These conceptions ranged from civic republicanism, with its faith in truth and authenticity, to the politics of experience and its call for psychic liberation and an end to hierarchy. As we have seen, his work also reflects some of the problems inherent in those notions: the early New Left's unreflective faith in singular truths of self and society and the counterculture's tendency toward anomic individualism. One might wish to blame him for this; yet, it is surely too much to ask of an artist that he or she single-handedly resolve the difficult tensions that arise in political action. And despite their limitations, Dylan's songs helped listeners toward new ways of being and thinking that were necessary, though clearly not sufficient, conditions for political transformation.

# *Conclusion*

## I

The political art of the fifties and sixties and the writings of the New York Intellectuals reveal the varied and subtle ways art educates citizens for democracy. In the service of a number of different visions of democracy—liberalism in the fifties, the "beloved community" of the civil rights movement, the civic republicanism of the early New Left, and the politics of experience of the late sixties—artworks brought political ideas and ideals into the realm of the senses and into the moral and emotional lives of individuals. More specifically, the critics and artists discussed in this book sought to expose the nature of political reality. The New York Intellectuals in their early writings thought that works of art could evoke and reveal the breakdown of modern capitalism. The dissonances of jazz helped listeners experience—more directly than an essay might—a society torn apart by racial tensions. Dylan in his early songs sought to expose the reality of political corruption and violence.

Artworks also educated by encouraging questioning. Trilling thought the novel could unsettle readers enough, by creating inner conflict, to get them to reevaluate deeply held moral prejudices. The later Dylan through surrealist juxtapositions and the dismantling of traditional song form hoped to free the unconscious forces of fantasy and free association, setting up an inner clash among id, ego, and socially internalized superego.

Finally, musicians in the sixties helped listeners imagine alternatives. "Free jazz" musicians created a musical beloved community, depicting racial equality and making accessible to the senses a vision of freedom reconciling individuality and group solidarity. The songs of the early Dylan embodied an ideal of authenticity that made its way into the everyday lives of many of his listeners. Dylan's later songs sought to produce in the listener a new consciousness for the counterculture.

These three facets of political education—revealing political reality, encouraging questioning, and imagining alternatives—were facilitated in subtle ways, through both content and form.[1] The New York Intellectuals showed how artworks educate through their content—in their case, the stories presented in novels. But in their early, Marxist embrace of modernism, they also saw form as educative: the dissolution of aesthetic form revealed bourgeois society's instability. The "Freedom Now Suite" told a political story, while "free jazz" musicians created political meaning through the form of free improvisation itself. Dylan's early songs conveyed a political message through lyrics, but the genre of folksinging itself, with its emphasis on "realness" over seamless technique, communicated the ideal of authenticity. His late sixties work used words to call up unconscious associations but also sought to loosen the hold of the ego through the dissolution of traditional structure.

My analysis of the diverse ways a work communicates political meaning suggests that current discussions of the arts' social impact are profoundly simplistic. Denunciations of rap, rock lyrics, and performance art focus solely on overt content without taking into account form, structure, or audience reception. A statement contained in a song's lyrics may be contradicted (or complicated) by its "formal" features. Clearly, the political meaning of a work of art is rarely a simple or unitary one.

The subtle and varied political meanings communicated by artworks and the complex, multilayered manner they embody those meanings call into question contemporary conservative attacks on political art, particularly that of the sixties. Conservatives see sixties art as profoundly antidemocratic. They argue that artworks encouraged anarchy rather than democracy, rejecting reason in favor of the unregulated unconscious. Daniel Bell, for example, contends that, in contrast to an earlier generation of radicals, including those who would become the New York Intellectuals, sixties activists' ideology represented "an attack on reason itself"; for Hilton Kramer, the activism of the decade constituted "an insidious assault on mind."[2] Similarly, according to a best-selling book by Allan Bloom, rock music is hostile to democracy because it encourages an anarchic liberation of desires, creating a protofascist community based on "shared feelings, bodily contact and grunted formulas."[3] Conservatives also argue that the sixties' warped concept of democracy obliterated distinctions between good and bad art, rejecting traditional aesthetic standards and in the process encouraging moral and political relativism. They contend that these attacks on tradition are incompatible with democracy because they lead to violence rather than debate and reject all rules and order in favor of individual desire.[4]

In this book, we have seen that important works of art in the sixties encouraged democracy rather than violence or antinomian individualism. The best works by free-jazz musicians and Bob Dylan contained a vision of community based on shared experience, but also on mutuality, respect for individuality, and (sometimes) authenticity. Even in the later Dylan, an attack on social conventions and a call for the liberation of individual consciousness is a precursor not to anarchy but to a new kind of community, although perhaps an unachievable one. Art that encouraged solipsism, antinomianism, and violence represented the breakdown of the sixties, not its culmination.

Conservatives' negative political evaluation of sixties art is primarily a function of their dislike of New Left politics. For them, "participatory democracy" can only lead to fascistic mob rule, and real democracy can only be liberal pluralist politics managed by elites. Theirs is a bifurcated world in which the only alternative to existing norms and institutions is the absence of norms and institutions; therefore, art that questions existing ways of thinking and acting can only be an invitation to anarchy. Conservative criticisms do not take into account the possibility that the rejection of what exists might be part of a project of building new ways of being, political and otherwise.

Based on their analysis of the sixties, conservatives argue that the arts should in some important way be disassociated from politics—"above politics," as it is sometimes put.[5] According to this perspective, critics and artists should be "disinterested," part of an "independent high culture" separate from popular culture and politics.[6] Conservatives like Kramer argue that when artworks serve political purposes, both art and politics become debased: aesthetic quality suffers by its subordination to political purpose, and political ideas are reduced to slogans and emotions. In their view, although artworks can safely address universal political themes like the dangers of radical change, when art is more directly tied to political goals or movements, it inevitably becomes propaganda.[7] This line of thought leads to the perverse conclusion that the only works that can safely have a political impact are those that disavow a political purpose.

My case studies show that the political visions contained in important sixties artworks are anything but simplistic and propagandistic. Works like "Free Jazz," the "Freedom Now Suite," "Folk Forms No. 1," "Ballad of Hollis Brown," "Bob Dylan's 115th Dream," and "Subterranean Homesick Blues" embody complex political ideas drawn from the civil rights movement, the New Left, and the counterculture without sacrificing artistic integrity. Indeed, the complexity of their political visions is an integral part of their aesthetic excellence. Citing George Orwell I would argue that a political purpose is precisely what gives these works their substance and richness:

> [L]ooking back through my work, I see that it is invariably where I lacked a *political* purpose that I was betrayed into purple passages, sentences without meaning, decorative adjectives and humbug generally.[8]

## II

In the introduction to this book I argued that while the capacity of artworks to engage the senses and the emotions gives them the ability to politically educate for democracy, this engagement can also bring people together in an antidemocratic manner or draw people away from politics altogether. To what extent did criticism and artworks in the fifties and sixties undermine democracy by encouraging an emotionally fused community that submerges individuality? Were the New York Intellectuals correct in their assertion that popular culture promotes conformity and discourages independent thought? To what degree do the artworks in this book draw audiences away from politics altogether? Let us now look at these issues in relation to the New York Intellectuals, sixties jazz musicians, and Bob Dylan.

The New York Intellectuals praised works of art that preserved individuality and criticized those that in their view promoted conformity; yet their critique of popular culture and their attempt to encourage independent thought ultimately failed. Their analyses of mass culture are flawed by ahistoricism, which is surprising coming from writers who sought to bring political concerns to criticism. An overestimation of the power of literature also led them (particularly Trilling) to neglect institutional and structural sources of conformity (e.g., consumer capitalism). More importantly, the very fear of communism and the "masses" that led them to criticize mass culture created its own conformity. Even in the Intellectuals' critiques of what they labeled "mass culture" they sometimes resorted to clichés and unexamined assumptions in the name of "realism." Their criticism could have helped readers examine dominant anticommunist assumptions but instead uncritically reproduced them.

Similarly, against the New Critics the Intellectuals argued for politically engaged literature, literature that would promote responsible political action. But although they sometimes thought art could encourage liberal values (tolerance, rationality, individuality) throughout society, in the end, like their hero Matthew Arnold, they abandoned politics because they saw society as beyond redemption: art could only preserve liberal values for detached elite intellectuals. Literature then became a means for intellectuals to preserve political ideas while remaining aloof from actual politics. The Intellectuals' criticism also drew citizens away from politics by overemphasizing literature's role as a teacher of the dangers of action rather than an aid to it. In a sense, this emphasis gives art a political role, but one that reinforces passivity toward the status quo.

By the sixties, artists and activists embraced the values of community and mass political action rejected by the New York Intellectuals. Community had become an ideal for both the civil rights movement and the New Left. Both movements drew on a vision of a society that could overcome the alienation of individuals from one another and from themselves, and artworks helped to articulate and elaborate this vision. Max Roach in the "Freedom Now Suite" constructed a narrative connecting African Americans with their past and future. "Free jazz" musicians through collective improvisation musically enacted a community that preserved and enhanced individuality in the manner of the "beloved community." However, in the wake of the de-emphasis of this ideal in favor of black power, jazz works in the later sixties submerged individuals into a whole. Aesthetically, a community that preserved individuality gave way to an embrace of uniformity. Society failed to support the beloved community because of liberalism's opposition to its basic tenets and, more importantly, because of resistance to racial equality.

Bob Dylan created a different kind of community. In his early, acoustic period, he helped construct a community of "folk" fans, centered around coffeehouses and small nightclubs. The music itself invited listeners into a republican community of authentic souls; if social masks and games were abandoned, it seemed to say, citizens would see and embrace each other as they really were. A politics of deception would give way to a politics of consensus. Dylan's realist narratives also encouraged empathy between races and classes. This notion of egalitarian community was undercut, however, by Dylan's star status, which grew at a rapid rate. Such star worship can lead individuals to lose themselves in the excitement of the crowd in a way that is in tension with democracy's notion of individual action.

Dylan's early songs also to some degree encouraged standardized, clichéd thinking by their use of stock symbols. Yet these songs are more than such symbols; thoughtful statements coexist with stock phrases. Against the New York Intellectuals and other critics of mass culture I would argue that the use of clichés does not paralyze the critical facilities of audiences; some may be seduced by them but others may pay more attention to thought-provoking features. It is true that less-popular works may embody political meaning in a more complicated and subtle form, but like works of "free jazz" their capacity for political education is severely limited by the small size of their audience.

Despite its limitations, Dylan's early music engaged more people than the works of any other artist or critic discussed in this book. His early songs urged people to think about political topics; many of their listeners also were involved in political movements. As with any artwork, it was possible to put a Dylan album on the stereo and remain politically passive, but the songs' clear and forceful message made that more difficult. The raw, even grating, quality of their singing and guitar playing, his refusal to soothe and lull the listener, also discouraged complacency.

Dylan's late-sixties electric songs sought to break down the rational ego and unite members of the counterculture in an ecstatic community of unmediated desire. Such a merging was problematic in that it seemed to obliterate the individuality and rationality necessary for democracy. Ironically, Dylan's songs ultimately adopted the private language of his unconscious, antithetical to the shared meaning they once presupposed. Like Coltrane's "Ascension," which could not balance individual and group but only alternate soloing and group merging, Dylan's late-sixties music both urged group fusion through the unconscious and isolated listeners within the confines of their own fantasies.

At the same time, Dylan's late-sixties songs did encourage individuals to live differently and ultimately change society through the counterculture. Whether such action was truly political or not is a more complicated question. Dylan's music reinforced the politics of experience, urging expression and the liberation of the unconscious. But to the extent that such politics easily degenerated into liberal gratification (on some level, even consumerism), these songs drew people away from the more difficult political battles against the Vietnam War, racism, and poverty, among others.

Put differently, in the sixties' closing years aesthetic experience that could have been a precursor to political thought and action too often became an end in itself, a substitute for politics. A statement in

1967 by Tuli Kupferberg of the underground rock group the Fugs is symptomatic:

> I consider rock and roll revolutionary. I consider the Stones and The Beatles very important revolutionaries. . . . If everybody could dance [in an "orgiastic" way] . . . then the revolution could be accomplished.[9]

The counterculture sought to extend the New Left's project to bring politics from the level of abstract theory into the experience of everyday life: the *Port Huron Statement* and the Yippie set of demands are remarkably similar.[10] Tom Hayden had called for a "reassertion of the personal" in order to create a politics that would connect with people's daily lives, but the personal came to replace the political. The New Left's Declaration of Independence, the *Port Huron Statement,* was superseded by the Haight-Ashbury "Declaration of Independence," which guaranteed its own "inalienable rights"—"freedom of the body, pursuit of joy, and the expansion of consciousness."[11] The New Left's vision of community and participatory democracy was supplanted by the "old liberal utopia" of private gratification.[12]

Ironically, this shift was predicted by one of the intellectual fathers of the counterculture, Herbert Marcuse. In his *Essay on Liberation,* Marcuse announced the emergence of a new revolutionary sensibility; the "rebels" of the sixties "link liberation with the dissolution of ordinary and orderly perception." Although seemingly private, the personal exploration of new forms of experience "anticipates, in a distorted manner," the "revolution in perception" that is a necessary part of social revolution. However, he warned that such a search for sensibility could become an end in itself and thereby be co-opted into the reigning ethic of consumption.[13] If the case studies in this book are representative, his fears seem to have been at least partly realized.

## III

Despite their potential for political education, democratic artworks are rare, the movements surrounding them short-lived. In each case studied here, artists and critics relatively quickly abandoned or downplayed the democratic features of their work or theory. The New York Intellectuals' promising ideas about the arts' role in encouraging genuine experience and critical thought too often gave way to their own ideological thinking. "Free jazz" music that made accessible a unique democratic vision was replaced by an enactment of solidarity at the expense of inclusiveness and individuality. Rock music that sought to liberate individuals from immoral and conformist politics for a better community ended up encouraging a retreat into private experience for its own sake.

In part, the reason for this retreat from politics is that the alternatives to democratic artworks are so seductive. The aesthetic qualities that can make artworks' political meaning effective also exert a lure away from politics. It is as if a democratic artwork is an unstable chemical compound, which easily transforms itself and can retain its structure only under very limited conditions.

Another explanation for this instability lies in the fragility of democracy itself. Democracy gives individuals a large responsibility for the collective good; it is easier to retreat into the order and stability of the crowd, to act vicariously through a strong leader. Perhaps, as Wolin has suggested, democracy is not so much a form of government as a series of infrequent moments of popular political action.[14]

In the sixties, disillusion with democracy grew out of society's resistance to change and a growing impatience on the part of activists.[15] Process often became less important than results, and sometimes frustration with the barriers to political transformation led to violence. Under such conditions, it is not surprising that artworks teaching democratic values became rarer.

This experience illustrates crucial limits on art's ability to further democracy: for art to perform this function, there must be a political environment to support it. Without an active citizenry and a society that encourages and facilitates democratic practice, no work of art can politically educate very effectively; its message falls on deaf ears. It is too much to ask of artworks that they maintain a democratic vision in the midst of an undemocratic society. As Theodor Adorno said of Schoenberg, "It is not the composer who fails in the work; history, rather, denies the work in itself."[16]

An awareness of the limitations of the power of artworks to politically educate for democracy should not discourage us, however, or blind us to art's capacity for such education. At its best, art can make complex political visions accessible to citizens, bringing them into the life of the mind and the emotions, encouraging tolerance, critical thinking, and empathy. Though the theorists and artists of the fifties and sixties ultimately were unable to hold onto their fragile democratic visions, when another movement for political renewal arises, it will undoubtedly be accompanied by the sights and sounds of democratic artworks.

# Notes

## *Introduction*

1. Timothy Dwight, "Introduction to *Greenfield Hill*," in *The American Literary Revolution, 1783–1837,* ed. Robert E. Spiller (Garden City, N.Y.: Doubleday-Anchor, 1967), pp. 18–19.

2. For an example of this thesis see Fredric Jameson, *The Political Unconscious: Narrative as a Socially Symbolic Act* (Ithaca: Cornell University Press, 1981). Rejecting "the distinction between those texts that are social and political and those that are not," Jameson asserts that "there is nothing that is not social and historical—indeed . . . everything is 'in the last analysis' political" (p. 20).

3. See Daniel Bell, *The Cultural Contradictions of Capitalism* (New York: Basic Books, 1978) and Allan Bloom, *The Closing of the American Mind* (New York: Simon & Schuster, 1987), among others. For a more detailed discussion of this perspective, see the conclusion to this book.

4. Ibid. as well as Joseph Epstein, "The Literary Life Today," *New Criterion* 1, no. 1 (September 1982): 6–15.

5. Hanna Pitkin persuasively argues, using Wittgenstein, that words only take on meaning from their context. The "meaning" of a term, then, consists of a cluster of related ideas, not reducible to one alone, that come out of its varying contexts. Hanna Pitkin, *Wittgenstein and Justice* (Berkeley: University of California Press, 1972), esp. p. 98.

6. See Adrian Henri, *Total Art: Environments, Happenings, and Performance* (New York: Oxford University Press, 1974); Edward Lucie-Smith, *Movements in Art since 1945* (London: Thames & Hudson, 1969); and Lucy Lippard, *Pop Art* (New York: Praeger, 1966).

7. These terms are not the only ones to suggest the two different approaches to democracy. Another way of putting it would be "representative" and "direct"

democracy. However, what I am interested in is not whether representation exists, but whether large numbers of citizens participate in ways other than voting. According to David Held, "The models could reasonably be divided into two broad types: direct or participatory democracy . . . and liberal or representative democracy . . . ." *Models of Democracy* (Stanford, Calif.: Stanford University Press, 1987), p. 4. See also Graeme Duncan, ed., *Democratic Theory and Practice* (Cambridge: Cambridge University Press, 1983), especially the essay by Carole Pateman, "Feminism and Democracy," which divides democracy into liberal and participatory modes.

The literature of democratic theory is vast. Works important to my thinking include Sheldon Wolin, *The Presence of the Past* (Baltimore: Johns Hopkins University Press, 1989); Wolin, "Fugitive Democracy," *Constellations* 1, no. 1 (April 1994); and Joshua Miller, *The Rise and Fall of Democracy in Early America, 1630–1789* (University Park: The Pennsylvania State University Press, 1991).

8. See John Stuart Mill, "Civilization" and "Inaugural Address" in *Mill's Essays on Literature and Society,* ed. J. B. Schneewind (New York: Collier, 1965).

9. For attempts to rethink liberalism in light of modern critics, see Alfonso J. Damico, ed., *Liberals on Liberalism* (Totowa, N.J.: Rowman & Littlefield, 1986) and Nancy L. Rosenblum, ed., *Liberalism and the Moral Life* (Cambridge: Harvard University Press, 1989).

10. Important modern exponents of this view include T. S. Eliot (see chapter 1); José Ortega y Gasset, *The Revolt of the Masses* (New York: Norton, 1932); and defenders of fascism—see Nathanael Greene, ed., *Fascism: An Anthology* (Arlington Heights, Ill.: AHM, 1968).

11. Plato, *Republic* 558c. The quotation is from Raymond Larson, trans., *The Republic* (Arlington Heights, Ill.: Harlan Davidson, 1979), p. 216.

12. The following paragraphs on the educative function of political theory are indebted to John H. Schaar, *Legitimacy in the Modern State* (New Brunswick, N.J.: Transaction, 1981), and four writings by Sheldon Wolin: *Politics and Vision* (Boston: Little, Brown, 1960), chapter 1; "Political Theory as a Vocation," *American Political Science Review* 63, no. 4 (December 1969); *International Encyclopedia of the Social Sciences*, s.v. "Political Theory: Trends and Goals"; and "Political Theory and Political Commentary," in *Political Theory and Political Education*, ed. Melvin Richter (Princeton: Princeton University Press, 1980), pp. 190–203. For other accounts of political theory as a source of political education see John Gunnell, *Between Philosophy and Politics* (Amherst: University of Massachusetts, 1986); John S. Nelson, ed., *What Should Political Theory Be Now?* (Albany: State University of New York Press, 1983); Leo Strauss, "What is Political Philosophy?" in *What is Political Philosophy?* (Glencoe, Ill.: Free Press, 1959); and Mark E. Warren, "What is Political Theory/Philosophy?," *PS* 22, no. 3 (September 1989): 606–12. Other claims that artworks function as a kind of political theory include J. Peter Euben, *The Tragedy of Political Theory* (Princeton: Princeton University Press, 1990), esp. pp. 50–59.

13. Wolin, "Political Theory and Political Commentary," p. 192.

14. Wolin, "Political Theory as a Vocation," p. 1075.

15. Schaar, *Legitimacy,* p. 9. On the role of culture in making what is conven-

tional seem natural, see also Roland Barthes, *Mythologies*, trans. Annette Lavers (New York: Hill & Wang, 1983).

16. Wolin, "Political Theory as a Vocation," p. 1073.

17. Ludwig Wittgenstein, *Philosophical Investigations*, trans. G. E. M. Anscombe (New York: Macmillan, 1968), par. 401; quoted in Pitkin, *Wittgenstein and Justice*, p. 295.

18. Clifford Geertz, *Local Knowledge* (New York: Basic Books, 1983), pp. 119–20.

19. Amiri Baraka, *The Autobiography of LeRoi Jones* (New York: Freundlich, 1984), pp. 57, 60.

20. It should be acknowledged that one's emotional responses can be isolated from the rest of one's existence as well. Here one thinks of Rousseau's discussion of the "sanguinary Sulla [who] cried at the account of evils he had not himself committed" and "the tyrant of Phera [who] hid himself at the theatre for fear of being seen groaning with Andromache and Priam, while he heard without emotion the cries of so many unfortunate victims slain daily by his orders." Jean-Jacques Rousseau, *Politics and the Arts* (*Letter to M. D'Alembert on the Theatre*), trans. Allan Bloom (Ithaca: Cornell University Press, 1960), p. 24.

21. James Boyd White, *When Words Lose Their Meaning* (Chicago: University of Chicago Press, 1984), pp. 15–17.

22. Raymond Williams, *Marxism and Literature* (London: Oxford University Press, 1977), p. 132. On the concept of "the emergent," see pp. 124–27.

23. It is true that many Intellectuals associated McCarthy with anti-intellectual mass culture, but they did not for that reason reject anticommunism; instead, they advocated a more responsible anticommunism.

24. Both jazz and rock have roots in earlier African American music and have a close relationship to the blues; the politics they sometimes expressed in the sixties had a common grounding in the civil rights movement.

25. Morris Dickstein, *Gates of Eden* (New York: Basic Books, 1977), p. 40.

26. Epstein, "Literary Life Today," p. 10.

27. Lionel Trilling, "The Liberal Mind: Two Communications and a Reply," *Partisan Review* 16, no. 6 (June 1949): 656. The fact that this piece was published six months before the start of the fifties does not, I believe, take away from its representativeness of the approach the New York Intellectuals would take during the coming decade.

28. Todd Gitlin, *The Sixties* (New York: Bantam, 1987), p. 81.

29. This is not to deny that the sixties helped spur the development of new kinds of criticism appropriate to its new kinds of art.

30. In the words of Walter Ong, "Oral communication unites people in groups. Writing and reading are solitary activities that throw the psyche back on itself." Similarly, according to Ong, "Sight isolates, sound incorporates. Whereas sight situates the observer outside what he views, at a distance, sound pours into the hearer." Walter J. Ong, *Orality and Literacy: The Technologizing of the Word* (London: Methuen, 1982), pp. 69, 72.

Lawrence Grossberg expresses similar sentiments: "Music has a unique and striking relationship to the human body, surrounding, enfolding and even invading it within its own rhythms and textures. It incorporates listeners into its own spaces, transforming passive reception into active production." Lawrence Grossberg, *We Gotta Get Out of this Place* (New York: Routledge, 1992), pp. 152–53. For a related analysis, see Simon Frith, "Towards an Aesthetic of Popular Music," in *Music and Society*, ed. Richard Leppert and Susan McClary (New York: Cambridge University Press, 1987), p. 139.

Part of music's capacity to create an environment is its ability, absent in reading, to coexist with other activities. See James Lull, "Listeners' Communicative Uses of Popular Music," in *Popular Music and Communication*, ed. James Lull (Newbury Park, Calif.: Sage, 1987), pp. 141–42.

31. Oral readings of literature can create a temporary community in much the same way that music can, and for brief periods in the Fifties this did occur for small audiences listening to the Beats.

Perhaps the most famous formulation of music's ability to create community is Nietzsche's analysis of the "Dionysian" element of art, which in *The Birth of Tragedy* he associated with music:

> Now the slave is a free man; now all rigid, hostile barriers that necessity, caprice, or "impudent convention" have fixed between man and man are broken. Now, with the gospel of universal harmony, each one feels himself not only united, reconciled, and fused with his neighbor, but as one with him, as if the veil of *maya* had been torn aside and were now merely fluttering in tatters before the mysterious primordial unity.

*The Basic Writings of Nietzsche*, ed. Walter Kaufmann (New York: Modern Library, 1968), p. 37.

32. In the words of Simon Frith, pop songs "give us a way of managing the relationship between our public and private emotional lives," and love songs can "give shape and voice to emotions that otherwise cannot be expressed without embarrassment or incoherence." "Toward an Aesthetic of Popular Music," 141.

33. See, for example, the following comments:

> The struggle between different discourses, different definitions and meanings within ideology is therefore always, at the same time, a struggle within signification: a struggle for possession of the sign which extends to even the most mundane areas of everyday life. . . . [S]uch commodities are indeed open to double inflection: to "illegitimate" as well as "legitimate" uses. These "humble objects" can be magically appropriated; "stolen" by subordinate groups and made to carry "secret" meanings: meanings which express, in code, a form of resistance to the order which guarantees their continued subordination.

Dick Hebdige, *Subculture: The Meaning of Style* (London: Methuen, 1979), pp. 17–18.

Similarly, Paul Willis shows how English "motorbike boys" used rock music for purposes not directly related to the lyrics. Willis argues that oppressed groups take the "profane" castoffs of capitalism and reclaim them, using them for their own purposes. "[T]hese cultures teach us that revolutionary cultural change will only come from reinterpretations, reformations of consciousness, and fermentation from below around the most trivial, everyday and commonplace items." Paul E. Willis, *Profane Culture* (London: Routledge & Kegan Paul, 1978), p. 7.

34. "Times Are A-Changin': It's Dylan at West Point," *New York Times*, 15 October 1990.

35. See Norman K. Denzin, "Problems in Analyzing Elements of Mass Culture: Notes on the Popular Song and Other Artistic Productions," and James T. Carey's reply, *American Journal of Sociology* 75 (1970): 1035–41. Denzin raises a number of important issues concerning the meanings of artworks and the popular song in particular. He argues that "the popularity of an art object may occur for reasons other than those directly extracted from its substantive content. There may be little correspondence between the intended and imputed meanings. Objects of art are often collected for reasons of prestige, status, or self-enhancement" (p. 1036). Earlier in the essay, he takes a less extreme view: "The meaning of a popular song . . . lies in the interactions brought to it. Its meaning resides only partly in the lyrics, the beat, or its mood" (p. 1036).

36. The Marxist idea of base and superstructure is a classic example, of course. For a critique, see Williams, *Marxism and Literature,* pp. 75–82.

37. Raymond Williams, *The Long Revolution* (New York: Pelican, 1961), p. 61, quoted in John Shepherd, *Music as Social Text* (Cambridge: Polity, 1991), p. 87. As Williams put it in *Marxism and Literature,*

> If "reality" and "speaking about reality" (the "material social process" and "language") are taken as categorically distinct, concepts such as "reflection" and "mediation" are inevitable. . . . The problem is different, from the beginning, if we see language and signification as indissoluble elements of the material social process itself, involved all the time both in production and reproduction. (P. 99)

38. As John Shepherd argues regarding music, "It can be asserted that because *people* create music, they reproduce in the basic qualities of their music the basic qualities of their own thought processes. If it is accepted that people's thought processes are socially mediated, then it could be said that the basic qualities of different styles of music are likewise socially mediated and so socially significant." *Music as Social Text,* p. 12.

39. Williams, *Marxism and Literature*, pp. 108–11.

40. Simon Frith, "Rock and the Politics of Memory," in *The 60s Without Apology*, ed. Sohnya Sayres et al. (Minneapolis: University of Minnesota Press, 1984), pp. 60–61; Frith, *Sound Effects* (New York: Pantheon, 1981), pp. 40–41.

41. Frith, *Sound Effects*, p. 11.

42. For more on this debate, particularly as it relates to rock music, see chapter 5.

## *Chapter 1. Literature and Democracy: The New York Intellectuals*

1. The archetypal Intellectual, Lionel Trilling, wrote his doctoral dissertation, and subsequently first book, on Arnold: *Matthew Arnold* (1939; reprint, New York: Harcourt Brace Jovanovich, 1954).

2. *The Portable Matthew Arnold*, ed. Lionel Trilling (New York: Penguin, 1980), p. 33. My analysis of Arnold is drawn from two works contained in this collection: most centrally, *Culture and Anarchy* (1869), pp. 469–573; and to a lesser degree, "Democracy" (1861), pp. 436–69.

3. Ibid., p. 442.

4. Ibid., p. 524.

5. Ibid., p. 499. Raymond Williams has argued that this conception of culture, generally associated at first with romanticism, was a response to industrialism and democratization, an attempt to preserve under the name of "art" all that was felt to be disappearing—creativity, freedom, and "higher" or "spiritual" values—under the pressure of the marketplace and the crowd. While every society has produced something like what we now call art, it is primarily since the Industrial Age that "aesthetic" activities and their products have been seen as fundamentally different and separate from the rest of life. Previously little or no differentiation was made between products of human skill that had a practical use (e.g., cabinets) and those that did not (e.g., violin sonatas). That is, the distinction between what we now call "art" and "craft" was minimal or nonexistent. But around this time "art," formerly a designation of "general human skill," came to refer to a special "imaginative" realm, while "aesthetic," previously referring to "general perception" came to designate "a specialized category of 'the artistic' and 'the beautiful.'" Williams, *Marxism and Literature*, p. 50.

For a history of this idea of culture, see Raymond Williams, *Culture and Society, 1780–1950* (New York: Columbia University Press, 1983). Williams also discusses this development in *Marxism and Literature*, pp. 11–20, 45–54. See also Terry Eagleton, *Literary Theory: An Introduction* (Minneapolis: University of Minnesota Press, 1983), pp. 1–53, for an account focusing on the category of "literature." Important documents in the development of this notion of art include Immanuel Kant, *Critique of Judgment*, trans. J. H. Bernard (New York: Macmillan-Hafner, 1951); Friedrich Schiller, *On the Aesthetic Education of Man*, trans. Reginald Snell (London: Routledge & Kegan Paul, 1954); Percy Bysshe Shelley, *A Defence of Poetry*, ed. John E. Jordan (Indianapolis: Bobbs-Merrill, 1965); and Mill, *Mill's Essays on Literature and Society*. Wordsworth and Coleridge are also important figures in this tradition. Finally, Eagleton in a later book takes Williams's thesis further, arguing that the concept of the aesthetic helped construct a growing middle-class sense of subjectivity, simultaneously allowing power to penetrate more deeply into individuals and providing a means of resistance to absolute power. Terry Eagleton, *The Ideology of the Aesthetic* (Cambridge, Mass.: Basil Blackwell, 1990), esp. pp. 1–27, 42–43.

6. *Portable Matthew Arnold*, p. 498.

7. Ibid., p. 543; cf. p. 537.

8. Ibid., p. 454.

9. Ibid., p. 505.
10. Ibid., p. 499.
11. Ibid., pp. 542–47.
12. Ibid., pp. 547–49.
13. See Williams, *Culture and Society*, pp. 127–28.
14. Sometimes it is argued that keeping too much power from the majority is a means of preserving democracy. If democracy is defined in minimalist terms—elections and individual rights—this argument may not be incoherent. Yet from the perspective of a fuller vision of democracy, the argument is profoundly anti-democratic.
15. I mostly rely on issues of *Partisan Review* for my understanding of the New York Intellectuals. Works dealing with the group include Alexander Bloom, *Prodigal Sons* (New York: Oxford University Press, 1986); Irving Howe, *A Margin of Hope* (New York: Harcourt Brace Jovanovich, 1982); idem, "The New York Intellectuals" in *Decline of the New* (New York: Harcourt, Brace & World, 1970); William Phillips, *A Partisan View* (New York: Stein and Day, 1983); William Barrett, *The Truants* (Garden City, N.Y.: Doubleday-Anchor, 1982); James Burkhart Gilbert, *Writers and Partisans* (New York: John Wiley and Sons, 1968); Grant Webster, *The Republic of Letters* (Baltimore: Johns Hopkins University Press, 1979); Alan M. Wald, *The New York Intellectuals* (New York: Oxford University Press, 1987); Terry A. Cooney, *The Rise of the New York Intellectuals* (Madison: University of Wisconsin Press, 1986); Neil Jumonville, *Critical Crossings* (Berkeley: University of California Press, 1991); and Harvey M. Teres, *Renewing the Left* (New York: Oxford University Press, 1996). Wald and Teres give the most emphasis to politics. However, neither of them focuses on the Intellectuals's ideas about the arts' potential for democratic political education; Wald emphasizes the writers' anti-Stalinism and their relationship to American radical politics, while Teres explores how the Intellectuals' insights might be used to improve Left politics by analyzing its failings, particularly what he sees as its neglect of personal experience.

For works on Trilling, see chapter 2. There have been two studies of Dwight Macdonald: Stephen J. Whitfield, *A Critical American: The Politics of Dwight Macdonald* (Hamden, Conn.: Archon, 1984) and Michael Wreszin, *A Rebel in Defense of Tradition: The Life and Politics of Dwight Macdonald* (New York: Basic Books, 1994).

Although I generalize about "the New York Intellectuals," there were differences between the members. This book focuses on the work of William Phillips and Philip Rahv, joint editors of *Partisan Review* from its founding in 1934 until Rahv's departure in 1969, and Lionel Trilling, with lesser emphasis on Dwight Macdonald and Robert Warshow. Though no one would dispute the preeminence of Phillips, Rahv, and Trilling, others might construct a slightly different account by putting more emphasis on other Intellectuals.

16. Despite their shift of emphasis in the postwar period from modernism to realism, they still supported modernism to some degree, mostly recast as "high culture." On the de-emphasis of modernism see Phillips, *Partisan View*, pp. 94–96, and (for Trilling) Jumonville, *Critical Crossings*, p. 122.

17. Joseph Freeman, introduction to *Proletarian Literature in the United States*, ed. Granville Hicks et. al (New York: International, 1935), p. 9.

18. Ibid., p. 18.

19. Michael Gold, "A Letter from a Clam-Digger," *New Masses* 5 (November 1929): 11; "Notes of the Month," *New Masses* 5 (January 1930): 7; "Notes of the Month," *New Masses* 6 (September 1930): 5; all quoted in Richard Pells, *Radical Visions and American Dreams* (Middletown, Conn.: Wesleyan University Press, 1973), pp. 176–77. For a defense of proletarian literature against the charges of, among other things, rejection of aesthetic excellence, see James F. Murphy, *The Proletarian Movement* (Urbana and Chicago: University of Illinois Press, 1991) and Barbara Foley, *Radical Representations* (Durham, N.C.: Duke University Press, 1993). Foley tries to show that "most CP critics, while not guided by anything resembling a party 'line' on aesthetic matters, were in fact uneasy with the view of literature as weaponry and repudiated the notion that proletarian literature should be written as 'propaganda'" (p. 37). She asserts that works of proletarian literature were often reviewed positively by mainstream reviewers and argues that the distorted view of these writers as propagandists is a result of the efforts of the New York Intellectuals (p. 14). Entering this debate is beyond the scope of this book; I am more interested in proletarian literature as understood by the New York Intellectuals in their attempts to develop their ideas about the arts' role in democratic political education.

20. Samuel Sillen, "The People, Yes," *New Masses* 31 (6 June 1939): 22, quoted in Pells, *Radical Visions and American Dreams,* p. 314.

21. Some Intellectuals did briefly embrace "proletarian literature," but combined it with an appreciation of modernism. See, e.g., Philip Rahv, "How the Waste Land Became a Flower Garden," *Partisan Review* 1, no. 4 (September–October 1934): 37–42.

22. See Marx's letter to Minna Kautsky, quoted in Maynard Solomon, ed., *Marxism and Art* (New York: Vintage, 1974), pp. 66–67, and Eugene Lunn, *Marxism and Modernism* (Berkeley: University of California Press, 1982), p. 17.

23. Schiller, *On the Aesthetic Education of Man,* pp. 27–28.

24. The word translated "remodel" is *umzuschaffen*, related to *schaffen*, to create. Elizabeth M. Wilkinson and L. A. Willoughby in their translation of Schiller's *Aesthetic Education of Man* (London: Clarendon, 1967) say "transform." *Werk* is like the English word "work" in that it can have artistic and nonartistic meanings. (My thanks to Leo Glueckselig for help with the analysis of German terms.)

Wilkinson and Willoughby support Williams's thesis that at the time this book was written the concept of art as something separate from craft and technical skill, or even the human ability to alter the world (as opposed to nature), was only beginning to appear (pp. 320–21). Thus Schiller uses the word *Kunst* (art) to also refer to technical skill (he calls a watchmaker a *Kunstler*), or even to (following Rousseau) civilization as opposed to nature. Wilkinson and Willoughby state that *Kunst* is cognate with *können*, to be able.

25. Karl Marx, *Early Writings*, ed. T. B. Bottomore (New York: McGraw-Hill, 1964), pp. 127–28.

26. Ibid., p. 159.

27. Ibid., p. 160.

28. Throughout this chapter and the next, the word "communism" refers to communist politics and ideology as viewed by the New York Intellectuals. A full discussion of whether their picture of communism represented an accurate account of Marxism, Soviet ideology and practice, or those who called themselves communists in America is beyond the scope of this book, although I do suggest later in this chapter that "communism" as used by the Intellectuals is more a construct with its own imperatives than a description of empirical reality.

29. See Harold Rosenberg, "The Pathos of the Proletariat," *Kenyon Review* 11, no. 4 (autumn 1949), reprinted in *Act and the Actor* (New York: World-NAL, 1970), pp. 14–57. (The reprinted version of the essay has some unacknowledged additions, however.) Although this essay was written at a time when many New York Intellectuals were beginning to reject Marxism, it vividly illustrates the vision of Marx from which their early work drew, and some continued to draw.

30. Although the editors wanted Trotsky to contribute to the journal, as indeed he did, he apparently wanted much more control over it than they were willing to give. In addition, Trotsky wanted the journal to take more of an explicit political position, accusing the editors in a letter of having "*nothing to say*" and wanting to create a "small cultural monastery." Letter from Trotsky to Dwight Macdonald, 20 January 1938, cited in Cooney, *Rise of the New York Intellectuals,* p. 130. On tensions between *Partisan Review* and Trotsky, see Cooney, *Rise of the New York Intellectuals,* pp. 126–33.

31. Wald, *New York Intellectuals,* p. 163, 93. Foley also notes, much less sympathetically, Trotsky's influence on Philip Rahv (*Radical Representations,* p. 16).

32. "Man will become immeasurably stronger, wiser, and subtler; his body will become more harmonized, his movements more rhythmic, his voice more musical. The forms of life will become dynamically dramatic." Leon Trotsky, *Literature and Revolution* (1923), excerpted in *Theories of Modern Art,* ed. Herschel B. Chipp (Berkeley: University of California Press, 1968), p. 466. In retrospect, this quotation evokes the kind of aesthetic politics that would culminate in fascism. See Walter Benjamin, *Illuminations,* ed. Hannah Arendt, trans. Harry Zohn (New York: Schocken, 1969), pp. 241–42 ("The Work of Art in the Age of Mechanical Reproduction"); Susan Sontag, "Fascinating Fascism," in *Under the Sign of Saturn* (New York: Vintage, 1981); and Rainer Stollmann, "Fascist Politics as a Total Work of Art: Tendencies of the Aestheticization of Political Life in National Socialism," *New German Critique* 14 (spring 1978): 41.

33. Trotsky, "Art and Politics," *Partisan Review* 5, no. 3 (August–September 1938): 10.

34. Ibid., p. 3.

35. André Breton and Diego Rivera, "Manifesto: Toward a Free Revolutionary Art," *Partisan Review* 6, no. 1 (fall 1938): 53. According to Wald, this manifesto was "largely written by Trotsky." Alan Wald, "Revolutionary Intellectuals: *Partisan Review* in the 1930's," in *Literature at the Barricades*, ed. Ralph F. Bogardus and Fred Hobson (University: University of Alabama Press, 1982), p. 199.

36. The Intellectuals' admiration for Trotsky was not hurt by the fact that he called New York the future "theoretical center of the international revolution." Letter to V. F. Calverton, 1932, cited in Wald, *New York Intellectuals*, p. 94. Originally in George Breitman and Sarah Lovell, eds., *Writings of Leon Trotsky* (New York: Pathfinder, 1973), p. 299.

37. On the influence of pragmatism on the Marxism of the Intellectuals at this time, mainly through Sidney Hook, who had studied with Dewey, see Alexander Bloom, *Prodigal Sons*, pp. 101–4; Cooney, *Rise of the New York Intellectuals*, pp. 64–66; and Wald, *New York Intellectuals*, pp. 118–27. In his important article "Form and Content" Phillips praises Dewey and his connection of art and experience, but he later seems to see him as insufficiently political and criticizes Hook later in the essay. Wallace Phelps [William Phillips], "Form and Content," *Partisan Review* 2 (January–February 1935): 32, 37. On Phillips and Rahv's disagreements with Dewey and Hook, see Cooney, *Rise of the New York Intellectuals*, pp. 32, 37–38. For an argument that the incorporation of pragmatism represented the "enfeeblement of American Marxism," see Wald, *New York Intellectuals*, pp. 228–30.

38. Phillips and Rahv, "Private Experience and Public Philosophy," 48 *Poetry* (May 1936): 103.

39. Clement Greenberg, "Avant-Garde and Kitsch" (1939), reprinted in *Art and Culture* (Boston: Beacon, 1961), pp. 3–21.

40. "Shakespeare was soaked in prevailing 'Elizabethan' attitudes and Dante did not seek poetic pastures fenced off from the blight of Catholic philosophy." Phillips and Rahv, "Private Experience," p. 102.

41. Ibid., p. 103.

42. Ibid., p. 104.

43. William Phillips, "The Esthetic of the Founding Fathers," *Partisan Review* 4, no. 4 (March 1938): 20.

44. See ibid., pp. 19–20; Phillips and Rahv, "Private Experience," p. 102; and Phillips, "Form and Content," p. 36.

45. William Phillips and Philip Rahv, "In Retrospect: Ten Years of *Partisan Review*," in *The Partisan Reader*, ed. William Phillips and Philip Rahv (New York: Dial, 1946), p. 683.

46. See, for example, Frederick Crews, "The Partisan," *New York Review of Books* 25, no. 18 (23 November 1978): 3–10. Wald also makes a version of the same argument, suggesting that the primary way the Intellectuals combined Marxism and modernism was by "housing both in the same journal for five or six years." Wald, *New York Intellectuals*, p. 222.

47. Gilbert, *Writers and Partisans*, pp. 173–74. Phillips also studied modernist literature in college. According to Gilbert, "Eliot in his poetry and criticism had made the literary world conscious of the meaning of modernity and tradition, just as Marx had seemed to do in politics" (p. 174).

48. T. S. Eliot, *Selected Essays* (New York: Harcourt, Brace, & World, 1932), pp. 246–47 ("The Metaphysical Poets"). See also pp. 115–17 ("Shakespeare and the Stoicism of Seneca") and his famous discussion of the "objective correlative" in the essay "Hamlet and His Problems" (p. 124).

49. See Max Horkheimer and Theodor W. Adorno, *Dialectic of Enlighten-*

*ment* (1944; reprint, New York: Continuum, 1988), pp. 54–55; and Theodor W. Adorno, *Prisms* (Cambridge: MIT, 1967), pp. 30–31.

50. Eliot, *Selected Essays,* p. 5 ("Tradition and the Individual Talent").

51. Webster, *Republic of Letters,* pp. 64–70; Eagleton, *Literary Theory*, pp. 38–41.

52. T. S. Eliot, "Notes Toward a Definition of Culture," *Partisan Review* 11, no. 2 (spring 1944): 145–57. This was later expanded into his book *Notes Toward the Definition of Culture* (New York: Harcourt, Brace, 1949).

53. Eliot, *Selected Essays*, p. 7 ("Tradition and the Individual Talent").

54. Ibid., p. 16 ("The Function of Criticism"). For the reference to Arnold, see *Portable Matthew Arnold*, pp. 500–505. Note that the title of Eliot's essay echoes Arnold as well. See "The Function of Criticism at the Present Time," in *Portable Matthew Arnold*, pp. 234–67. Whatever else their differences, both critics see the order of art as an antidote to the dangers of democratization and a potentially anarchic working class.

55. Phillips, "Form and Content," p. 36. For another favorable analysis of Eliot by an Intellectual at this time, see Philip Rahv, "A Season in Heaven," *Partisan Review and Anvil* 3, no. 5 (June 1936): 11–14.

56. Phillips, "Form and Content," p. 34.

57. Philip Rahv, "Dostoevsky and Politics," *Partisan Review* 5, no. 2 (July 1938): 25–36.

58. Marx, "The Communist Manifesto," in *The Marx-Engels Reader,* ed. Robert Tucker (New York: Norton, 1972), p. 338.

59. "[Some] may wish to get rid of modern arts, in order to get rid of modern conflicts. Or they may imagine that so signal a progress in industry wants to be completed by as signal a regress in politics. . . . [B]ut to work well the new-fangled forces of society, they only want to be mastered by new-fangled men—and such are the working men." Marx, "Speech at the Anniversary of the People's Paper," in Solomon, *Marxism and Art,* p. 42. See Lunn and Marshall Berman, *All That is Solid Melts into Air* (New York: Simon & Schuster, 1982) for more on the relationship between Marxism and modernism.

60. Dwight Macdonald, "The Soviet Cinema: 1930–1938," *Partisan Review* 5, no. 2 (July 1938): 37. Another important article in the New York Intellectuals' Marxist criticism is William Phillips and Philip Rahv, "Some Aspects of Literary Criticism," *Science and Society* 1, no. 2 (winter 1937): 212–20.

61. See Eagleton, *Ideology of the Aesthetic*, p. 202.

62. For a dissenting view on the Intellectuals' analysis of the Popular Front, see Stanley Aronowitz, *Roll Over Beethoven* (Hanover, N.H.: Wesleyan University Press, 1993), pp. 131–66.

63. The exception to this neglect is Teres, although he does not discuss the important essay "Private Experience and Public Philosophy."

64. Philip Rahv, "Twilight of the Thirties," *Partisan Review* 6, no. 4 (summer 1939): 595. After the Stalin-Hitler pact of 23 August 1939, the Popular Front died out, for obvious reasons. Some New York Intellectuals argued that the frame of mind associated with it did not, however. See Cooney, *Rise of the New York Intellectuals,* p. 174.

65. Rahv, "Twilight of the Thirties," p. 8.

66. Ibid., p. 15.

67. Ibid., p. 10.

68. Ibid., p. 12.

69. William Phillips, "The Intellectuals' Tradition," *Partisan Review* 8, no. 6 (November–December 1941): 491.

70. Ibid., p. 493.

71. Rahv, "Twilight of the Thirties." Greenberg's "Avant-Garde and Kitsch" makes a similar argument.

72. Thomas Hill Schaub, *American Fiction in the Cold War* (Madison: University of Wisconsin Press, 1991), pp. 3–15. Trilling's work constituted a key force in developing these ideas and translating them into literary criticism. (See chapter 2.)

73. "Our Country and Our Culture," *Partisan Review* 10, no. 3 (May–June 1952): 284.

74. Although the material in this paragraph is not for the most part drawn from the Intellectuals themselves, these arguments heavily influenced their understanding of culture. See, for example, Dwight Macdonald, "A Theory of Mass Culture," in *Mass Culture*, ed. Bernard Rosenberg and David Manning White (New York: Free Press, 1957), p. 69. The essay was originally published in *Diogenes* 3 (summer 1953).

75. On Eliot's influence on the New Critics, see James Breslin, *From Modern to Contemporary* (Chicago: University of Chicago Press, 1983), pp. 13–16. Other early influences include T. E. Hulme, I. A. Richards, and Ezra Pound. See Arnold L. Goldsmith, *American Literary Criticism, 1905–1965*, vol. 3 (Boston: Hall-Twayne, 1979), pp. 103–4.

76. On the Agrarian movement, see John M. Bradbury, *The Fugitives: A Critical Account* (Chapel Hill: University of North Carolina, 1958); Paul K. Conkin, *The Southern Agrarians* (Knoxville: University of Tennessee Press, 1988); Louise Cowan, *The Fugitive Group: A Literary History* (Baton Rouge: Louisiana State University Press, 1959); Alexander Karanikas, *Tillers of a Myth: Southern Agrarians as Social and Literary Critics* (Madison: University of Wisconsin Press, 1969); and Thomas Daniel Young, *Waking Their Neighbors Up: The Nashville Agrarians Rediscovered* (Athens: University of Georgia Press, 1982).

77. Twelve Southerners, *I'll Take My Stand* (1930; reprint, New York: Harper Torchbooks, 1962), pp. xxii, xxiv, xxvii.

78. See also Donald Davidson's contribution: "The furious pace of our working hours is carried over into our leisure hours, which are feverish and energetic. We live by the clock" (ibid., p. 34). Like Marx, Davidson argues that our existence is split into work and leisure, with the latter just a relief from the former.

79. Ibid., p. 29.

80. Ibid., pp. 33–35.

81. Ibid., p. 36.

82. Ibid., p. 43. Davidson continued to support racial segregation into the postwar period. However others, notably Robert Penn Warren, supported civil rights. On the Agrarians' attitudes toward African Americans, see Karanikas, *Tillers of a Myth*, pp. 88–94 and Conkin, *Southern Agrarians*, pp. 150–61.

83. Breslin, *From Modern to Contemporary,* pp. 13–16. On the New Critics see, among many others, William J. Handy, *Kant and the Southern New Critics* (Austin: University of Texas Press, 1963); Murray Krieger, *The New Apologists for Poetry* (Minneapolis: University of Minnesota Press, 1956); John Crowe Ransom, *The New Criticism* (Norfolk, Conn.: New Directions, 1941); Webster, *Republic of Letters;* and W. K. Wimsatt Jr., *The Verbal Icon* (Lexington: University Press of Kentucky, 1967).

84. William K. Wimsatt Jr., and Cleanth Brooks, *Literary Criticism: A Short History* (Chicago: University of Chicago Press, 1957), p. 748.

85. Shirley F. Staton, *Literary Theories in Praxis* (Philadelphia: University of Pennsylvania Press, 1987), pp. 12–13.

86. Wimsatt and Brooks, *Literary Criticism,* p. 748.

87. Cleanth Brooks, *The Well Wrought Urn* (New York: Reynal and Hitchcock, 1947), p. 194.

88. Allen Tate, *The Man of Letters in the Modern World: Selected Essays, 1928–1955* (Cleveland and New York: World-Meridian, 1955), p. 32. According to Tate, language provides us with "genuine knowledge of our human community . . . that we have not had before" (p. 20). The poet should convey "the reality of man's experience, not what his experience ought to be, in any age" (p. 32).

89. Brooks, *Well Wrought Urn,* p. 8.

90. Ibid., p. 180.

91. Ibid., p. 189. See also p. 178.

92. Vincent B. Leitch, *American Literary Criticism from the Thirties to the Eighties* (New York: Columbia University Press, 1988), p. 31.

93. Ibid., p. 16.

94. John Crowe Ransom, *Selected Essays of John Crowe Ransom* (Baton Rouge: Louisiana State University Press, 1984), p. 60.

95. Ibid., p. 61.

96. Ibid., p. 60.

97. Allen Tate, "Poetry Modern and Unmodern," in *Essays of Four Decades* (Chicago: Swallow, 1968), quoted in Breslin, *From Modern to Contemporary,* p. 28.

98. Philip Rahv, *The Myth and the Powerhouse* (New York: Farrar, Straus and Giroux, 1965), p. 44. This and the following paragraph draw on three essays from this collection: "The Myth and the Powerhouse" (1953), "Fiction and the Criticism of Fiction" (1956), and "Criticism and the Imagination of Alternatives" (1956–58).

99. Ibid., p. 14.

100. Ibid., p. 66.

101. Ibid., pp. 56, 59.

102. Ibid., p. 20.

103. Ibid., p. 180.

104. Ibid., p. 44.

105. On Trilling's response to the New Critics, see "The Meaning of a Literary Idea," in *The Liberal Imagination* (New York: Doubleday-Anchor, 1950) and my discussion of it in chapter 2.

106. Philip Rahv, "Notes on the Decline of Naturalism" (1942), in *Literature*

*and the Sixth Sense* (Boston: Houghton Mifflin, 1969), p. 86. Trilling, *Liberal Imagination*, p. 205.

107. Philip Rahv, "Concerning Tolstoy," *Partisan Review* 13, no. 4 (September–October 1946): 430.

108. Rahv, *Literature and the Sixth Sense*, p. 36.

109. Harold Rosenberg, "A Herd of Independent Minds," *Commentary*, September 1948, p. 246. See also Rahv's interpretation of Henry James as both a modernist and a realist in "The Cult of Experience in American Writing" (1940) and "Notes on the Decline of Naturalism" (1942) in *Literature and the Sixth Sense*. Finally, there is Christopher Lasch, "Modernism, Politics, and Philip Rahv," *Partisan Review* 47, no. 2 (1980): 183–94.

110. On the linkage between realism and naturalism, see J. A. Cuddon, *A Dictionary of Literary Terms* (New York: Penguin, 1982), p. 416.

111. Leslie Fiedler, "The State of American Writing," *Partisan Review* 15, no. 8 (August 1948): 871.

112. For an account that distinguishes realism and naturalism but with a less disparaging view of the latter, see Donald Pizer, *Realism and Naturalism in Nineteenth-Century American Literature* (Carbondale: Southern Illinois University Press, 1984).

113. Lionel Trilling, *The Opposing Self* (New York: Viking, 1955), p. 166. See also pp. 90–91.

114. Leslie Fiedler in "The State of American Writing" (a symposium), *Partisan Review* 15, no. 8 (August 1948): 875.

115. Ibid.

116. William Barrett, "The End of Literature," *Partisan Review* 16, no. 9 (September 1949): 945.

117. According to Lawrence Levine, "Arnold was perhaps the single most significant disseminator of such attitudes and had an enormous influence in the United States." Some said Arnold had more readers in America than England; one commentator remarked in 1927 that no one ever mentioned Arnold because his ideas had become so much a part of American thought. Lawrence W. Levine, *Highbrow/Lowbrow* (Cambridge: Harvard University Press, 1988), p. 224.

118. Ibid., pp. 175, 173.

119. Regarding the protection of the arts, in 1867 George Henry Lewes said that unless there was "a decided separation of the drama which aims at art from those theatrical performances which only aim at amusement of a lower kind," "the final disappearance of the art is near at hand" (ibid., p. 75). Regarding high culture as a response to fears of immigrants and people of color, in 1870 John Sullivan Dwight said music was "a civilizing agency," a "beautiful corrective of our crudities," bringing order to "a great mixed people of all races" (p. 200). Levine points out that the terms "highbrow" and "lowbrow" came from phrenology, which put Caucasians and western Europeans above other races and peoples (pp. 219–23).

120. Representative works include three essays collected in Daniel Bell, *Radical Right*: Seymour Martin Lipset, "The Sources of the Radical Right" (1955), David Riesman and Nathan Glazer, "The Intellectuals and the Discontented

Classes" (1955); and Richard Hofstadter, "The Pseudo-Conservative Revolt" (1955).

121. Ibid., p. 293 (Bell).

122. Ibid., p. 196 (Riesman and Glazer).

123. Ibid., p. 70 (Hofstadter).

124. Norman Jacobs, ed., *Culture for the Millions?* (Boston: Beacon, 1959), pp. 192–93. (This was a symposium on mass culture featuring leading intellectuals of the fifties.) For more optimistic viewpoints, see Daniel Bell, *The End of Ideology* (Glencoe, Ill.: Free Press, 1960), p. 25. For a later version of the argument for cultural pluralism, see Herbert J. Gans, *Popular Culture and High Culture* (New York: Basic Books, 1974).

125. Macdonald, "A Theory of Mass Culture," p. 72.

126. Robert Warshow, *The Immediate Experience* (1962; reprint, New York: Atheneum, 1979), pp. 189–203.

127. Ibid., pp. 194–95.

128. Ibid., p. 53.

129. Ibid., pp. 77, 200.

130. Ibid., p. 76.

131. Ibid., p. 72.

132. Dwight Macdonald, "Masscult and Midcult," reprinted in *Against the American Grain* (New York: Random House, 1962), pp. 37–55. The latter essay was originally published in *Partisan Review,* spring 1960. For an analysis of Warshow's essay in terms of "Popular Front" culture see Andrew Ross, *No Respect* (New York: Routledge, 1989).

133. Warshow, *Immediate Experience,* pp. 75–76.

134. Ibid., p. 76.

135. Ibid., pp. 79–80.

136. David Suchoff suggests that the Intellectuals in condemning the Rosenbergs were conducting an internal purge of their own leftist Jewish origins. David Suchoff, "The Rosenberg Case and the New York Intellectuals," in *Secret Agents: The Rosenberg Case, McCarthyism, and Fifties America*, ed. Marjorie Garber and Rebecca Walkowitz (New York: Routledge, 1995), pp. 155–69.

137. Levine, *Highbrow/Lowbrow,* pp. 21, 107–8. Levine shows how the division of artworks into high and low also mandated a change in the way (high) art was to be consumed by audiences. Elites enforced a series of unwritten rules regarding the consumption of high art, so that even if nonelites took part, they had to do so in a prescribed manner (p. 177). Previous to the shift audiences, by clapping and vocalizing, became virtually part of theatrical and musical performances, often causing a particular scene or piece of music to be changed or terminated; afterwards, they were expected to sit in reverent silence (p. 146).

138. Ibid., pp. 25–29.

139. See the sources listed in the introduction, note 33, above.

140. For a view of popular culture as potentially democratic and emancipating, see Iain Chambers, *Popular Culture: The Metropolitan Experience* (London: Routledge, 1988).

141. Warshow, *Immediate Experience,* p. 77.

142. Ibid., pp. 72–73.
143. Ibid., p. 81.
144. Alexander Bloom, *Prodigal Sons,* p. 213.
145. See Bell, *Radical Right.*
146. Alexander Bloom, *Prodigal Sons,* pp. 226, 240–42, 249.
147. Leslie Fiedler, *An End to Innocence* (Boston: Beacon, 1952), esp. pp. 23, 25. For a more sympathetic view of Trilling's role regarding questions of communism and academic freedom, see William M. Chace, *Lionel Trilling: Criticism and Politics* (Stanford, Calif.: Stanford University Press, 1980), p. 99n.
148. Dwight Macdonald, "A Theory of 'Popular Culture,'" *Politics*, February 1944, pp. 20–23; idem, "A Theory of Mass Culture," pp. 59–73; and idem, "Masscult and Midcult," pp. 11–12.
149. Interestingly, in light of future developments, the title was suggested to him by C. Wright Mills, after Macdonald had considered and rejected "New Left." Dwight Macdonald, "Publisher's Preface," to 1968 reprint of *Politics* (New York: Greenwood Reprint Corp., 1968).
150. Dwight Macdonald, "Why *Politics*?" *Politics*, February 1944, p. 6.
151. Macdonald, "A Theory of 'Popular Culture,'" p. 23.
152. Ibid.
153. Dwight Macdonald, "Introduction: Politics Past," in *Memoirs of a Revolutionist* (New York: Farrar, Straus, & Cudahy, 1957), p. 6. Macdonald also opined that "no one has a duty to interest himself in politics except a politician" (p. 4).
154. Macdonald, "Masscult and Midcult," p. 64. Now he uses the term "mass culture" rather than "popular culture," relying on the ideas of the "mass society" theorists outlined earlier in this chapter. The language of class has disappeared, replaced by the notion of "mass." (See, e.g., p. 8.) The 1960 version also introduced the idea of "midcult."
155. Ibid., p. 12.
156. Ibid., p. 56.
157. Ibid., p. 72.
158. Ibid., p. 70.
159. Ibid. As Macdonald had said earlier in agreeing with Allen Tate that Ezra Pound should have received the Bollingen Prize, in America "clear distinctions [are] maintained between the various spheres, so that the value of an artist's work . . . is not confused with the value of [his] politics." Dwight Macdonald "Homage to Twelve Judges" in *Politics Past* (New York: Viking, 1957); originally published in *Politics*, winter 1949. Other Intellectuals disagreed with Macdonald's view that the spheres of politics and art could or should be so separate. For the controversy surrounding the award, see William Barrett, "A Prize for Ezra Pound," *Partisan Review* 16, no. 4 (April 1949): 344–47; Clement Greenberg, "The Question of the Pound Award," *Partisan Review* 16, no. 5 (May 1949): 512–22; Allen Tate, "Further Remarks on the Pound Award," *Partisan Review* 16, no. 6 (June 1949): 666–70.
160. Tate, "Further Remarks on the Pound Award."
161. On New York Intellectual attacks on mass culture as themselves symptomatic of formulaic thinking, see Rosenberg, "A Herd of Independent Minds."

## *Chapter 2. Liberalism, The Novel, and the Self: Lionel Trilling and the Dilemmas of Political Action*

1. Howe, *Margin of Hope,* p. 229. Webster calls Trilling the New York Intellectuals' "Representative Man" (*Republic of Letters,* p. 252). For other accounts of Trilling, none of them from the point of view of political theory, see Mark Krupnick, *Lionel Trilling and the Fate of Cultural Criticism* (Evanston, Ill.: Northwestern University Press, 1986); Stephen L. Tanner, *Lionel Trilling* (New York: G. K. Hall, 1988); Chace, *Lionel Trilling;* and Mark Edmundson, "On Lionel Trilling," *Salmagundi* 74–75 (spring–summer, 1987): 161–68. See also Cornel West's interesting analysis of Trilling in relation to the tradition of American pragmatism in *The American Evasion of Philosophy* (Madison: University of Wisconsin Press, 1989), pp. 164–81. Nicolaus Mills, *American and English Fiction in the Nineteenth Century* (Bloomington: Indiana University Press, 1973), challenges Trilling's thesis that American novelists have avoided society and politics in their work. For a harsher dissenting view, see Russell Jacoby, *The Last Intellectuals* (New York: Basic Books, 1987): "The cadence of his prose and his measured liberalism distinguished Trilling, but not the brilliance, originality, or force of his thought. His reach, in fact, was limited, no further than Anglo-American literature; his social theory, thin; his philosophy, weak" (p. 25). Finally, see the works on the New York Intellectuals in chapter 1.

2. Michael Walzer, "The Communitarian Critique of Liberalism," *Political Theory* 18, no. 1 (February 1990): 15. See also Charles Larmore, "Political Liberalism," *Political Theory* 18, no. 3 (August 1990): 331–60, in which he argues for "political liberalism," which is not as individualistic as classical liberalism. This "political liberalism," according to Larmore, incorporates the romantic values of "tradition and belonging" (p. 357).

3. Mill, *Mill's Essays on Literature and Society,* pp. 161, 404. For a more recent approach to the relationship between liberalism and the arts, see Richard Rorty, *Contingency, Irony, and Solidarity* (New York: Cambridge University Press, 1989).

4. Trilling, *Liberal Imagination* , p. ix.

5. Ibid., p. 215.

6. Ibid., p. 94. By reading modern literature so monolithically, it should be noted, Trilling glosses over important political differences between the authors he cites. For a contemporary attack on Trilling's condemnation of modernism, see Delmore Schwartz, "The Duchess' Red Shoes," *Partisan Review* 10, no. 1 (January–February 1953): 55–73.

7. Trilling, *Liberal Imagination,* p. 215.

8. The book's influence is detailed by Thomas Schaub in *American Fiction in the Cold War,* p. 20: "There is widespread agreement among recent critics that Trilling's collection of essays represented, in Gene Wise's words, 'one of those threshold moments marking the transition from Progressive explanations to counter-Progressive ones.' In Russell Reising's view, the ideas Trilling set forth in *The Liberal Imagination* emerged as 'the dominant interpretation of American culture and literature' (93). Alexander Bloom argues that this book, more than

any other, 'marks the emergence of the New York Intellectuals into the postwar' (190)." He is citing Gene Wise, *American Historical Explanations: A Strategy for Grounded Inquiry* (Homewood, Ill.: Dorsey, 1973); Russell Reising, *The Unusable Past: Theory and the Study of American Literature* (New York: Methuen, 1986); and Alexander Bloom, *Prodigal Sons.*

9. Trilling, *Liberal Imagination*, pp. 93–94, viii.

10. Ibid., p. xii.

11. See Hannah Arendt, *On Revolution* (New York: Viking, 1965), chapter 2, particularly her discussion of the dangers of Billy Budd's attempt to bring absolute goodness into the public realm and her claim that the "boundlessness" of the French Revolution's passion for social justice led to the Terror (p. 87).

12. Trilling, *Liberal Imagination*, p. viii.

13. Ibid., p. xii.

14. Ibid., p. 213.

15. Ibid., pp. 273, 283.

16. Ibid., p. 276.

17. Ibid., p. 278.

18. Ibid., p. 279.

19. Ibid., p. 293.

20. Ibid., p. 282.

21. Ibid., p. 215.

22. Ibid., pp. ix, 288.

23. Ibid., p. ix. Trilling cites Wordsworth's remark, "Our continued influxes of feeling are modified and directed by our thoughts, which are indeed the representatives of our past feelings."

24. See Eliot, *Selected Essays*, pp. 124–25.

25. Trilling, *Liberal Imagination,* p. 94.

26. Ibid., p. 288.

27. Ibid., p. 107.

28. Ibid., p. 108. As we shall see, Trilling will come to criticize the subversion of values that he here praises.

29. Terry Eagleton has argued that such thinking is circular. In relation to another reception theorist, Wolfgang Iser, he has said, "He writes that a reader with strong ideological commitments is likely to be an inadequate one, since he or she is less likely to be open to the transformative power of literary works. What this implies is that in order to undergo transformation at the hands of the text, . . . [the] reader would *already* have to be a liberal." *Literary Theory: An Introduction*, p. 79, cited in Peter J. Rabinowitz, "Whirl without End: Audience-Oriented Criticism," in *Contemporary Literary Theory*, ed. G. Douglas Atkins and Laura Morrow (Amherst: University of Massachusetts Press, 1989), p. 93. While there is some truth to this argument, it is perhaps too much to ask of any theory that posits a change of consciousness that even the most recalcitrant be converted by the agent of change. Marxists certainly have argued that only those ready for a certain change in consciousness will participate in that change.

30. "From the Notebooks of Lionel Trilling," in *Partisan Review: The 50th Anniversary Edition*, ed. William Phillips (New York: Stein & Day, 1985), p. 14. The entry is from 1927.

31. Ibid., p. 24.
32. Lionel Trilling, *The Middle of the Journey* (New York: Avon-Equinox, 1976).
33. Ibid., p. 31.
34. Ibid., p. 13.
35. Ibid., p. 303 (cf. p. 55).
36. Ibid., p. 75.
37. Ibid., p. 55.
38. Ibid., p. 120.
39. Ibid., pp. 301, 303.
40. Ibid., pp. xix–xxi.
41. For a critique by a fellow New York Intellectual of the novel's distance from experience, see Warshow, "The Legacy of the Thirties," in *The Immediate Experience*, pp. 42–48.
42. Trilling, *Liberal Imagination,* pp. vii–xi.
43. Trilling, *Middle of the Journey*, p. 301.
44. Ibid., p. 300.
45. Ibid., p. 266.
46. Ibid.
47. Ibid., pp. 25–26.
48. Ibid., p. 193.
49. Ibid., pp. 13, 26.
50. Mikhail Bakhtin, *Problems of Dostoevsky's Poetics* (Minneapolis: University of Minnesota Press, 1984), p. 87.
51. Robert Penn Warren, *All the King's Men* (New York: Bantam, 1946), p. 45.
52. Ibid., p. 31.
53. Ibid., p. 38.
54. As he puts it, "[W]hat folks claim is right is just a couple of jumps short of what they need to do business." Ibid., p. 257.
55. Ibid., pp. 246–48.
56. Hannah Arendt, *The Human Condition* (Chicago: University of Chicago Press, 1958), p. 185.
57. Warren, *All the King's Men,* p. 353.
58. Ibid., pp. 311, 314.
59. Ibid., p. 202.
60. Ibid., p. 438.
61. Another possibility is that New Critics were less strict in the application of their principles with novels than with poetry, upon which their theories mostly focused.
62. On the latter, see Krupnick, *Lionel Trilling,* p. 105.
63. Lionel Trilling, *A Gathering of Fugitives* (Boston: Beacon, 1956), p. 66.
64. Trilling, *Opposing Self*, pp. 163, 166.
65. Lionel Trilling, *Beyond Culture* (New York: Viking, 1965), p. 114.
66. Ibid., p. 98. Though his concern with death was heightened and took on a particular form in the fifties, it was present from nearly the beginning of his career. In Trilling's first published story a character calls death "life's best pal and

severest critic." Lionel Trilling, "Impediments," *Menorah Journal* 11, no. 3 (June 1925): 286–90, quoted in Chace, *Lionel Trilling,* p. 22.

67. Trilling, *Beyond Culture*, p. 108.

68. Ibid., p. 115.

69. In *The Opposing Self* he argues that the "spirit" is limited by circumstances and conditions, but only because of these limitations "does spirit have virtue and meaning" (p. 207).

70. Chace shows how for Trilling Jewishness was also a means of maintaining a certain distance from society (though Trilling rarely discussed his heritage publicly). As Trilling himself put it: "If the anti-Semitism that we observed did not arouse our indignation, this was in part because we took it to be a kind of advantage: against this social antagonism we could define ourselves *and* our society, we could discover who we were and who we wished to be." Lionel Trilling, "Young in the Thirties," *Commentary* 41, no. 5 (May 1966): 43, quoted in Chace, *Lionel Trilling,* p. 11. One could argue that being Southerners served a similar function for the Agrarians/New Critics.

71. Trilling, *Beyond Culture,* p. 112.

72. Ibid., pp. 5–6. This essay, "On the Teaching of Modern Literature," was first published in *Partisan Review*, January–February 1961, yet still represents the line of thought he had developed in the Freud piece.

73. Trilling, *Opposing Self*, p. 205. From "Flaubert's Last Testament" (1953).

74. Personal communication.

75. Trilling, *Liberal Imagination,* p. ix.

76. Ibid.

77. For a contemporary criticism of Trilling's shifting use of the word "social" and his contention that American novels do not have the "social texture" of European ones, see Schwartz, "The Duchess' Red Shoes," esp. p. 58.

78. The quote continues, "it is . . . [the novelist's] assumption that the individual who accepts . . . 'his station and its duties' is pretty sure to have a quality of integral selfhood. Whether he be Mr. Knightley or Sam Weller or Plantagenet Palliser, the country gentleman or the cockney servant or the Prime Minister, heir of the Duke of Omnium, a man is what he is by virtue of his class membership. His sentiment of being, his awareness of discrete and personal existence, derives from his sentiment of class." Lionel Trilling, *Sincerity and Authenticity* (Cambridge: Harvard University Press, 1971), p. 115. Similarly, in *The Liberal Imagination* he argues that "social class is so real that it produces actual differences of personality" (p. 209). See also *Liberal Imagination*, p. 207, and *Sincerity and Authenticity*, pp. 77, 81, 38–39.

79. Trilling, *Liberal Imagination*, pp. 89–91.

## *Chapter 3. The Sixties: Politics, Aesthetics, and Everyday Life*

1. In generalizing across various art forms, my account glosses over significant differences between them. The purpose of this chapter is not to discuss every connection between politics and art in the sixties, but only to discern some general

principles that provide the context for the case studies involving music in subsequent chapters.

2. Herbert Marcuse, *Eros and Civilization* (New York: Vintage, 1962), p. 174. Though Marcuse's study was originally published in 1955, it did not gain popularity until its reissue, with a new preface, in 1962.

3. See also David Kettler, "A Note on the Aesthetic Dimension in Marcuse's Social Theory," *Political Theory* 10, no. 2 (May 1982): 267–75.

4. Herbert Marcuse, *An Essay on Liberation* (Boston: Beacon, 1969), pp. 32, 45.

5. Ibid., pp. 46–47. Nine years later, in *The Aesthetic Dimension* (Boston: Beacon, 1978), Marcuse repudiated this call for a synthesis between art and life, instead (like Adorno) arguing that art is best able to criticize society by remaining autonomous, separate from politics (pp. 13, 18, 22, 37).

6. Though Marcuse did not approve of everything done under the banner of the New Left in the sixties, in 1968 he called the movement "the only hope we have." Herbert Marcuse, "On the New Left," in *The New Left: A Documentary History*, ed. Massimo Teodori (Indianapolis: Bobbs-Merrill, 1969), p. 472.

7. The dividing line between the two parts of the decade is necessarily somewhat arbitrary. Some see 1968 as the turning point, while I follow Wini Breines in seeing 1965 as more crucial. Winifred Breines, "Whose New Left?", *Journal of American History* 75, no. 2 (September 1988): 529 n.3. Breines cites, among other incidents in 1965, the first antiwar demonstration organized by SDS and the first Selma march of the same year, in which many demonstrators were beaten, leading to continued disillusionment with King and nonviolence. Julius Lester speaks of the "new militancy that entered The Movement in 1965," influenced by Malcolm X. Julius Lester, "The Angry Children of Malcolm X," in *Black Protest Thought in the Twentieth Century*, ed. August Meier, Elliot Rudwick, and Francis L. Broderick, 2d ed. (New York: Macmillian, 1985), p. 479. The year 1966 saw the election of Stokely Carmichael as chairman of SNCC and the subsequent elimination of whites from the organization. See Clayborne Carson, *In Struggle* (Cambridge: Harvard University Press, 1981), pp. 191–211. Obviously, there were commonalities between the two halves of the decade; the shift was one of emphasis.

8. Sympathetic overviews include Gitlin, *The Sixties* and Milton Viorst, *Fire in the Streets* (New York: Simon & Schuster, 1979); more specific accounts include Wini Breines, *Community and Organization in the New Left* (New Brunswick, N.J.: Rutgers University Press, 1989); James Miller, *Democracy is in the Streets* (New York: Simon & Schuster, 1986); Carson, *In Struggle;* Taylor Branch, *Parting the Waters* (New York: Touchstone, 1988); and James H. Cone, *Malcolm & Martin & America* (Maryknoll, N.Y.: Orbis, 1991). For conservative accounts critical of the sixties, see Bell, *Cultural Contradictions of Capitalism* and Allan Bloom, *Closing of the American Mind.*

9. Gitlin, *The Sixties,* pp. 81–82. Pat Watters refers to "the historic sit-in at Greensboro, North Carolina, that set the movement in motion." Pat Watters, *Down to Now: Reflections on the Southern Civil Rights Movement* (New York: Pantheon, 1971), p. 52. For interviews with sit-in participants, see Howell Raines, *My Soul is Rested* (New York: Penguin, 1977), pp. 75–108. Gitlin acknowledges

that there had been direct actions before 1960—earlier sit-ins and the Montgomery Bus Boycott—yet points out that the actions of 1960 brought the movement to a new level of intensity.

10. Gitlin, *The Sixties,* p. 81.

11. On the relationship of the New Left to liberalism, see ibid., pp. 54–60, 127–33.

12. My view of the new vision of politics arising out of the civil rights movement is indebted to Michael Rogin, "In Defense of the New Left," *democracy* 3, no. 4 (fall 1983): 106–16. Although in his otherwise fine book, *Democracy is in the Streets,* James Miller attempts to "lay to rest the misconception that the idea of participatory democracy was a product of [the civil rights movement]" (p. 103), he presents statements to the contrary by New Left activists themselves. (See, e.g., pp. 144, 225).

13. On connections between SDS and SNCC, see Gitlin, *The Sixties,* p. 128. For Savio's account of his involvement, see David Lance Goines, *The Free Speech Movement* (Berkeley, Calif.: Ten Speed Press, 1993), pp. 93–99. For Hoffman's story, see Abbie Hoffman, *Soon to Be a Major Motion Picture* (New York: Berkley, 1982), pp. 63–68.

14. On the relationship between representative democracy and "participatory democracy," see James Miller, *Democracy is in the Streets,* pp. 94, 142–43.

15. Ella J. Baker, "Bigger Than a Hamburger," in *Eyes on the Prize: America's Civil Rights Years,* ed. Clayborne Carson et al. (New York: Penguin, 1987), p. 88. Originally published in *The Southern Patriot,* June 1960. Cf. Bob Moses: "Leadership is there in the people. . . . [T]he leadership will emerge from the movement that emerges." Carson, *In Struggle,* p. 303. According to Viorst, the concept of "group-centered" decision making began in the late fifties in James Lawson's nonviolence workshops (*Fire in the Streets,* p. 190).

16. Richard King, *Civil Rights and the Idea of Freedom* (New York: Oxford University Press, 1992), p. 150.

17. On participatory democracy and its ambiguities, see James Miller, *Democracy is in the Streets,* pp. 92–102, 141–56.

18. Gitlin, *The Sixties,* p. 134.

19. Harold D. Lasswell, *Politics: Who Gets What, When, How* (New York: McGraw-Hill, 1938). For a sampling of pluralist writers, including Daniel Bell, Richard Hofstadter, David Riesman, and Seymour Martin Lipset, see Bell, *The Radical Right.* This volume, most of which was originally published in 1955, chronicles the threat to traditional interest group politics by the ideological, "status politics" exemplified (in the authors' view) by McCarthy. For an account that disputes the pluralists' view of McCarthy and presents an insightful critique of pluralism in general, see Michael Paul Rogin, *The Intellectuals and McCarthy* (Cambridge: MIT Press, 1967).

20. The fullest account of prefigurative politics is Breines's *Community and Organization in the New Left.* See also Mitchell Cohen and Dennis Hale, eds. *The New Student Left: An Anthology* (Boston: Beacon, 1966), p. 95, and Joshua Miller, "No Success Like Failure: Existential Politics in Norman Mailer's *The Armies of the Night,*" *Polity* 22, no. 3 (spring 1990): 379–96. See also the statement of one

Free Speech Movement participant that "the means the students used *were* the ends of the movement." Gerald Rosenfield, "Generational Revolt and the Free Speech Movement," *Liberation*, December 1965–January 1966, cited in *The New Radicals*, ed. Paul Jacobs and Saul Landau (New York: Vintage, 1966), p. 214. On prefigurative elements of the early New Left, see Gitlin, *The Sixties,* p. 107.

21. See King, *Civil Rights,* pp. 54–58.

22. Carson, *In Struggle*, pp. 17, 21.

23. For further discussion of the idea of authenticity, its embodiment in the art of the sixties, and its political implications, see chapter 5.

24. *Port Huron Statement* in James Miller, *Democracy is in the Streets,* p. 332.

25. On "mutual regard" see Carson, *In Struggle*, p. 23. Carson quotes James Lawson, but Martin Luther King supported the idea as well. (See chapter 4.)

26. See Christopher N. Reiner, "Politics as Art: the Civic Vision," in Cohen and Hale, *New Student Left,* pp. 27–33.

27. Interview with Trilling by Stephen Donadio, "Columbia: Seven Interviews," *Partisan Review* 35 (summer 1968): 386–87, cited in Krupnick, *Lionel Trilling,* p. 147.

28. "Ultimately, one can define the modern state sociologically only in terms of the specific *means* peculiar to it, as to every political association, namely, the use of physical force." Max Weber, "Politics as a Vocation," in *From Max Weber*, ed. H. H. Gerth and C. Wright Mills (New York: Oxford University Press, 1976), pp. 77–78.

29. Rogin, "In Defense of the New Left," p. 110. For the early American roots of this ideal, beginning with the Puritans, see Joshua Miller, *Rise and Fall of Democracy*. For an interpretation of King in light of African American culture, arguing that these roots have been overlooked in favor of white scholars and philosophers, see Lewis V. Baldwin, *There is a Balm in Gilead: The Cultural Roots of Martin Luther King, Jr.* (Minneapolis: Fortress, 1991).

30. Manning Marable, *Race, Reform, and Rebellion* (Jackson: University Press of Mississippi, 1991), p. 25.

31. James Miller, *Democracy is in the Streets,* pp. 145–46. Miller calls this experience-oriented philosophy "existentialism" (p. 146). Whereas civic republicanism calls for order and community, existentialism values "spontaneity, imagination, passion, playfulness, *movement*—the sensation of being on the edge, at the limits of freedom" (p. 147). Achieving a particular goal becomes less important than the fact that one has made a commitment; in an impersonal, empty society, action becomes a means of self-discovery and self-destination, a "reassertion of the personal" (pp. 59, 144, 101).

On the tension between existential and political goals, see also Richard Flacks, "Some Problems, Issues, Proposals," in Jacobs and Landau, *New Radicals,* pp. 162–65.

32. Stokely Carmichael and Charles V. Hamilton, *Black Power* (New York: Vintage, 1967), p. 44. William Van Deburg divides black power advocates into two groups: "pluralists" saw black solidarity as a prelude to black participation in political bargaining with other groups, while "nationalists" emphasized separatism.

William Van Deburg, *New Day in Babylon: The Black Power Movement and American Culture, 1965–1975* (Chicago: University of Chicago Press, 1992), pp. 25–26.

33. Black power had roots in opposition and resistance to slavery. See Floyd B. Barbour, ed., *The Black Power Revolt* (Boston: Porter Sargent, 1968), Wilson Jeremiah Moses, *The Golden Age of Black Nationalism, 1850–1925* (Hamden, Conn.: Archon Books, 1978), and John T. McCartney, *Black Power Ideologies* (Philadelphia: Temple University Press, 1992). After emancipation, there were calls for African Americans to take charge of their own communities, sometimes by armed struggle. See the statement of 1880 concerning the burning of a town by blacks who had been wronged (Barbour, *Black Power Revolt,* p. 50) and A. Philip Randolph's call in 1919 for armed resistance and black use of economic power to stop lynching. Meier, Rudwick, and Broderick, *Black Protest Thought,* pp. 95–100. The long black nationalist tradition culminating, in a sense, in Malcolm X contributed to the idea of black power.

The term itself did not gain currency until the latter half of the sixties, as its ideas gained in popularity. Marable designates 1965–70 as the era of black power, arguing that "by 1967 and early 1968, Black Power had become the dominant ideological concept among a majority of black youth, and significant portions of the black working class and middle strata" (*Race, Reform, and Rebellion,* p. 96). Obviously other ideologies, such as nonviolence, continued to be present. For African American critiques of black power from an integrationist perspective in the late sixties, see Meier, Rudwick, and Broderick, *Black Protest Thought,* pp. 584–629.

34. Van Deburg, *New Day in Babylon,* p. 195.

35. Van Deburg calls "soul" "the folk equivalent of the black aesthetic." Ibid.

36. Pierre Bourdieu, *Language and Symbolic Power* (Cambridge: Harvard University Press, 1991), p. 51.

37. Van Deburg, *New Day in Babylon,* pp. 197–204.

38. Bourdieu, *Language and Symbolic Power*, pp. 37, 86.

39. See M. M. Bakhtin, "Discourse in the Novel," in *The Dialogical Imagination*, ed. Michael Holquist (Austin: University of Texas Press, 1981), esp. pp. 270–73.

40. Van Deburg, *New Day in Babylon,* pp. 216–24.

41. Huey Newton, "Huey Newton Talks to the Movement," in Meier, Rudwick, and Broderick, *Black Protest Thought,* pp. 495–96.

42. Larry Neal, "Any Day Now: Black Art and Black Liberation," *Ebony*, August 1969, p. 56; quoted in Jennifer Jordan, "Cultural Nationalism in the 1960s: Politics and Poetry," in *Race, Politics, and Culture: Critical Essays on the Radicalism of the Sixties*, ed. Adolph Reed Jr. (New York: Greenwood, 1986), p. 31.

43. Black power itself has been criticized for positing a black community with a single consciousness and perspective so that African Americans who feel differently are not authentically black. For criticism from this perspective see Adolph Reed Jr., "The 'Black Revolution' and the Reconstitution of Domination," in Reed, *Race, Politics, and Culture,* esp. pp. 73–74. For an attempt to point toward a more inclusive and philosophically grounded black aesthetic, see Houston A. Baker

Jr., "On the Criticism of Black American Literature: One View of the Black Aesthetic," in *Philosophy Born of Struggle*, ed. Leonard Harris (Dubuque, Iowa: Kendall/Hunt, 1983), pp. 252–71.

Others have argued that black power was antidemocratic, because its politics consisted primarily of leaders acting in the name of all blacks without representing the diversity within the African American community. Reed, *Race, Politics, and Culture,* pp. 74–75. Cornel West also criticizes the notion of "black authenticity," arguing that it is a form of cultural conservatism, ignoring divisions of gender, sexual orientation, and class. Cornel West, "Black Leadership and the Pitfalls of Racial Reasoning," in *Race-ing Justice, En-gendering Power*, ed. Toni Morrison (New York: Pantheon, 1992), pp. 390–401.

44. To a lesser extent, Norman O. Brown's *Life Against Death* (New York: Vintage, 1959) was also representative and influential.

45. Marcuse, *Eros and Civilization.*

46. Lionel Trilling, *Liberal Imagination*, p. 47 ("Freud and Literature").

47. Ibid., p. 35.

48. Ibid., pp. 170, 169.

49. Marcuse, *Eros and Civilization*, p. 18.

50. Although Marcuse speaks of a "non-repressive civilization" (ibid., p. vii), the concept of "surplus repression" suggests that some amount of (nonsurplus) repression will always be present. He does not resolve this ambiguity, although he does tell us that repression is "largely surplus repression" (p. 140).

51. Ibid., p. 135. On the relationship between surrealism and Marcuse, see Frederic Jameson, *Marxism and Form* (Princeton: Princeton University Press, 1971), pp. 83–116.

52. Norman Podhoretz referred in *Partisan Review* to the Beat "bohemians" of the fifties as worshipers of "primitivism, instinct, energy, [and] 'blood,'" who were "hostile to civilization." He claimed "bop language" exhibited the "primitive vitality and spontaneity [the Beats] find in jazz" and expressed "contempt for coherent, rational discourse." Norman Podhoretz, "The Know-Nothing Bohemians," in *Doings and Undoings* (New York: Farrar, 1964), p. 147, quoted in Webster, *Republic of Letters*, p. 246. Trilling, referring to Ginsberg et al. in *The Opposing Self* (p. 96), spoke of

> a group of my students who have become excited over their discovery of the old animosity which Ezra Pound and William Carlos Williams bear to the iamb, and have come to feel that could they but break the iambic shackles, the whole of modern culture could find a true expression. The value of form must never be denigrated.

Cited in Webster, *Republic of Letters,* p. 245. For a fuller analysis of the Beats as precursors of the counterculture of the sixties, see chapter 5.

53. Norman Mailer, "The White Negro," in *Advertisements for Myself* (New York: NAL-Signet, 1959), pp. 302–22. For a contemporary attack on that essay's view of African Americans, see James Baldwin, "The Black Boy Looks at the White Boy," in *Nobody Knows My Name* (New York: Dial, 1961), pp. 216–41.

54. Ed Ward, Geoffrey Stokes, and Ken Tucker, *Rock of Ages: The Rolling*

*Stone History of Rock and Roll* (New York: Rolling Stone Press/Summit Books, 1986), p. 174.

55. On the values of the counterculture, see Jerry Hopkins, ed., *The Hippie Papers* (New York: NAL-Signet, 1968), a collection of writings from "underground" papers, and Charles Perry, *The Haight-Ashbury: A History* (New York: Vintage, 1984).

56. Rogin, "In Defense of the New Left," p. 115.

57. Gitlin, *The Sixties,* pp. 222–25; "The Digger Papers: The Post-Competitive, Comparative Game of a Free City," in Teodori, *New Left,* pp. 376–80. The latter essay was originally published in the *Realist,* August 1968. For some of the more destructive aspects of the Diggers, see Gitlin, *The Sixties,* pp. 225–30.

58. David Horowitz, Michael Lerner, and Craig Pyes, eds., *Counterculture and Revolution* (New York: Random House, 1972), p. 46.

59. Perry, *Haight-Ashbury,* p. 252.

60. Ibid., p. 114.

61. Ibid., p. 252.

62. Thad Ashby and Rita Ashby, "Ecstatic Living," in Hopkins, *Hippie Papers,* pp. 205–7. Originally published in the *Oracle of Southern California* (Los Angeles), October 1967.

63. A counterculture "Declaration of Independence" declares that "We hold these experiences to be self-evident, that all is equal. . . ." Perry, *Haight-Ashbury,* p. 96.

64. Hoffman, *Soon to Be a Major Motion Picture,* p. 84.

65. Ibid., p. 161.

66. Abbie Hoffman, *Revolution for the Hell of It* (New York: Pocket Books, 1970), pp. 70, 174.

67. Ibid., pp. 101, 99.

68. Quoted in *Our Time: An Anthology of Interviews from the East Village Other,* ed. Allen Katzman (New York: Dial, 1972), p. 291.

69. Horowitz, Lerner, and Pyes, *Counterculture and Revolution,* p. 36. Testimony of Abbie Hoffman at the Chicago Seven trial.

## *Chapter 4. "Let Freedom Ring!": Jazz and African American Politics, 1950–1970*

1. W. E. B. DuBois, *The Souls of Black Folk* (New York: Dover, 1994), p. 2.

2. Langston Hughes, "The Negro Artist and the Racial Mountain," *Nation* 122 (23 June 1926), in Meier, Rudwick, and Broderick, *Black Protest Thought* , p. 111.

3. Barbour, *Black Power Revolt,* p. 23.

4. Ibid., p. 46.

5. Marcus Garvey, "Aims and Objects of Movement for Solution of Negro Problem" in Meier, Rudwick, and Broderick, *Black Protest Thought,* p. 105.

6. DuBois, *Souls of Black Folk,* pp. 2–3.

7. Quoted in Arna Bontemps, "The Negro Renaissance: Jean Toomer and

Beyond" in *Anger and Beyond*, ed. Herbert Hill (New York: Harper & Row, 1966), p. 25.

8. Although this chapter is in the "sixties" half of the book, jazz's representation of political ideas, culminating in the sixties, began in the mid-fifties. Similarly, the modern civil rights movement began in the fifties. Indeed, Manning Marable has argued that it if were not for the cold war, the movement could have taken off in the 1940s. Marable, *Race, Reform, and Rebellion*, p. 18. Thus the dividing line between the two decades does not work nearly as well for African American culture and politics as for whites. Yet 1960 is still a crucial turning point. Culturally, the jazz works of the fifties were only precursors to more fully realized performances like Max Roach's "Freedom Now Suite," Charles Mingus's *Charles Mingus Presents Charles Mingus*, and Ornette Coleman's "Free Jazz," all issued in 1960. Politically, as I noted in chapter 3, that year saw the influential sit-ins in North Carolina and the birth of SNCC.

9. Works consulted for this chapter include Amiri Baraka (LeRoi Jones), *Blues People* (New York: William Morrow, 1963), one of the first studies to connect changes in black music with changes in black politics (see, e.g., p. 65); idem, *Black Music* (New York: William Morrow, 1970), which analyzes jazz from 1959 to 1967; Rob Backus, *Fire Music: A Political History of Jazz* (Chicago: Vanguard, 1976); Valerie Wilmer, *As Serious as Your Life* (Westport, Conn.: Lawrence Hill, 1977); Frank Kofsky, *Black Nationalism and the Revolution in Music* (New York: Pathfinder, 1970); Ortiz Walton, *Music: Black, White & Blue* (New York: William Morrow, 1972); and Ben Sidran, *Black Talk* (New York: Da Capo, 1971). In "Afro-American Musical Adaptation" in *Afro-American Anthropology: Contemporary Perspectives*, ed. Norman E. Whitten Jr. and John F. Szwed (New York: Free Press, 1970), pp. 219–28, John Szwed explores the social functions of earlier black music, arguing perceptively that "*song forms and performances are themselves models of social behavior that reflect strategies of adaption to human and natural environments*" (p. 220; emphasis in original). Charles Keil's *Urban Blues* (Chicago: University of Chicago Press, 1966) and Albert Murray's *Stomping the Blues* (New York: Vintage, 1982) are also useful, although they are more concerned with the function of blues music within the black community than within the larger political context. (Keil critiques Baraka on pp. 39–44.) Parts of Ralph Ellison's *Shadow and Act* (New York: Vintage, 1972) place jazz in a social and political context in an interesting way. (For Ellison's critique of Baraka, see pp. 247–58.) Lawrence W. Levine, *Black Culture and Black Consciousness* (London: Oxford University Press, 1977), pp. 3–80, 195–297, 407–40, discusses the social role of black music, focusing mostly on an earlier period. Shepherd, *Music as Social Text*, contains interesting examples of structural analysis of music's political meaning; in particular, see chapter 7 on differences between European and African American music reflective of larger political differences. For an overview of musical developments during the period of this chapter, although with a superficial analysis of jazz's political meaning, see Michael J. Budds, *Jazz in the Sixties*, exp. ed. (Iowa City: University of Iowa Press, 1990). Other studies contain a purely musical analysis of "free jazz." See, for example, Ekkehard Jost, *Free Jazz* (New York: Da Capo, 1981). Though all these studies have merit, none of them attempts

to show systematically how jazz has contained political meaning. Finally, for an interesting look at music's social meaning that focuses on relationships between sounds and among performers in a group, see Christopher Small, *Music of the Common Tongue* (London: John Calder; New York: Riverrun, 1987).

This chapter confines itself to jazz, as a case study of music's political education in the civil rights era, recognizing that there were other kinds of music (blues, gospel, soul, "freedom songs") expressing the African American quest for freedom. On the social role of the blues, see Keil and Murray. For references to works about "freedom songs" see note 12, below.

10. Polyphony is opposed to homophony or monophony in which there is only one melodic line. "Row, row, row your boat" and other such "rounds" are a type of polyphony, in which one melody is staggered at different times (technically, "imitative counterpoint"). The more equal in prominence the different melodic lines are, the closer one gets to true polyphony. Polyphony is also used in classical music, but without the freedom of "free jazz."

Others who have connected polyphony and politics include Theodor Adorno and Mikhail Bakhtin. Adorno emphasized the collective nature of polyphony, seeing its source in the "collective practices of cult and dance." Theodor W. Adorno, *Philosophy of Modern Music*, trans. Anne G. Mitchell and Westley V. Blomster (New York: Seabury, 1980), p. 18. See also idem, *Introduction to the Sociology of Music,* trans. E. B. Ashton (New York: Continuum, 1976), p. 97. Bakhtin saw in Dostoevsky's "polyphonic novel" a kind of political equality that opposes hierarchy and monologic authoritarianism:

> *A plurality of independent and unmerged voices and consciousnesses, a genuine polyphony of fully valid voices is in fact the chief characteristic of Dostoevsky's novels.* What unfolds in his works is not a multitude of characters and fates in a single objective world illuminated by a single authorial consciousness; rather, *a plurality of consciousnesses, each with equal rights and each with its own world,* combine but are not merged in the unity of the event. Dostoevsky's heroes are, by the very nature of his creative design, *not only objects of authorial discourse but also subjects of their own directly signifying discourse.*

Mikhail Bakhtin, *Problems of Dostoevsky's Poetics*, trans. Caryl Emerson (Minneapolis: University of Minnesota Press, 1984), pp. 6–7. (Emphasis in original.) Bakhtin here uses a musical metaphor to describe a literary text; I take Bakhtin's understanding of polyphony, with its extramusical implications, and apply it to music.

11. For an overview of the political, social, and spiritual role of black music from slave days to the blues and freedom songs, with a particular emphasis on usually neglected kinds of religious music, see Jon Michael Spencer, *Protest & Praise* (Minneapolis: Fortress, 1990).

12. Bernice Johnson Reagon, booklet accompanying *Voices of the Civil Rights Movement: Black American Freedom Songs, 1960–1966,* Smithsonian Collection R023, p. 4. Reagon says she saw freedom songs "pull together sections of the

Black Community at times when other means of communication were ineffective." In another instance, she argues, through song "We became visible, our image was enlarged" (p. 4). See also the interview with Reagon in *They Should Have Served That Cup of Coffee*, ed. Dick Cluster (Boston: South End, 1979), esp. pp. 19–22. For another participant's account of the importance of freedom songs for the movement, see Mary King, *Freedom Song* (New York: William Morrow, 1987), pp. 23–24. Finally, cf. Richard King, *Civil Rights*, pp. 41–42. Similarly, Sidran, though perhaps overstating the case, argues that "black music is—and always has been—the most important single socializing element of black culture . . ." (*Black Talk*, pp. xxiii).

13. "Without These Songs," *Newsweek*, 31 August 1964, p. 74, cited in Spencer, *Protest & Praise*, p. 90.

14. Sidran, *Black Talk*, p. 129.

15. For an analysis of African culture's effect on African American visual arts, see Robert Ferris Thompson, *Flash of the Spirit* (New York: Random House, 1983). For a view challenging Thompson's thesis, see Mary Jo Arnoldi and Ivan Karp, review of *Flash of the Spirit*, *Art in America* 73 (November 1985): 23–27. Henry Louis Gates Jr., *The Signifying Monkey* (New York: Oxford University Press, 1988), analyzes African American literature in terms of African "trickster" figures.

16. This section draws upon Levine, *Black Culture and Black Consciousness*, p. 6; Sidran, *Black Talk*, pp. 1–29; and Baraka, *Blues People*, pp. 1–31. For an argument that there is a "West African core" uniting all African American music, see Olly Wilson, "The Significance of the Relationship Between Afro-American Music and West African Music," *Black Perspective in Music* 2, no. 1 (spring 1974): 3–22, esp. p. 19. John Szwed has pointed out that "Africa presents itself as an incredibly complex spectrum of cultural variety." John Szwed, "Discovering Afro-America" in *Black America*, ed. John Szwed (New York: Basic Books, 1970), p. 289. There is undoubtedly such a variety in West African music; this section only seeks to highlight common features.

17. Baraka, *Blues People*, pp. 28–29.

18. All musical performances have an element of improvisation. There is an element of improvisation even in the playing of the written melody by a "classical" musician, as he or she can interpret that melody using dynamics, tone, phrasing, and (sometimes) embellishment. Yet such improvisation is minimal compared to a jazz musician's creation of the melody he or she is playing.

19. Baraka, *Blues People*, p. 19.

20. Baraka states some of the ways slaves transformed the hymns: "Rhythmic syncopation, polyphony, and shifted accents, as well as the altered timbral qualities and diverse vibrato effects of African music were all used by the Negro to transform most of the 'white hymns' into Negro spirituals" (ibid., p. 47). For a classic account of the spirituals as expressions of sorrow as well hope, see DuBois, *Souls of Black Folk*, pp. 155–65 ("On the Sorrow Songs"). Levine shows how slave songs expressed a longing for justice, covertly commented on whites, served as an outlet for individual feelings, and created group solidarity. Levine, *Black Culture and Black Consciousness*, pp. 5–55. As an example of the songs' use as

covert instructions, Levine describes how "Steal away, steal away, steal away to Jesus!" could act as the announcement of a secret meeting (p. 52). Spencer argues, in contradiction to those who see the spirituals as a form of passive acceptance, that they teach "*confrontation* and *conflict*" (*Protest & Praise,* p. 13).

21. Kofsky, *Black Nationalism,* p. 211.

22. Sidran, *Black Talk,* pp. 47–48.

23. "Feet Can't Fail Me Now," *Village Voice,* 3 January 1984, p. 59.

24. Other works by Ellington in this vein include "Creole Rhapsody" (1931); "Black, Brown, and Beige" (1943), and "Tone Parallel to Harlem" (1950). See Budds, *Jazz in the Sixties,* p. 99.

25. G. E. Lambert, *Duke Ellington* (New York: A. S. Barnes, 1959), p. 22, quoted in Walton, *Music,* p. 79. Ellington was also among the first to take a dislike to the word "jazz" with its sexual connotations, preferring the term "Negro Music." Nat Hentoff, *Jazz Is* (New York: Avon, 1976), p. 30.

26. Ellington is quoted in Hentoff, *Jazz Is,* p. 30–31.

27. Thelonious Monk once called bebop "something they can't play," presumably referring to white popular musicians. "The Loneliest Monk," *Time,* June 1964, p. 86, quoted in Walton, *Music,* p. 95.

28. This music, unfortunately, contained rather bland, Muzak-like string arrangements. It would have been interesting to have heard, as Charles Mingus did, Parker improvising over Stravinsky's "Firebird Suite." Jacket notes to *Let My Children Hear Music,* Columbia KC 31039 (1971). See also Lennie Tristano's statement that "[o]ne of the main things in Bird's life was that he wanted to be recognized as an artist, not as an entertainer. . . ." Rob Reisner, ed., *Bird: The Legend of Charlie Parker* (New York: Da Capo, 1979), p. 224.

29. Sidran, *Black Talk,* p. 95. For examples of the same dilemma with a later avant-garde (the Association for the Advancement of Creative Musicians), see Ronald M. Radano, *New Musical Figurations* (Chicago: University of Chicago Press, 1993), pp. 100, 104.

30. Parker could react assertively, and sometimes violently, to racist behavior. See Reisner, *Bird,* pp. 51, 126.

31. Walton, *Music,* p. 97; cf. Sidran, *Black Talk,* p. 109.

32. On the beginnings of rhythm and blues in Los Angeles and New York, see Arnold Shaw, *Honkers and Shouters* (New York: Collier, 1978), pp. xvi–xvii; and idem, *Black Popular Music in America* (New York: Schirmer, 1986), pp. 187–92.

33. Kofsky, *Black Nationalism,* pp. 41–49. On evocations of Africa in jazz, see Norman C. Weinstein, *A Night in Tunisia: Imaginings of Africa in Jazz* (New York: Limelight, 1993). For an interesting argument that hard bop (or "soul jazz"), aided by the stereotype of blacks as "natural" musicians, promoted black solidarity, see John F. Szwed, "Musical Style and Racial Conflict," *Phylon* 27, no. 4 (winter 1966): 358–66.

34. Marable, *Race, Reform, and Rebellion,* pp. 48–49.

35. Kofsky, *Black Nationalism,* p. 227.

36. Ibid.

37. C. O. Simpkins, *Coltrane* (New York: Herndon House, 1975), p. 160.

Thelonious Monk said something similar: "The best thing about jazz is that it makes a person appreciate freedom. Jazz and freedom go hand in hand."*Esquire's World of Jazz,* ed. James Poling (New York: Thomas Crowell, 1975), p. 202.

38. "Freedom" is a composition by Charles Mingus (*Reevaluation: The Impulse Years*, Impulse/ABC AS-9234-2 [20 September 1963]); *The Freedom Rider* and *Free for All* are both albums by Art Blakey and the Jazz Messengers (Blue Note BLP-4156/84156 [27 May 1961] and Blue Note BST-84170 [1964], respectively); Max Roach performed the *Freedom Now Suite* (Columbia JC 36390 [31 August and 6 September 1960]); and Sonny Rollins recorded *The Freedom Suite* (Milestone SMJ-6044M, [February 1958]). Rollins made the political nature of his work clear in a statement, set off in a box, on the back cover of the album:

> America is deeply rooted in Negro culture: its colloquialisms, its humor, its music. How ironic that the Negro, who more than any other people can claim America's culture as his own, is being persecuted and repressed, that the Negro, who has exemplified the humanities in his very existence, is being rewarded with inhumanity.

In his liner notes the producer downplayed the political implications of the music, claiming it was about "freedom in general," personal and aesthetic freedom, rather than political liberation. Despite the disclaimer, the record was soon pulled from the shelves and reissued without Rollins's statement and given the title of a three minute-piece that ends the album: "The Shadow Waltz." (Michael Rogin suggested to me that this retitling should be read symbolically: African Americans, instead of gaining "freedom" are thrown back into the "shadow.")

39. The album *Let Freedom Ring!* is by saxophonist Jackie McLean (Blue Note BST 84106 [19 March 1962]).

40. In a telephone interview (29 April 1997), lyricist Oscar Brown Jr. told me that the suite was originally to be entitled "The Beat," tracing the transplantation of the African beat to America. However, unbeknownst to Brown, Max Roach, who unlike the lyricist favored Malcolm X over Martin Luther King, issued the album under the current title. Brown claims he only found out about the new title when Nat Hentoff called him for a biographical statement for the jacket notes. There is also a live recording of the suite, but it is from 1964 and features different personnel. Max Roach Group with Abbey Lincoln, *Freedom Now Suite*, Magnetic Records, MRCD 110 (January 1964).

41. Max Roach, interview with author, Amherst, Mass., 17 July 1991.

42. The blues form is six measures rather than twelve, but following the same harmonic movement among tonic, subdominant, and dominant keys.

43. On the arbitrariness, even randomness, of slave whippings, see Frederick Douglass, *The Narrative and Selected Writings* (New York: Modern Library, 1984), p. 36.

44. In his interview with me, Roach said that since they realized freedom had not been attained in 1960, they were unsure how to end the song, so just finished on an "upbeat" note.

45. Roach interview.

46. Liner notes to *Freedom Now Suite.*

47. Roach interview.

48. Liner notes.

49. The interest by American blacks in Africa had begun by at least 1957, when Ghana became independent. John Lewis has said about that period, "Sure we identified with the blacks in Africa, and we were thrilled by what was going on. Here were black people, talking of freedom and liberation and independence, thousands of miles away. We could hardly miss the lesson for ourselves. They were getting their freedom, and we still didn't have ours in what we believed was a free country." Quoted in Viorst, *Fire in the Streets*, p. 102.

50. Roach interview.

51. Martin Luther King, *Where Do We Go from Here: Chaos or Community?* (Boston: Beacon, 1967), p. 125.

52. This statement and the rest of the section are not meant to imply that there was not conflict among the various actors in the civil rights movement. While King brought about change through his influence on national politics and the national media, SNCC was more localist, trying to transform race relations by empowering ordinary citizens. See Carson, *In Struggle.* In addition, competing with King's integrationism was an increasing nationalist sentiment, represented largely by the Nation of Islam, which grew tremendously in the fifties, numbering 65,000 to 100,000 members by 1960. See Marable, *Race, Reform, and Rebellion,* pp. 55–57. The most famous product of the Nation of Islam, of course, was Malcolm X, who grew increasingly influential until his death in 1965 by rejecting the vision of community of King and the early SNCC. See Malcolm X, *The Autobiography of Malcolm X* (New York: Ballantine, 1965) and *Malcolm X Speaks,* ed. George Breitman (New York: Grove Weidenfeld, 1965). An important symbol of the ultimate triumph of nationalism came in 1966 when Stokely Carmichael was elected executive secretary of SNCC and used it to promote "black power." See Carson, *In Struggle*, pp. 200–228. For a classic, if opinionated, history of the dialectic between nationalism and integrationism in African American thought, see Harold Cruse, *The Crisis of the Negro Intellectual* (New York: Quill, 1984).

Despite the differences between King and SNCC, and the growing nationalist trend, I have constructed an ideal type of the movement around 1960. Although Malcolm X would come to influence jazz musicians later in the decade (see Kofsky's 1966 interviews with Coltrane and McCoy Tyner in *Black Nationalism,* pp. 186–87, 209), the works of Mingus and Coleman analyzed in this chapter, encompassing the years 1955–60, have an earlier political context.

53. For an Arendtian account of the civil rights movement's notion of freedom, see Richard King, *Civil Rights*.

54. *This is SCLC* , in Meier, Rudwick, and Broderick, *Black Protest Thought,* p. 306. The idea of the beloved community goes at least as far back as Josiah Royce's *Problem of Christianity* and was utilized in Walter Rauschenbusch's *Theology of the Social Gospel*, which influenced King. See Ira G. Zepp Jr., *The Social Vision of Martin Luther King, Jr.* (Brooklyn, N.Y.: Carlson, 1989), p. 209. However, King had his own understanding of the beloved community, and that is what is relevant for this chapter. See also Kenneth L. Smith and Ira G. Zepp Jr., *Search*

*for the Beloved Community* (Valley Forge, Pa.: Judson, 1974), esp. pp. 119–20; John A. Ansbro, *Martin Luther King, Jr.* (Maryknoll, N.Y.: Orbis, 1982), pp. 187–97; and Cone, *Martin & Malcolm & America*, pp. 120–35. SNCC's founding creed also mentions this term. Carson, *In Struggle*, p. 23.

55. Carson, *In Struggle*, p. 23; King, *Where Do We Go From Here?*, p. 101. By interpreting King's concept of the beloved community politically, I do not deny its important religious underpinnings. However, I think it is an overstatement to say, as Smith and Zepp do, that "King's conception of the Beloved Community was grounded, in the final analysis, not in the tradition of the enlightenment or secular democratic political theory, but in the millennial hope of Judeo-Christian religion" (*Search for the Beloved Community*, p. 128). In fact, elsewhere in their book, Smith and Zepp analyze the close relationship between politics and religion for King.

56. King, *Where Do We Go From Here?*, p. 101.

57. Ibid., p. 124. In his critique of Plato, Aristotle also used a musical metaphor at *Pol.* 2.5.14 to argue against uniformity, which he saw as undermining real solidarity: "It was as if you were to turn harmony into mere unison, or to reduce a theme to a single beat." Aristotle, *Politics*, trans. Ernest Barker (London: Oxford University Press, 1976), p. 51.

58. Howard Zinn, *SNCC: The New Abolitionists* (Boston: Beacon, 1964), p. 37.

59. King, *Where Do We Go From Here?*, p. 180. King obviously does not address the postmodern insight that any group marginalizes some individuals. Perhaps he would envision a group that continually recreates its identity in response to the awareness of such marginalization; presumably, politics might then continually strive toward, though never completely achieve, inclusiveness.

60. William R. Beardslee, *The Way Out Must Lead In*, 2d ed. (Westport, Conn.: Lawrence Hill, 1983), p. 8; cited in Richard King, *Civil Rights*, p. 57.

61. King, *Where Do We Go From Here?*, p. 58; cited in Richard King, *Civil Rights*, pp. 104–5.

62. Quoted in Nat Hentoff, "Archie Shepp: The Way Ahead," *Black Giants* (New York: World, 1970), p. 119.

63. Wilfrid Mellers, *Music in a New Found Land* (New York: Knopf, 1965), p. 301, quoted in Levine, *Black Culture and Black Consciousness*, p. 238. Although Dodds is speaking specifically of the drummer's role, much of what he says applies to all the members of a group that is "swinging."

64. Two other relevant examples are worth noting here, even though they are beyond the scope of this chapter. First, in 1949 Lennie Tristano recorded two tracks in which the group was told to improvise without preset parameters. (*Crosscurrents*, Capitol M-11060). This early instance of "free jazz," however, sounded nothing like the music to later bear that name; in particular, it lacked the connection with the blues that would characterize the music of the late fifties and early sixties. Second, in a series of albums beginning in 1965, Miles Davis's group, though not completely abandoning traditional harmony, stretched it to its limits, while simultaneously experimenting with tempo, meter, and, to some degree, polyphony. Though important and influential, this music, coming as it did five years

after Mingus's "Folk Forms #1" and Coleman's "Free Jazz," is not central to an understanding of the way free jazz came to embody the vision of the developing civil rights movement.

Harvey Pekar cites recordings by Django Reinhardt ("Improvisation" [1937]); Shorty Rogers, Jimmy Guiffre, and Shelly Manne ("Abstract #1" [1954]); and Chico Hamilton ("Free Form" [1955]), as other precursors of the "free jazz" of the sixties. Harvey Pekar, "Father of Free Jazz," *Northern Ohio Live*, May 1994, pp. 16–18.

65. "Work Song" is on *Chazz!* (Fantasy F-86002 [23 December 1955]); "Haitian Fight Song" is on *The Clown* (Atlantic 910 42-1 [12 March 1957]; the original "Fables of Faubus" is on *Mingus Ah Um* (Columbia CS 8171 [1959]); "Prayer for Passive Resistance" is on *Pre-Bird* (Limelight/Polygram EXPR 1015 [24–25 May 1960]) as well as *Mingus at Antibes* (Atlantic SD 2-3001 [13 July 1960]); and "Meditations on Integration" is on *Mingus at Monterey* (Fantasy JWS 001 and 002 [20 September 1964]). Mingus's comment about the alternative title to "Haitian Fight Song" is on the jacket notes to *The Best of Charles Mingus* (Atlantic SD 1555).

66. *Charles Mingus Presents Charles Mingus* (Barnaby/Candid BR-5012 [October 20, 1960]). Mingus's record company would not allow him to record the lyrics, so the original recording of this piece was purely instrumental. Mingus was able to release the vocal version because he started his own record company.

67. Liner notes to *The Best of Charles Mingus*.

68. Paul Oliver, foreword to *The Meaning of the Blues* (New York: Collier, 1963), p. 9. The blues is in one sense a chord progression, usually twelve measures, featuring movement among tonic, subdominant, and dominant. However, blues feeling can be injected into any progression by the use of "bent" or flatted notes, or even a certain tonal quality. See also Murray, *Stomping the Blues*, pp. 68–69.

69. "Percussion Discussion" is on *Chazz!* and "Conversation" is on Charlie Mingus Sextet, *East Coasting* (Affinity 86 [August 1957]).

70. On the blurring of rhythm and melody in the jazz avant-garde, see Baraka, *Black Music*, p. 76.

71. I know of only one other example of this practice, again around the same period: the exchange between Clifford Brown and Harold Land, as part of the Max Roach–Clifford Brown group, in "Blues Walk" in 1955. (*The Quintet*, vol. 2; Mercury EMS-2-407.)

72. Liner notes to *The Best of Charles Mingus*.

73. According to Ronald Radano, the title of this piece referred to Louis B. Leakey's theory, publicized in 1959, that the human race originated in Africa (*New Musical Figurations*, p. 65 n. 96).

74. Whitney Balliet, "Mingus," *New Yorker*, 18 June 1979, p. 105.

75. For example, ex-sideman Mal Waldron said, "I was copying Bud Powell for a time, and then Horace Silver, but if I did it in the middle of a tune, Mingus would yell at me, 'Stop that! That's Horace Silver!'" Bob Blumenthal, "Mal Waldron," *Down Beat*, April 1981, p. 29.

76. Bret Primack, "The Gospel according to Mingus: Disciples Carry the Tune," *Down Beat*, 7 December 1978, p. 41.

77. Ibid., p. 40. The article gives evidence that Dannie Richmond, John Handy, and Charles McPherson went through a similar process of development. For other such testimonials, see Blumenthal, "Mal Waldron," p. 29, and Dan Morgenstern, "Inside Mingus with Bobby Jones," *Down Beat*, 11 May 1972, p. 18.

78. According to saxophonist Bobby Jones, "With Mingus you have the freedom to give the cue yourself if you think the group is ready, but you really have to know when. It's exhilarating when you do it, to have everybody jump in with you." Morgenstern, "Inside Mingus," p. 18.

79. Radano calls Coleman "perhaps the first among the free players to introduce the idea of improvisational freedom signifying cultural freedom, albeit in terms more poetic than overtly ideological" (*New Musical Figurations*, p. 70). The last part of this sentence, dichotomizing "poetic" and "overtly ideological" notions of freedom, leaves little room for an artistic representation of freedom like Coleman's that derives from his experience as an African American and his hopes for a more harmonious society yet does not allude to a fully developed political theory or movement.

80. See A. B. Spellman, *Four Lives in the Bebop Business* (New York: Pantheon, 1966), pp. 93–94 and the interview with Coleman in Arthur Taylor, *Notes and Tones* (New York: Perigee, 1982), pp. 35–36, 40–41. See also the interview with Coleman in *The Jazz Musician*, ed. Mark Rowland and Tony Scherman (New York: St. Martin's, 1994), esp. pp. 45–46. Finally, there is a biography of Coleman: John Litweiler, *Ornette Coleman: A Harmolodic Life* (New York: Da Capo, 1992).

81. Interview with Coleman in Taylor, *Notes and Tones*, pp. 40–41. The word "human" shows up repeatedly in his song and album titles. See also Spellman, *Four Lives*, pp. 93–94.

82. On Coleman's early experiences playing rhythm and blues in Texas, see Spellman, *Four Lives*, pp. 85–90 and Litweiler, *Ornette Coleman*.

83. Ornette Coleman, *Free Jazz* (Atlantic 1364 [December 1960]). The other musicians are Don Cherry (trumpet), Freddie Hubbard (trumpet), Eric Dolphy (bass clarinet), Scott Le Faro (bass), Charlie Haden (bass), Billy Higgins (drums), and Ed Blackwell (drums). Because the name of the piece became the name of a style, I refer to the musical piece in uppercase ("Free Jazz") and the style in lowercase ("free jazz").

84. Quoted in John Litweiler, *The Freedom Principle* (New York: William Morrow, 1984), pp. 33–34. It is true that a person could play patterns based on chords or scales even if there was no preset harmony, but it is less likely; and even if he did he would have to make sure his implied harmony fit in with that of the rest of the group.

85. Liner notes to *Free Jazz*.

86. Spellman, *Four Lives*, pp. 143–44.

87. Jacket notes to *Change of the Century* (Atlantic SD-1327). Later in the liner notes, Coleman adds, "I don't tell the members of my group what to do. I want them to play what they hear in the piece for themselves. I let everyone express himself just as he wants to. The musicians have complete freedom, and so, of course, our final result depends entirely on the musicianship, emotional make-up and taste of the individual members. Ours is at all times a group effort and it is

only because we have the rapport that we do that our music takes on the shape that it does. A strong personality with a star-complex would take away from the effectiveness of our group, no matter how brilliantly he played. . . ."

88. When I use the word "conversation" I am not being totally metaphorical. At one point in Hubbard's "solo" section, there is a musical dialogue between Coleman and Dolphy that imitates speech patterns in the manner of "What Love" (which Dolphy had earlier played with Mingus, although it was not recorded until after *Free Jazz*). The vocalized tone of saxophonists Coleman and Dolphy in general contributes to the air of "conversationality." Dolphy himself said that he tried "to get the instrument to more or less speak" (jacket notes to *Free Jazz*).

89. Martin Luther King, *The Words of Martin Luther King*, (New York: Newmarket Press, 1983), p. 97.

90. *Ascension,* Impulse AS-95 (28 June 1965), reissued as MCA-29020, features Coltrane, Archie Shepp, and Pharoah Sanders (tenor sax), Dewey Johnson and Freddie Hubbard (trumpet), Art Davis and Jimmy Garrison (bass), Marion Brown and John Tchicai (alto sax), McCoy Tyner (piano), and Elvin Jones (drums). There were two versions of the piece recorded and released. Biographies of Coltrane include Bill Cole, *Coltrane* (New York: Schirmer, 1976), and Simpkins, *Coltrane,* as well as J. C. Thomas, *Chasin' the Trane* (Garden City, N.Y.: Doubleday, 1975); Brian Priestley, *John Coltrane* (London: Apollo, 1987); and Eric Nisenson, *Ascension: John Coltrane and his Quest* (New York: St. Martin's, 1993). See also David Wild, *The Recordings of John Coltrane: A Discography*, 2d ed. (Ann Arbor, Mich.: Wildmusic, 1979).

91. On *Coltrane's Sound* (Atlantic 1419 [26 October 1960]); *Olé Coltrane* (Atlantic 1373 [25 May 1961]); *Africa/Brass* (Impulse 6 [7 June 1961]); and *Coltrane "Live" at Birdland* (Impulse 50 [18 November 1963]), respectively. The meaning of "Alabama" is discussed in Cole, *Coltrane,* p. 150.

92. *The Africa Brass Sessions, Vol. 2* (MCA Impulse 29008 [23 May and 7 June 1961]). The same year, 1961, Coltrane had agreed to play a benefit for SNCC at the University of California, but the concert was canceled after the chancellor said that students could not raise funds for political organizations. Kofsky, *Black Nationalism,* pp. 221–22.

93. See the comments of Rashied Ali in Rowland and Scherman, *Jazz Musician,* p. 184. Compare, however, the views of some older musicians: Milt Jackson claimed Coltrane was "was not involved in politics," while Sonny Rollins said, "I can't draw any parallels between the social times of the Sixties and John's playing," while adding that "it may be relevant to somebody that grew up in the Sixties and heard Coltrane in the Sixties, and was into whatever movements were going on at the time" (pp. 183–84).

94. The quote is from Archie Shepp's jacket notes.

95. According to Simpkins, the players were sometimes given four notes to play, and they could play them in any order and rhythmic arrangement (p. 189).

96. As Spellman puts it in the liner notes, "This is impact and release, communion and response; the emphasis is on the unmentionable, on what I call the Marvelous. . . ." Despite Spellman's reference to "the Marvelous," "Ascension" has little in common with the playful spirit of surrealism.

97. Jost makes a similar point about the two works, though without ascribing a political connotation to the difference, on p. 89 of *Free Jazz.*

98. Indeed, this is stated explicitly in the liner notes by Shepp: "The emphasis was on textures rather than the making of an organizational entity. There was a unity, but it was a unity of sounds and textures rather than an ABA approach. You can hear, in the saxophones especially, a reaching for sound and an exploration of the possibilities of sound." Recalling Coleman's statement about his music, Shepp compares "Ascension" to New Orleans jazz: "The precedent for what John did goes all the way back to New Orleans, where the voicings were certainly separate even though the group idea held. This is like a New Orleans concept but with 1965 people." Yet given its emphasis on unified texture, "Ascension" resembles New Orleans jazz very little. Unlike "Free Jazz," one is hard pressed to hear "the voicings [being] separate" in "Ascension." See Jost, *Free Jazz,* p. 90 for discussion of this development ("[T]he dense sound of the group improvisation hardly permits such individual stylistic traits to stand out . . .").

It is important to note that a group sound virtually subsuming individuals was not a feature of Coltrane's work with smaller groups, which constituted the vast majority of his recordings and concerts. Yet it is revealing that when he did create a large "free jazz" recording along the lines of Coleman's "Free Jazz," the sections featuring group improvisation (as opposed to the "soloist with rhythm" segments) created a texture in which individual musicians can only with difficulty be distinguished. According to Cole, *Ascension* "had been the number one album of 1966 in the polls" (*Coltrane,* p. 195); Jost argues that the "increasing trend in collective improvisation (especially in larger groups) toward playing with tone colour and away from motivic improvisation, is probably due in some measure to the extraordinary effect *Ascension* had on late Sixties' jazz" (*Free Jazz,* p. 90).

Finally, one must acknowledge that both musically and as a symbol of the free-jazz movement, Coltrane was far more influential than Coleman throughout the entire decade. By devoting more space to Coleman I am not questioning that fact; rather, I am using Coleman as an example of the musical exploration of the ideas of the civil rights movement in the early sixties. Coltrane himself for a period was enamored with Coleman's music, taking lessons from him, asking him to join his band, and recording with his sideman Don Cherry. See John Coltrane, *The Avant-Garde,* Atlantic LP 1451 (8 July 1960); and Rowland and Scherman, *Jazz Musician,* p. 176.

99. Radano sees in Coltrane's later music a "manic freneticism" reminiscent of "tribal West African drumming" as well as a "ritualistic intensity" calling to mind "Christian . . . spiritualism" (*New Musical Figurations,* p. 72) While not disagreeing with these descriptions, I emphasize the group fusion, submerging individuality, that is characteristic of the kind of rituals Radano refers to.

100. Len Lyons, *The 101 Best Jazz Albums* (New York: William Morrow, 1980), p. 406. Braxton later repudiated his earlier rejection of emotion in music (ibid.). For an analysis of Braxton as a postmodernist, calling into question dichotomies like black/white, high art/low art, and art/entertainment, using modernism to express black spiritual aspirations, see Radano, *New Musical Figurations.*

101. John Coltrane featuring Pharoah Sanders, *Live in Seattle*, Impulse AS 9202-2 (30 September 1965) ("Evolution").

102. Ross, *No Respect*, p. 72. For an analysis of the lyrics of soul music as a vehicle for black political thoughts and feelings, see Van Deburg, *New Day in Babylon*, pp. 204–16.

103. Quoted in Godfrey Hodgson, *America in Our Time* (New York: Vintage, 1978), p. 310.

104. Thus Coltrane said that "the audience, in listening, is in an act of participation. And when you know that somebody is maybe moved the same way you are . . . it's just like having another member of the group." Kofsky, *Black Nationalism*, p. 226.

105. For examples of opposition to free jazz by established musicians, see the statements of Randy Weston, Philly Joe Jones, and Johnny Griffin in Taylor, *Notes and Tones*, pp. 27, 45–46, 67.

106. On this subculture see Gitlin, *The Sixties*, pp. 52–53.

## *Chapter 5. Authenticity and Surreality: Bob Dylan, the New Left, and the Counterculture*

1. Gitlin, *The Sixties*, pp. 197–98. Ray Pratt calls Dylan "the most important American popular musical figure of the 1960s." Ray Pratt, *Rhythm and Resistance: The Political Uses of American Popular Music* (Washington, D.C.: Smithsonian, 1990), p. 122. On a purely musical level, Dave Harker overstates only somewhat: "Dylan has influenced more songwriters, singers, poets and musicians—not to mention more audiences—than almost any other living person." Dave Harker, *One for the Money: Politics and Popular Song* (London: Hutchinson, 1980), p. 112.

2. Quoted in James Miller, *Democracy is in the Streets*, p. 161. "Only half-joking" is Miller's comment.

3. Andrew Kopkind, "Looking Backward," *Ramparts*, February 1973, p. 29; quoted in ibid., p. 238.

4. I use the term "rock and roll" to refer to music tending toward short, popular, danceable songs. Although the term "rock" could encompass "rock and roll" and what came after it, I use it to designate the later music that allowed for longer songs, expanded harmonies and forms, and the claim to be "art." The best illustration can be seen in the development of the Beatles: *Meet the Beatles* is rock and roll; *Sgt. Pepper* is a rock album. Like everything else in the sixties, the dividing line comes somewhere around 1965. Simon Frith claims that Dylan made the first rock LP in 1965. Frith, "Rock and the Politics of Memory," in Sayres, *The 60s Without Apology*, p. 60.

5. As Iain Chambers has pointed out, it was this routine quality of work, rather than "mass culture" that threatened to turn the public into an unthinking "mass." Chambers, *Urban Rhythms*, pp. 16–17.

6. Peter Wicke, *Rock Music: Culture, Aesthetics, and Sociology* (New York: Cambridge University Press, 1990), p. 32.

7. Ibid., p. 10; Chambers, *Urban Rhythms,* p 17.

8. Wicke, *Rock Music,* p. 11.

9. One might cite here the famous story that Elvis Presley's hip movements were so suggestive that when he appeared on the Ed Sullivan Show he was filmed only from the waist up, in the interests of "decency."

10. See James Baldwin, *The Fire Next Time* (New York: Dell, 1962).

11. Ward, Stokes, and Tucker, *Rock of Ages,* p. 129.

12. Steve Perry points out that early rock-and-roll songs often simultaneously did well on white popular, rhythm and blues, and country play lists. Steve Perry, "Ain't No Mountain High Enough: The Politics of Crossover," in *Facing the Music,* ed. Simon Frith (New York: Pantheon, 1988), p. 68. Eventually, there was an integration of groups and music production. The Stax record company, which in the early sixties produced many rhythm and blues hits, was owned by whites, but many of the songs were written and performed by integrated groups (p. 73).

13. John Goldrosen, *The Buddy Holly Story* (New York: Music Sales, 1979), p. 97, cited in George Lipsitz, *Time Passages: Collective Memory and American Popular Culture* (Minneapolis: University of Minnesota Press, 1990), p. 122. Lipsitz argues that the interactions between working-class blacks and whites that helped create rock and roll were a result of the migration of rural Americans to industrial cities due to defense production jobs coming out of World War II (p. 116).

14. Lipsitz, *Time Passages,* pp. 122–23.

15. Charlie Gillett, *The Sound of the City* (New York: Outerbridge and Dienstfrey, 1970), p. vii.

16. David Pichaske, *A Generation in Motion* (New York: Schirmer, 1979), pp. 44–56.

17. Quoted in Ward, Stokes, and Tucker, *Rock of Ages,* p. 143.

18. Pichaske, *Generation in Motion,* pp. 44–56.

19. See Wicke, *Rock Music,* chapter 2, and Grossberg, *We Gotta Get Out of this Place,* pp. 144, 155. "[T]here is little evidence (even in the songs themselves) that rock rejected the dominant liberal consensus or the major ideological assumptions (sexism, racism and classism) of that consensus. It is not merely that many if not most rock fans lived somewhere inside the vast center of U.S. society; it is also that they imagined themselves remaining within it." (Grossberg, *We Gotta Get Out of this Place,* p. 144.)

20. Grossberg, *We Gotta Get Out of this Place,* p. 145.

21. See ibid., p. 155: "In a way, rock is always trying to escape the prison of its own everyday life, although it never understands what is on the 'other side,' as it were, or even that there is another side. It never faces the realities of another realm of economic and political power." Grossberg claims that there is no evidence, for example, that Tracy Chapman's political songs, though commercially successful, have "won anyone to an ideologically different position, or to any form of political resistance" (p. 168). This may be true, but as I will argue in the conclusion to this book, it is an impossible standard to hold a work of art to that it singlehandedly spur someone to activism.

Grossberg does believe rock can help create "affective empowerment"; that is, it can give people a kind of energy with which to be more active participants in their lives and world (p. 86). As he puts it elsewhere, "Rock and roll is not revolutionary but is a form of struggle against a certain debilitating organization of pessimism." Lawrence Grossberg, "Rock and Roll in Search of an Audience," in Lull, *Popular Music and Communication*, p. 180.

22. Lipsitz, *Time Passages*, p. 113.

23. Lipsitz: "[R]ock and roll music has been and continues to be a dialogic space, an arena where memories of the past serve to critique and change the present" (ibid., p. 100). Lipsitz also sees the music as having "democratic and egalitarian propensities" because of its origins in urban, working-class culture. Chambers argues along somewhat similar lines: "Music can be considered an important 'counter-space' (Henri Lefebvre) in our daily lives. Its power lies in a temporary suspension of the division between the 'private' and the 'public,' between imagination and the routines, social roles and social relations in which we regularly find ourselves locked. As such, music is not an 'escape' from 'reality,' but an interrogative exploration of its organizing categories. Imagination and 'reality' are brought together in a significant friction and exchange. And the major site of this encounter is the frequently repressed zone of the body" (*Urban Rhythms*, p. 209).

24. Frith, *Sound Effects*, p. 9.

25. Quoted in Gillett, *Sound of the City*, pp. 13–14.

26. Folk music is often defined as traditional, anonymously written songs, passed on orally with individual variations. Pratt, *Rhythm and Resistance*, p. 103. Most of the music discussed in this section does not fit this definition, but instead consists of songs written in that style, often by urban singers for urban audiences. The reader should keep this in mind, imagining quotation marks around the term "folk music." The term "folk music" itself took on political significance, as we shall see. For debates in early sixties music circles about what "authentic" folk was, see David A. DeTurk and A. Poulin Jr., eds., *The American Folk Scene* (New York: Dell, 1967).

27. Those who trace American political folk music back to the Wobblies cite the *Little Red Songbook* handed out to new members with their union cards. See Jerome L. Rodnitzky, *Minstrels of the Dawn: The Folk-Protest Singer as a Cultural Hero* (Chicago: Nelson-Hall, 1976), pp. 3–16. Others argue that this early protest music was grounded in European models without the subsequent idolization of the "folk." See R. Serge Denisoff, *Great Day Coming: Folk Music and the American Left* (Urbana: University of Illinois Press, 1971), p. 9. For an analysis of American Communist Party culture, focusing on the People's Songs movement, see Robbie Lieberman, *"My Song Is My Weapon: People's Songs, American Communism, and the Politics of Culture, 1930–1950* (Urbana: University of Illinois Press, 1989). Ian Watson, *Song and Democratic Culture in Britain* (New York: St. Martin's, 1983), looks at social and political aspects of folk songs in Britain beginning in the nineteenth century.

28. Frith, *Sound Effects*, p. 28; see also Denisoff, *Great Day Coming*, pp. 11–15, and Pratt, *Rhythm and Resistance*, pp. 99, 106, 109. Pratt argues that although this vision is compatible with conservatism, often positing a single culture and erasing racial and class conflict, it represents a potentially emancipatory search for alternatives.

29. Denisoff, *Great Day Coming,* pp. 16, 46–48, 107–8.

30. Ward, Stokes, and Tucker, *Rock of Ages,* p. 252.

31. Ibid.

32. On the government attack on folk music as communist, see Denisoff, *Great Day Coming,* pp. 138–44. Such attacks had a brief revival in the early sixties (pp. 152–59).

33. Indeed, some clubs like the Village Vanguard hosted all three types of acts. Ibid. and Max Gordon, *Live at the Village Vanguard* (New York: Da Capo, 1980).

34. Ward, Stokes, and Tucker, *Rock of Ages,* p. 254.

35. Ibid., pp. 254–55.

36. Ibid., p. 140.

37. Chambers, *Urban Rhythms,* p. 87.

38. On the Beats, see *The New American Poetry, 1945–1960,* ed. Donald Allen (New York: Grove, 1960); Ann Charters, *Beats and Company* (Garden City, N.Y.: Doubleday, 1986); idem, *Kerouac* (New York: Warner, 1974); Bruce Cook, *The Beat Generation* (New York: Scribner, 1971); *On the Poetry of Allen Ginsberg,* ed. Louis Hyde (Ann Arbor: University of Michigan Press, 1984); Jane Kramer, *Allen Ginsberg in America* (New York: Random House, 1969); Barry Miles, *Ginsberg: A Biography* (New York: Simon & Schuster, 1989); Fred McDarah, *Kerouac and Friends: A Beat Generation Album* (New York: William Morrow, 1985); Gregory Stephenson, *The Daybreak Boys: Essays on the Literature of the Beat Generation* (Carbondale and Edwardsville: Southern Illinois University Press, 1987); John Tytell, *Naked Angels: The Lives and Literature of the Beat Generation* (New York: McGraw-Hill, 1976); and Regina Weinreich, *The Spontaneous Poetics of Jack Kerouac* (Carbondale and Edwardsville: Southern Illinois University Press, 1987).

Though they celebrated the self, there was a "transcendental" element in their ethos as well, like their American "transcendentalist" ancestors whom they so admired. Influenced by Gary Snyder, who had studied Buddhism and Zen, as well as by Blake and Coleridge, they sought to explore their inner experience in order to become part of a universal consciousness, a kind of mystic oneness.

39. Allen Ginsberg, *Howl and Other Poems* (San Francisco: City Lights, 1956), p. 9.

40. Ginsberg actually made extensive revisions on much of his work, although he tried to create the myth that "Howl" was written in one night. His work, in any case, has a feeling of spontaneity. Breslin, *From Modern to Contemporary,* pp. 78, 96 n.

41. See, for example, Jack Kerouac, *On the Road* (New York: NAL-Signet), pp. 148–49. ("At lilac evening I walked with every muscle aching among the lights of 27th and Welton in the Denver colored section, wishing I were a Negro, feeling that the best the white world had offered was not enough ecstasy for me, not enough life, joy, kicks, darkness, music, not enough night. . . . I was only myself, Sal Paradise . . . wishing I could exchange worlds with the happy, true-hearted, ecstatic Negroes of America.") On the relationship between blacks and Beats in Greenwich Village, see Cruse, *Crisis of the Negro Intellectual,* pp. 273–75. For an

account by an African American involved with the Beats, see Baraka, *Autobiography of Leroi Jones*, pp. 149–63. In a different kind of connection between the Beats and jazz, Charles Mingus and his wife were married in 1975 by Allen Ginsberg. Janet Coleman and Al Young, *Mingus/Mingus* (New York: Limelight, 1996), p. 30.

42. The championing by some New York Intellectuals—notably Rosenberg and Greenberg—of experiential "action painting" is an exception to the principle I have been describing. Part of the explanation might have to do with differences between the Intellectuals; Rosenberg was more sympathetic to the New Left than most of his cohorts. Differences between the traditions of literature and painting might also help explain this phenomenon.

43. Tytell, *Naked Angels*, p. 227.

44. Cited in Viorst, *Fire in the Streets*, p. 75.

45. James Miller, *Democracy is in the Streets*, pp. 45, 36. On the relationship between the Beats, jazz, and the FSM, see Gerald Rosenfield, "Generational Revolt and the Free Speech Movement," in Jacobs and Landau, *New Radicals*, pp. 214–15.

46. James Miller, *Democracy is in the Streets*, p. 160.

47. Booklet accompanying Dylan's album *Biograph*, Columbia C5X 38830 (November 1985), p. 5. The first ellipsis is Dylan's own.

48. Robert Shelton, *No Direction Home: The Life and Music of Bob Dylan* (New York: Morrow-Beech Tree, 1986), p. 39. Other biographies of Dylan include Anthony Scaduto, *Bob Dylan: An Intimate Biography* (Secaucus, N.J.: Castle, 1971); and William McKeen, *Bob Dylan: A Bio-Bibliography* (Westport, Conn.: Greenwood, 1993). McKeen also provides an exhaustive bibliography of works about Dylan. There are two useful collections of essays about Dylan: *Bob Dylan: The Early Years*, ed. Craig McGregor (New York: Da Capo, 1972); and *The Dylan Companion*, ed. Elizabeth Thompson and David Gutman (New York: Delta-Bell, 1990).

49. Wilfrid Mellers, *A Darker Shade of Pale: A Backdrop to Bob Dylan* (New York: Oxford University Press, 1985), p. 115.

50. Notes to *Biograph*, p. 26.

51. *Bob Dylan*, Columbia CS 8579 (March 1962).

52. Mellers, *Darker Shade of Pale*, p. 122.

53. *The Freewheelin' Bob Dylan*, Columbia KCS 8786 (May 1963) and *The Times They Are A-Changin'*, Columbia KCS 8905 (January 1964).

54. I classify as political "Blowin' in the Wind," "Masters of War," "A Hard Rain's A-Gonna Fall," "Oxford Town," "Talkin' World War III Blues" (all from *The Freewheelin' Bob Dylan*), "The Times They Are A-Changin,'" "Ballad of Hollis Brown," "With God on Our Side," "Only a Pawn in Their Game," and "The Lonesome Death of Hattie Carroll" (all from *The Times They Are A-Changin'*). Dylan at this time also wrote and performed "The Death of Emmett Till," though it was not commercially released until 1991 on Bob Dylan, *The Bootleg Series, Volumes 1-3 [Rare and Unreleased] 1961–1991*, Columbia C3K 47382.

55. James Miller, *Democracy is in the Streets*, p. 145.

56. For an analysis of the origins of authenticity in eighteenth- and nineteenth-century romanticism, see Marshall Berman, *The Politics of Authenticity* (New York: Atheneum, 1972). For a less historical defense of authenticity, see Charles Taylor, *The Ethics of Authenticity* (Cambridge: Harvard University Press, 1991). On the dangers of the politics of authenticity, see Arendt, *On Revolution*, pp. 96–106.

57. On the role of discussion in the New Left, see Breines, *Community and Organization in the New Left*, pp. 37, 41.

58. "Blowin' in the Wind."

59. "Masters of War."

60. Shelton, *No Direction Home*, p. 191.

61. "Ballad of Hollis Brown."

62. "The Lonesome Death of Hattie Carroll."

63. Hannah Arendt has emphasized the political importance of being able to view reality from the point of view of others, to (as Kant puts it) "put . . . ourselves in the place of any other man." See Hannah Arendt, *Lectures on Kant's Political Philosophy*, ed. Ronald Beiner (Chicago: University of Chicago Press, 1982), p. 43. Arendt quotes Kant's *Critique of Judgment*, sec. 40. It should be acknowledged that Arendt is here speaking of aesthetic judgment (taste) rather than empathy. She argued that compassion is too intimate to be politically relevant, although she praises the political virtues of the more general and rational "solidarity." Arendt, *On Revolution*, pp. 81–84.

64. From Dylan's jacket notes to the album *Joan Baez in Concert, Part 2*, in Bob Dylan, *Writings and Drawings* (New York: Knopf, 1973), p. 77.

65. The first two are from ibid., pp. 76, 82; the last one is from "11 Outlined Epitaphs," which was printed on the back of *The Times They Are A-Changin'* and is reprinted in *Writings and Drawings*, p. 107.

66. Quoted in Jesse Lemisch, "I Dreamed I Saw MTV Last Night," *Nation*, 18 October 1986, p. 375.

67. Dwight Macdonald, "Masscult & Midcult," in *Against the American Grain*, pp. 14, 34. Interestingly, if incorrectly, Macdonald saw jazz as an example of authentic folk art and rock a form of mass culture (p. 14 n).

68. Pratt, *Rhythm and Resistance*, p. 116.

69. Dylan later recognized the problems of presenting himself as one of the common folk in the whimsical "I Shall Be Free no. 10": "I'm just average, common too / I'm just like him, the same as you . . . / It ain't no use a-talking to me / It's just the same as talking to you." *Freewheelin' Bob Dylan.*

70. Charles Taylor in *The Ethics of Authenticity* argues, against critics of the idea like Allan Bloom, that authenticity does not necessarily represent either a rejection of moral standards or of connection with others. Taylor defends authenticity as a moral ideal that presupposes community. He sees relativistic notions of authenticity that define themselves against morality as postmodern perversions of the ideal. See esp. pp. 65–66.

71. Originally available only on a "bootleg," the song now can be heard on *The Bootleg Series, Volumes 1–3*.

72. Cf. Dada's "found objects." Mellers, *Darker Shade of Pale*, pp. 32, 46, 66.

73. For a consideration of some of the problems of the left folk aesthetic, see Lemisch, "I Dreamed"; the letters in response to that article (*Nation*, 13 December 1986); and Lemisch's reply (*Nation*, 20 December 1986).

74. Henry Louis Gates Jr., "'Authenticity' or the Lesson of Little Tree," *New York Times Book Review*, 24 December 1991, p. 26.

75. "Blowin' in the Wind."

76. "Masters of War."

77. "My Back Pages," *Another Side of Bob Dylan*, Columbia CS 8993 (August 1964).

78. "Seven breezes a-blowin'/All around the cabin door / Seven shots ring out / Like the ocean's pounding roar." "There's seven people dead / On a South Dakota farm / There's seven people dead / On a South Dakota farm / Somewhere in the distance / There's seven new people born" ("Hollis Brown"). For another example of the mystical use of numbers, see "A Hard Rain's A-Gonna Fall": "I've stumbled on the side of twelve misty mountains, / I've walked and I've crawled on six crooked highways, / I've stepped in the middle of seven sad forests. . . ."

79. "A Hard Rain's A-Gonna Fall."

80. The best example of this is Whitman's "Song of Myself," parts of which are reminiscent of Dylan's "A Hard Rain's A-Gonna Fall":

> Where the she-whale swims with her calf and never forsakes it,
> Where the steam-ship trails hind-ways its long pennant of smoke,
> Where the fin of the shark cuts like a black chip out of the water,
> Where the half-burn'd brig is riding on unknown currents . . .

Walt Whitman, "Song of Myself," in *Leaves of Grass*, ed. Emory Holloway (Garden City, N.Y.: Doubleday, 1926), p. 53.

81. "Ballad of Hollis Brown."

82. Jean Starobinski illustrates this very well in his famous study of Rousseau:

> Authentic speech is speech that does not limit itself to mimicking something that already exists; it is free to deform and to invent, as long as it remains obedient to its own inner law. That law is subject to no outside control or discussion. The law of authenticity prohibits nothing, but it is never satisfied. It requires not that language *reproduce* a preexisting reality but that it *produce* truth freely and without interruption. The law of authenticity tolerates, even requires, that the writer give up looking for a 'true self' in an unvarying past and seek instead to create a self through writing. Hence it exalts as truth an act that, in strict morality, might be condemned as fiction, as a product of unverifiable fancy.

Jean Starobinski, *Jean-Jacques Rousseau: Transparency and Obstruction* (Chicago: University of Chicago Press, 1988), pp. 198–99.

83. Some of the themes of the surrealists began earlier with the dada movement; however, while dada was primarily destructive of established ideas about art, the surrealists developed a positive vision as well. See Robert Short, "Dada

and Surrealism," in *Modernism*, ed. Malcolm Bradbury and James McFarlane (New York: Penguin, 1976), pp. 301–4.

84. André Breton once said, "Only liberty still thrills me." Herbert Gershman, *The Surrealist Revolution in France* (Ann Arbor: University of Michigan Press, 1969), p. 11.

85. Quoted in Short, "Dada and Surrealism," p. 303.

86. Gershman, *Surrealist Revolution in France,* p. 28. See also Mary Ann Caws, *André Breton* (New York: Twayne, 1971), p. 35.

87. See André Breton, *Manifestoes of Surrealism* (Ann Arbor: University of Michigan Press, 1972), pp. 28–29: "But we, who have made no effort whatsoever to filter, we who in our works have made ourselves into simple receptacles of so many echoes, modest *recording instruments* who are not mesmerized by the drawings we are making, perhaps we serve an even nobler cause."

88. Gershman, *Surrealist Revolution in France,* p. 12.

89. Salvador Dali, "The Object as Revealed in Surrealist experiment" (1931), in Chipp, *Theories of Modern Art,* pp. 421–24.

90. Patrick Waldberg, *Surrealism* (New York: Oxford University Press,1965), pp. 24–25 (quoting Lautréamont).

91. As an early draft of "Subterranean Homesick Blues," reproduced on the inside cover of *Writings and Drawings* shows, however, some of these songs were heavily revised, though they retained an improvised feeling.

92. Ralph J. Gleason, "Bob Dylan: 'What Do You Want Me to Say?'" interview with Dylan, 1967–68, in *The Rolling Stone Interviews*, ed. Ben Fong-Torres, vol. 2 (New York: Warner, 1973), p. 25.

93. "Talkin' World War III Blues."

94. *Bringing It All Back Home*, Columbia CS 9128 (March 1965).

95. *Highway 61 Revisited*, Columbia CS 9189 (August 1965), and *Blonde on Blonde*, Columbia C2S 841 (May 1966).

96. Ginsberg himself has acknowledged the connections among surrealism, the Beats, and Dylan: "It's like the thing Bob Dylan picked up on from me and Kerouac, the chain of images that you get in 'motorcycle black madonna two-wheeled gypsy queen' in 'Gates of Eden,' which is basically a surrealistic conjunction, concatenation." Roger Anderson, "Allen Ginsberg: Poetry from Outside Pale" (interview), *Calendar Magazine* (San Francisco), May 1987, p. 8.

97. Shelton, *No Direction Home,* p. 187.

98. Ibid., p. 201. For Dylan's own account of this incident see Nat Hentoff, "The Crackin', Shakin', Breakin' Sounds" in McGregor, ed., *Bob Dylan,* pp. 59–60.

99. Quoted in Pichaske, *Generation in Motion,* p. 63. Dylan uses the terms "message type" and "finger pointing" in Mellers, *Darker Shade of Pale,* p. 138 and Hentoff, "Crackin', Shakin', Breaking' Sounds," p. 47.

100. "Gates of Eden," *Bringing It All Back Home.*

101. For an account of Dylan focusing on questions of identity and Dylan's decentering of the ego, see Aidan Day, *Jokerman: Reading the Lyrics of Bob Dylan* (Cambridge, Mass.: Basil Blackwell, 1988).

102. "It's Alright Ma (I'm Only Bleeding)," *Bringing It All Back Home.*

103. "Ballad of a Thin Man," *Highway 61 Revisited.*

104. Ginsberg, *Howl and Other Poems*, pp. 21–22.

105. "Where Ma Rainey and Beethoven once unwrapped the bed roll." "Tombstone Blues," *Highway 61 Revisited.*

106. "Desolation Row," *Highway 61 Revisited.*

107. Gleason, "Bob Dylan," p. 12.

108. "Bob Dylan's 115th Dream," *Bringing It All Back Home.*

109. Jacket notes to *Bringing It All Back Home*. Sontag, *Under the Sign of Saturn*, p. 72.

110. Jacket notes to *Bringing It All Back Home*. Whitman, "Song of Myself," p. 76.

111. Richard Poirer argues that the Beatles in their use of allusions, clichéd formulas, and the wax models on the cover of *Sgt. Pepper's Lonely Hearts Club Band* exhibit a "fascination with the invented aspects of everything around them." Richard Poirer, "Learning from the Beatles," in *The Performing Self* (New York: Oxford University Press, 1971), p. 131. Interestingly, this essay first appeared in *Partisan Review* in 1967.

112. Paul Willis sees the evocation of timelessness as central to rock and roll. Paul Willis, "The Golden Age," in *On Record*, ed. Simon Frith and Andrew Goodwin (New York: Pantheon, 1988), pp. 54–55.

113. "Subterranean Homesick Blues," *Bringing It All Back Home.*

114. "It's Alright Ma (I'm Only Bleeding)." Although the quoted section is written in *Writings and Drawings* as three lines, on the record it sounds like one continuous line, squeezed into one breath.

115. "Leopard-Skin Pill-Box Hat," *Blonde on Blonde.*

116. "Rainy Day Women #12 & 35," *Blonde on Blonde.*

117. In fact the underground guerilla group that formed in 1969 from the remnants of SDS, the Weathermen, took their name from a line from this song: "You don't need a weather man / To know which way the wind blows."

118. Cf. Kerouac's novel, *The Subterraneans.*

119. In the film *Cool Hand Luke*, the rebel played by Paul Newman is first seen sawing parking meters off their poles.

120. "Only a Pawn in Their Game."

121. "A Hard Rain's A-Gonna Fall."

122. "Tombstone Blues," *Highway 61 Revisited.*

123. Dali, "The Object as Revealed," p. 421; Benjamin, *Illuminations,* p. 178.

124. From "Bob Dylan's 115th Dream" and "Stuck Inside of Mobile with the Memphis Blues Again" (*Blonde on Blonde*), respectively. Interestingly, some children's songs employ this same reversal. For example, "Polly Wolly Doodle" contains the line "curly eyes and laughing hair." "Polly Wolly Doodle" performed by Burl Ives on *A Child's Celebration of Song*, Warner Brothers CD 9 42519-2.

125. Benjamin, *Illuminations*, p. 181. This nostalgic mood is also present in many of the Beatles' songs or albums which present a pastiche of different styles (*The White Album, Sgt. Pepper's Lonely Hearts Club Band*). In the fading ending of "All You Need is Love," one hears bits of thirties ballroom music, the "Marseillaise," "She Loves You," boogie-woogie, "In the Mood," "Greensleeves," and Indian music. Pichaske, *Generation in Motion,* p. 101.

126. Waldberg, *Surrealism,* p. 18.

127. See Gershman, *Surrealist Revolution in France,* pp. 80–116, and the excerpts from *Political Position of Surrealism* in Breton, *Manifestoes of Surrealism,* pp. 207–78.

128. Quoted in Gershman, *Surrealist Revolution in France,* pp. 87–88.

129. "Desolation Row."

130. Gleason, *The Rolling Stone Interviews*, pp. 17, 21.

131. Ibid., pp. 21–22.

132. Benjamin, p. 189.

133. Ibid., p. 179.

134. David Pichaske suggested to me by letter that in the subsequent albums *John Wesley Harding*, *Nashville Skyline*, and *New Morning*, Dylan retreated from this individualism into the conservative communitarianism of "country" music.

## *Conclusion*

1. The distinction between form and content is somewhat problematic, because on some level they blur into one another. There is no content without form and no form without content. (On form as "sedimented content," carrying its own meaning, see Jameson, *Political Unconscious*, p. 99) However, by "content" I refer to representational aspects of a work: in literature, words, sentences, and stories; in music, lyrics, notes, and melodies. By "form" I refer to a work's structure and syntax—that is, the way the manifest content is presented and arranged—acknowledging that such features have their own meaning or "content."

2. Bell, *Cultural Contradictions of Capitalism*, p. 143; Hilton Kramer, "A Note on *The New Criterion*," *New Criterion* 1, no. 1 (September 1982): 2. It should be noted that in contrast to Kramer and his colleagues at the *New Criterion*, Bell sees the excesses of sixties' culture as an extension of modernism rather than a falling away from it. Bell is also one of the few conservatives to argue for a continuity between the fifties and sixties (pp. 41–45).

3. Allan Bloom, *Closing of the American Mind*, p. 75. As he puts it a few pages later, referring to rock music and Marcuse's ideas, "Free sexual expression, anarchism, the mining of the irrational unconscious and giving it free reign are what they have in common" (p. 78).

4. Bell, *Cultural Contradictions of Capitalism*, pp. 142, 37.

5. See Epstein, "Literary Life Today," p. 13.

6. Kramer, "A Note," pp. 1–4.

7. From the conservative point of view, artworks can be vehicles for political education; however, "politicized" artworks, those with an avowedly political purpose, rarely have a healthy political impact (or constitute good art, for that matter). The distinction, although not entirely clear, seems to be between those works that have a political subject matter yet speak to universal themes and those whose primary purpose is narrowly political. See Epstein, "Literary Life Today," p. 13.

8. George Orwell, "Why I Write," in *A Collection of Essays* (New York: Harbrace, 1946), p. 316.

9. Interview with the Fugs, *Berkeley Barb*, 12 May 1967, in Hopkins, *Hippie Papers*, pp. 213–14.

10. See Rogin, "In Defense of the New Left," p. 115. Abbie Hoffman stated at the Chicago 7 trial that his movement was dedicated to "cooperation versus competition, to the idea that people should have better means of exchange than property or money, that there should be some other basis for human interaction." Later, he said that the Yippies demanded "a society based on humanitarian cooperation and equality, a society which allows and promotes the creativity present in all people and especially of youth." Quoted in Horowitz, Lerner, and Pyes, *Counterculture and Revolution*, pp. 28, 45.

Though the rock musician Country Joe McDonald described the New Left (centered in Berkeley) and the counterculture (centered in San Francisco) as "two distinctly different communities," he said that "the average participant took the best of both worlds and put them together." Katy Butler and Jim Brewer, "In the Shadow of the War," *San Francisco Chronicle*, 9 April 1987, p. 27.

11. Perry, *Haight-Ashbury*, p. 96.

12. Wilson Carey McWilliams, *The Idea of Fraternity in America* (Berkeley: University of California Press, 1973), p. 620. In the words of Michael Lerner, "Youth culture had rebelled against the ethic of production, but not . . . the ethic of consumption." Horowitz, Lerner, and Pyes, *Counterculture and Revolution,* p. 180.

13. Marcuse, *Essay on Liberation*, p. 37.

14. Wolin, "Fugitive Democracy." See also Arendt, *On Revolution*, pp. 225ff. on the tension between democratic movements and the requirements for stable and durable government.

15. James Miller in *Democracy is in the Streets* argues that the growth of the movement into a mass phenomenon lessened the emphasis on issues of democratic process.

16. Quoted in Martin Jay, *Adorno* (Cambridge: Harvard University Press, 1984), p. 163.

# Index

abolitionism, 83
action, political, 4, 77, 141, 171
  in *All the King's Men*, 65–67
  and civil rights movement, 81
  and counterculture, 91
  and Dylan, 144, 162
  and New Left, 80, 83, 195n. 31
  and New York Intellectuals, 30, 40, 48, 75, 167; movement away from art as an aid to, 20, 70
  Trilling's ambivalence about, 53, 59–64, 67, 70, 72
Adams, Ansel, 4
Adorno, Theodor, 15, 171, 200n. 10
*Aesthetic Dimension, The* (Marcuse), 193n. 5
"Africa" (Coltrane), 100, 122
"African Violets," 101
"Alabama" (Coltrane), 121
"All Africa" (Roach), 104
*All the King's Men* (Warren), 64–67
Almanac Singers, 131
anarchy, 17–19, 27, 165, 183n. 54
  represented in Dylan's music, 150, 158
  represented in jazz, 113, 124–25
Anderson, Eric, 152
*Another Side of Bob Dylan*, 152
"anti-anti-communism," 47
anticommunism, 42, 47, 132
Apollinaire, Guillaume, 134, 147
*Appeal to the Colored People of the World* (Walker), 95
Arendt, Hannah, 56, 66, 190n. 11, 215 n. 63
Aristotle, 48, 83, 205n. 57
Arnold, Matthew, 17–20, 42, 49, 154
  and Eliot, 27–28, 183n. 54
  influence in America, 186n. 117
  and New York Intellectuals, 21, 38, 167
art, 13, 166, 178n. 5, 180n. 24, 186n. 119
  definitions of, 3–4, 150
  and everyday life, 134–35, 152, 159
  as escape, 14–16, 64, 71, 169
  as political educator, 7–9, 12–14, 71, 158
  traditional European conception of, 98, 146, 153
  as unmasking, 138
Artaud, Antonin, 92, 153
"Ascension" (Coltrane), 122–24, 169, 208n. 96, 209n. 98
authenticity, 9, 74, 120, 215n. 70, 216 n. 82
  black, 197n. 43
  and folk music, 133, 137–38
  and the New Left, 78, 82
  in work of Dylan, 128, 140–43, 145, 162, 164–65
automatic writing, 146–47

Baez, Joan, 132, 140, 149
Baker, Ella, 81
Bakhtin, Mikhail, 200n. 10
"Ballad of a Thin Man" (Dylan), 151, 157
"Ballad of Hollis Brown" (Dylan), 139–40, 144–45, 166
Balliet, Whitney, 114
"Bantu," 101
Baraka, Amiri, 7, 201n. 20
Barrett, William, 41
Baudelaire, Charles, 147
Beatles, 92, 127, 170, 218n. 111
Beats, 89, 126, 130, 133, 176n. 31
  influence on Dylan, 134–35, 147, 149, 152, 154, 217n. 96
Beethoven, Ludwig van, 98, 152
Bell, Daniel, 165, 219n. 2
"beloved community," 1, 80–84, 125,
  King on, 106, 204nn. 52 and 54, 205 n. 55
  represented in jazz, 113, 121–22, 123, 163–64, 168
Benjamin, Walter, 149, 157, 161
Bentham, Jeremy, 54
Berry, Chuck, 129
*Billy Budd, Sailor* (Melville), 190n. 11
*Birth of Tragedy, The* (Nietzsche), 176n. 31
black aesthetic, 85, 196n. 35
Black Arts movement, 86
black English, 86
Black Panthers, 83
black power, 83–86, 122, 168, 195n. 32, 196n. 33, 196n. 43
Blake, William, 213n. 38
Blakey, Art, 100
*Blonde on Blonde* (Dylan), 149, 152
Bloom, Alexander, 189–90n. 8
Bloom, Allan, 165, 215n. 70, 219n. 3
blues, 86, 110–11, 115–17, 205n. 64
  defined, 206n. 68
  in Dylan's work, 136, 154
  rock and, 129, 175n. 24
"Blue Suede Shoes," 130, 137
*Bob Dylan*, 137
"Bob Dylan's 115th Dream," 152, 166
body
  counterculture's emphasis on, 79, 90, 145, 170
  music's relation to, 12, 156, 212n. 23
Bollingen Prize for poetry, 50, 188n. 159
Boone, Pat, 132
Boudin, Leonard, 135
Bourdieu, Pierre, 85
Bourne, Randolph, 83
Brando, Marlon, 89, 136
Braxton, Anthony, 124, 209n. 100
Breton, André, 24, 146, 157
*Bringing it All Back Home* (Dylan), 148–49, 152–53
Brooks, Cleanth, 36
*Brown v. Board of Education* (1954), 80
Brown, James, 86, 124
Brown, Oscar, Jr., 102, 203n. 40
Bruce, Lenny, 92, 132
Buber, Martin, 107
Burroughs, William, 133

"call and response," 98, 104
*Cantos* (Pound), 50
Carmichael, Stokely, 84
Carter Family, 132
Cassady, Neal, 133
*Catch-22* (Heller), 11
Chace, William M., 192n. 70
"Chain Gang," 130
Chambers, Iain, 210n. 5, 212n. 23
Chambers, Whittaker, 60
*Charles Mingus Presents Charles Mingus*, 113–15
Cherry, Don, 117
Chicago Seven, 92
Cicero, 107
cinema, 29, 43, 44
citizenship, 20
"civic republicanism," 83, 195n. 31
  represented in Dylan's music, 128, 137, 143, 154, 162–63
civil rights and liberties, 4, 43, 47–48, 50
civil rights movement, 1, 163, 166, 175 n. 24, 199n. 8
  conceptions of politics, 75, 79–83, 106–7, 168; represented in jazz, 116, 120–21, 123–25, 209n. 98
  diversity within, 204n. 52
  and folk music, 131
  and participatory democracy, 194 n. 12
  and youth culture of fifties, 135–36
Cohn-Bendit, Daniel, 92
Coleman, Ornette, 125, 207nn. 79 and 87
  "Free Jazz," 1, 116–21, 209n. 88
  vocalized tone, 98, 116, 118, 208n. 88

Coleridge, Samuel Taylor, 213n. 38
Coltrane, John, 86, 208nn. 92 and 93, 209n. 99, 210n. 104
"Ascension," 122–24, 169, 208nn. 95 and 96, 209n. 98
on political meaning of jazz, 101
comic books, 43
communism, 89, 135, 175n. 23, 181n. 28
Marx on, 23
and mass culture, 33, 42–48, 51
New York Intellectuals on, 9, 20–21, 32, 40, 167
Trilling on, 56, 61, 67–70
*Communist Manifesto*, 34
Communist Party, 60, 89, 158
and early New York Intellectuals, 24–26, 29–31, 180n. 19
and postwar Intellectuals, 47–48
communitarianism, 54, 219n. 134
community, 18, 84, 131
and authenticity, 215n. 70
Dylan's ultimate rejection of, 159–60, 171
and folk music of Bob Dylan, 128, 141–43, 148–49, 165, 168
and individuality, 1, 15, 79, 84, 106, 169–70
and literature, 176n. 31
and music, 176n. 31
and New Critics, 35, 185n. 88
and New Left, 78, 187, 109.31
represented in jazz, 97, 121, 123–25
*Coney Island of the Mind* (Ferlinghetti), 135
conformity, 69, 133, 145, 150–51, 167, 171
Congress of Racial Equality (CORE), 83
conservatism, 21, 25, 31, 33, 37, 73
contemporary, 10, 164–66, 219n. 7
liberalism's borrowing from, 54, 58
and modernism, 55
and New Critics, 36–37
"Conversation" (Mingus), 111–12
"Cookin,'" 100
*Cool Hand Luke*, 218n. 119
Corso, Gregory, 135
counterculture, 9, 78, 86–93, 220n. 10
and Bob Dylan, 126–28, 145, 150–51, 158–59, 164, 169
political vision of, 75, 170, 198n. 63
creativity, 156, 220n. 10
and the Beats, 133
and the counterculture, 90–91, 145–46
and European conception of art, 178 n. 5
Marcuse on, 87
in New Left's political vision, 82–83
*Crucible* (Miller), 44
cultural nationalism, 84–86
"cultural pluralism," 43
"cultural studies," 13
culture, 178n. 5
Arnold's analysis of, 17–20
"high" and "low," 19, 166; in Dylan's work, 150–52; roots of the split between, 19, 186n. 119, 187n. 137; in thought of New York Intellectuals, 33, 42–51, 179n. 16
"middlebrow," 45, 49, 188n. 154
popular, 20, 151, 157–58, 166–67, 188n. 154
*Culture and Anarchy* (Arnold), 17–20, 28, 42
Curson, Ted, 114

"Dahomey Dance" (Coltrane), 122
Davidson, Donald, 34, 184nn. 78 and 82
Davis, Miles, 205n. 64
Dean, James, 89, 136
death, 60, 64, 69–72, 191n. 66
deconstruction, 36
democracy, 163, 165, 167–69, 171, 179 n. 14
Arnold's ambivalence about, 17–20
and black power movement, 197n. 43
in civil rights movements' idea of freedom, 107
and counterculture, 91
definitions of, 3–5, 173n. 7
in Dylan's works, 150, 158–59
Eliot's view of, 27–28, 183n. 54
liberal, 2, 9, 11, 20, 141, 165; as alternative to totalitarianism, 32; defined, 4–5; mass culture as a threat to, 69; postwar threats to, 42–46; and realist novels, 40; Trilling on, 53, 68–69, 73–74
and Marx, 23
and mass culture, 42–51, 178n. 5
and modernism, 30
and New Critics, 36–37
participatory, 9, 80–81, 140–43, 161, 165, 170; defined, 5; and civil rights movement, 194n. 12

democracy *(continued):*
represented in jazz, 116, 121
sensibility required for, 8
Southern Agrarians on, 34–35
Yippies' view of, 92–93
"democratic artworks," 2
Denzin, Norman K., 177n. 35
Depression, 21–22, 131
"Desolation Row" (Dylan), 152, 159–60
determinism, 23–24, 40, 67
Dewey, John, 25, 182n. 37
dialogue
between citizens, 5
inner, 8
in jazz, 98, 104, 111–16, 118–21, 123–24, 208n. 88
Dickstein, Morris, 10
Diggers, 90
"Dis Hyeah," 100
diversity, 9, 55, 73–74, 86
Dolphy, Eric, 114, 117
Donne, John, 27
Dostoevsky, Fyodor, 29, 58, 155, 200 n. 10
"Driva' Man" (Roach), 102–3
drugs, 89, 100
DuBois, W. E. B., 95–96
Duchamp, Marcel 4
Dupee, F. W., 26
Dwight, Sullivan, 186n. 119
Dwight, Timothy, 2
Dylan, Bob, 9, 13, 14, 163–69, 210n. 1
attack on conformity, 150–51, 171
attack on cultural and aesthetic valuations, 150–55
and counterculture, 126–28, 145, 150–51, 158–59, 164, 169
early influences of, 136–37
"folk music" of, 128, 136–45, 153, 168; and authenticity, 127, 140–43, 145, 162, 164–65; realist narratives, 139–40; unmasking function of, 138–40
and "high culture," 150–52
influence of Beats on, 134–35, 147, 149, 152, 154, 217n. 96
and New Left, 126–28, 143, 145, 151, 154, 161–62
on popular culture, 151, 157–58
psychic liberation in the music of, 155–58
retreat into private consciousness, 159–62
rock music of, 149–62
and surrealism, 147–49, 155–59, 161–63
works: *Another Side of Bob Dylan*, 152; "Ballad of a Thin Man," 151, 157; "Ballad of Hollis Brown," 139–40, 144–45, 166; *Blonde on Blonde*, 149, 152; *Bob Dylan*, 137; "Bob Dylan's 115th Dream," 152, 166; *Bringing it All Back Home*, 148–49, 152–53; "Desolation Row," 152, 159–60; *The Freewheelin' Bob Dylan*, 137, 147–48; "Gates of Eden," 217n. 96; "A Hard Rain's A-Gonna Fall," 142, 144–45; *Highway 61 Revisited*, 149, 152; "I Shall Be Free no. 10," 215n. 69; "It's Alright Ma (I'm Only Bleeding), 154; "The Lonesome Death of Hattie Carroll," 139; "Masters of War," 140, 142, 156; "My Back Pages," 144; "Rainy Day Women #12 & 35," 154, 157–58; "Subterranean Homesick Blues," 153–56, 166; "Talkin' World War III Blues," 147–49, 160; *The Times They Are A-Changin'*, 137, 140, 144, 153; "The Times They Are A-Changin'," 156; "Tombstone Blues," 157; "Who Killed Davey Moore?", 141–42; "With God On Our Side," 142

Eagleton, Terry, 190n. 29
Eliot, T. S., 15, 21, 26–30, 48–49, 55, 182n. 47
and Arnold, 183n. 54
New Critics and, 33, 36
"objective correlative," 57, 182n. 48
Ellington, Duke, 99, 116
Elliot, Ramblin' Jack, 136
Ellison, Ralph, 155
emotions, 104, 166–67
artworks' engagement of, 159, 163, 172
and community, 79
and the counterculture, 92
and literature, 27, 56–59, 61, 134, 190n. 23

and mass culture, 44
and music, 22, 110, 124, 142–43, 176n. 32
in thought of New York Intellectuals, 25
empathy, 125, 172
and the beloved community, 106
in Dylan's music, 139, 168
in jazz improvisation, 108, 113, 115, 119, 121
Enlightenment values, 55–56
equality, 125, 164, 200n. 10
in Arnold's cultural theory, 18
in beloved community, 1, 106, 164
and counterculture, 145
in Dylan's work, 168
and participatory democracy, 9
represented in jazz, 1, 109, 111–12, 164
*See also* hierarchy
*Eros and Civilization* (Marcuse), 78
*Essay on Liberation, An* (Marcuse), 78, 170
everyday life, 81, 87, 90, 170, 177n. 33
art and, 85, 134–35, 146, 159
experience,
Beats' pursuit of, 133
and community, 14–15, 79, 165
in contrast to abstract ideas, 56
independent, mass culture's threat to, 44–46
literature's engagement of, 16, 25, 27–30, 38, 75; Trilling on, 57–58, 61
and New Critics, 35, 185
and New York Intellectuals, 25–26, 28–31, 134, 171
pursuit of, in the sixties, 78, 84, 91, 171, 195n. 31; represented in Dylan's music, 128, 142–43, 149–50, 158–59

"Fables of Faubus" (Mingus), 109–10, 113
*Famous All Over Town* (Santiago), 143
Faulkner, William, 26, 58
Ferlinghetti, Lawrence, 135
Fiedler, Leslie, 41, 48
Fields, W. C., 92
film. *See* cinema
*Finnegans Wake* (Joyce), 41
Flacks, Richard, 127, 135
Foley, Barbara, 180n. 19
"Folk Forms #1" (Mingus), 114–15, 117, 166
folk music, 46, 126, 131–33, 153
defined, 212n. 26
Dylan's, 9, 128, 135–45, 168
Forster, E. M., 70
Frank, Waldo, 96
Frankfurt School, 13
Franklin, Aretha, 86
free association, 134, 146–47, 156, 160, 164
freedom, 9, 88, 125, 164, 195n. 31
acknowledgment of limits leads to, 70
in *All the King's Men*, 65
civil rights movement's notions of, 1, 106–7, 116, 120–21
as a component of democracy, 17–18
and counterculture, 145, 149, 155–56, 158–59, 198n. 63
and European conception of art, 178 n. 5
in liberalism, 56, 121
in realist novels, 38–40
relationship between creativity and, 23
represented in jazz, 96–97, 101–25, 133, 203n. 37, 207nn. 79 and 87
resignation as, 60, 63–64
songs, 97, 200n. 12
surrealist notion of, 145–47, 161–62
"Freedom Day" (Roach), 103–4
"Freedom Now Suite," 102–6, 124, 164, 166, 168, 203n. 40
"Free Jazz" (Coleman), 116–21, 166, 209n. 98
*Freewheelin' Bob Dylan, The*, 137, 147–48
Freud, Sigmund, 59, 69–71, 87–88, 145–46
"Freud: Within and Beyond Culture" (Trilling), 69–71
Frith, Simon, 14, 176n. 32
Fugs, 91, 170

Garvey, Marcus, 96
"Gates of Eden" (Dylan), 217n. 96
Gates, Henry Louis, 143
Geertz, Clifford, 7
"Get a Job," 130
Ginsberg, Allen, 89, 133–35, 213n. 40
and Bob Dylan, 134, 145, 152, 217 n. 96

Gitlin, Todd, 10, 81, 127
Goethe, Johann Wolfgang von, 57
Gold, Michael, 22, 131
"Goodnight Irene," 132
gospel music, 100
Greenberg, Clement, 214n. 42
Greenwich Village, 132, 136
Grossberg, Lawrence, 175n. 30, 211nn. 19 and 21
"group-centered leadership," 80–83, 194 n. 15,
Guthrie, Woody, 136–37, 141

"Haitian Fight Song" (Mingus), 109–10
Haley, Bill, 136
Hamilton, Charles V., 84
Handy, John, 207n. 77
"happenings," 4, 90, 146
"hard bop," 100
Harker, Dave, 210n. 210
Harlow, Jean, 152
Hawkins, Coleman, 103, 105
Hayden, Tom, 80, 82, 127, 135, 170
Hebidge, Dick, 176n. 33
Held, David, 174n. 7
"He's a Rebel," 130
hierarchy, 145, 150, 153, 158, 161–62, 200n. 10
*Highway 61 Revisited* (Dylan), 149, 152
Hiss, Alger, 48
Hitler, Adolf, 15
Hoffman, Abbie, 80, 91–92, 220n. 10
Holiday, Billie, 100
Holly, Buddy, 129, 136
Hook, Sidney, 182n. 37
Howe, Irving, 53
*Howl* (Ginsberg), 133, 135, 152, 213n. 40
Hubbard, Freddie, 117
*Huckleberry Finn*, 58, 69
Hughes, Langston, 95
Hulme, T. E., 184n. 75
Hunter, Tab, 132
Hurt, Mississippi John

ideas, 56, 71, 74, 77
ideology, 61, 67, 176n. 33, 194n. 19
  and literature, 56–58
  and mass culture, 44, 46–47
*I'll Take My Stand*, 33–35
imagination, 6, 146, 157–58, 195n. 31, 212n. 23
immigrants, 42, 186n. 119
Impressions, 152
improvisation, 98–99, 108–9, 164, 201 n. 18
  collective, 111–25, 168, 209n. 98
  as self-expression, 115
individualism, 9, 17–18, 22, 79, 84, 165
  and Beats, 134
  and civil rights movement's idea of freedom, 107
  in Dylan's work, 148–49, 154, 161–62, 219n. 134
  liberalism's tendency toward, 54
  and New Left, 141
individuality, 89, 164–65, 167–69
  and civil rights movement, 82, 106
  and community, 1, 15, 79, 84, 106, 169
  and democracy, 5, 20, 169
  in Dylan's work, 142, 149, 161–62, 169
  in jazz, 2, 98, 107–9, 111–25, 171, 209n. 99
  and literature, 12
  J. S. Mill on, 54
  threats to by mass culture, 9
  Trilling on, 57, 74
industrialism, 27, 33–35, 43, 178n. 5
intellectuals, political role of, 31, 68, 74, 141, 167
intention of the artist, 14, 35
International Workers of the World ("Wobblies"), 131
Iser, Wolfgang, 190n. 29
"I Shall Be Free no.10" (Dylan), 215n. 69
"It's Alright Ma (I'm Only Bleeding)" (Dylan), 154

Jackson, Milt, 208n. 93
Jacoby, Russell, 189n. 1
"Jailhouse Rock," 130
James, Henry, 42
Jameson, Frederic, 173n. 2
jazz, 34, 126, 175n. 24, 199n. 8
  African roots of, 97–98, 105, 209n. 99
  bebop, 7, 89, 100, 133, 135, 202n. 27
  Ornette Coleman, 98, 116–21, 125, 207nn. 79 and 87
  John Coltrane, 86, 208nn. 92 and 93, 209n. 99, 210n. 104; "Ascension," 122–24, 169, 208nn. 95 and 96, 209n. 98; on political meaning of jazz, 101

dialogue in, 98, 104, 111–16, 118–21, 123–24, 208n. 88
Duke Ellington, 99
and fifties folk culture, 132
and freedom, 96–97, 101–25, 133, 203n. 37, 207nn. 79 and 87
"Freedom Now Suite" (Roach), 102–6, 124, 164–68, 203nn. 40 and 44
"free jazz," 1–2, 106, 109, 116–25, 164–69; Coltrane's influence on, 209n. 98; displacement of, by other kinds of jazz, 171; early attempts at, 205n. 64
"Free Jazz" (Coleman), 116–21, 166, 209n. 98
improvisation, meaning of, 98–99, 108–9, 164, 201n. 18; collective, 111–25, 168, 209n. 98
individuality and solidarity in, 107–9, 111–25, 171, 209n. 99
Charles Mingus, 109–16, 120–21, 125, 202n. 27, 206n. 75
New Orleans, 99, 112, 114, 118, 209 n. 98
Charlie Parker, 100, 107, 115, 133, 135
polyphony in, 97–99, 111–16, 118–20, 122–23, 125, 200n. 10
Max Roach, 102–6, 111, 124, 168, 203nn. 40 and 44
as self-expression, 97, 99, 104, 107–8, 120–21; in Coleman's music, 117–18; in Mingus's music, 111, 114–15, 206n. 75
Jefferson, Blind Lemon, 132
Johnson, Robert, 152
Joyce, James, 55

Kant, Immanuel, 78, 215n. 70
Kennedy, John, 80
Kerouac, Jack, 89, 133, 135, 217n. 96
King, B. B., 98
King, Martin Luther, 83, 102, 105–7, 121, 124, 204n. 52
idea of beloved community, 1, 80, 97, 106, 113
Kingston Trio, 132
Kopkind, Andrew, 127
Kovacs, Ernie, 92
Kramer, Hilton, 165–66, 219n. 2
Krassner, Paul, 91
Kupferberg, Tuli, 170

Laine, Frankie, 132
Laing, R. D., 83
Larmore, Charles, 189n. 2
Lawrence, D. H., 26, 55
Lawson, James, 194n. 15
Leadbelly, 132
"Leader of the Pack," 130
Lefebvre, Henri, 212n. 23
Lenya, Lotte, 152
Lerner, Michael, 220n. 12
Levine, Lawrence, 42, 46, 186nn. 117 and 119, 201n. 20
Lewes, George Henry, 186n. 119
Lewis, John, 107, 204n. 49
*Liberal Imagination, The* (Trilling), 55–59, 69–71, 189n. 8
liberalism, 12, 34, 37, 163, 167–69, 189 n. 2
dichotomization of group and individual in, 97, 109, 115
idea of freedom, 106, 121
in *The Middle of the Journey*, 60–64
"new," 32
novels as an aid to, 38
protean nature of, 53–54
and the sixties, 80
threats to, 33
Trilling's definition of, 55–56
"Liberia" (Coltrane), 122
liberty. *See* freedom
Lincoln, Abbey, 102–4
Lipsitz, George, 211n. 13, 212n. 23
Little, Booker, 105
Little Richard, 136
"Lonesome Death of Hattie Carroll, The" (Dylan), 139

Macdonald, Dwight, 43, 46–49, 141, 188nn. 154 and 159
Mailer, Norman, 11, 89
Malcolm X, 101, 204n. 52
Malraux, André, 39
"Man of Constant Sorrow, A," 137
Mann, Thomas, 72
Mantilla, Raymond, 105
Marable, Manning, 101
Marcuse, Herbert, 87–88, 91–92, 158
*Aesthetic Dimension, The*, 193n. 5
*Essay on Liberation, An*, 78, 170
on repression, 197n. 50
and surrealism, 145

"marvelous," 146, 155–59, 208n. 96
Marx, Karl, 27, 38, 48
  early writings of, 22–24, 87
  and modernism, 29, 182n. 47, 183n. 59
  and New Critics, 34, 184n. 78
  and surrealists, 158
Marx Brothers, 92
Marxism
  and early New York Intellectuals, 20–26, 181n. 29
  and modernism in thought of New York Intellectuals, 24–26, 28–32, 164, 182nn. 37, 46, and 47
  New York Intellectuals' postwar retreat from, 49–51
Maslow, Abraham, 91
"mass culture," 15, 128, 210n. 5
  New Critics on, 33–35
  New York Intellectuals on, 9, 20, 31–33, 42–51, 188n. 154; and folk culture, 141; Clement Greenberg, 25; problems with, 167–68; and separation of art and politics, 77
  rock music as, 13
  Trilling on, 59
"mass society," 87, 188n. 154
"Masters of War" (Dylan), 140, 156
McCarthy, Joseph, 135, 194n. 19
  and New York Intellectuals, 21, 33, 47, 51, 175n. 23
McDonald, Country Joe, 220n. 10
McLean, Jackie, 115
McPherson, Charles, 207n. 77
"Meaning of a Literary Idea, The" (Trilling), 56–57
"Meditations on Integration" (Mingus), 109
Memphis Jug Band, 132
*Middle of the Journey, The* (Trilling), 60–64, 71
Mill, John Stuart, 4, 54
Miller, Arthur, 44
Miller, James, 83, 135, 194n. 12, 220n. 15
Mingus, Charles, 109–16, 120–21, 125, 202n. 27, 206n. 76
  *Charles Mingus Presents Charles Mingus*, 113–15
  "Conversation," 111–12
  "Fables of Faubus," 109–10
  "Folk Forms #1," 114–15, 117
  "Haitian Fight Song," 109–10
  "Meditations on Integration," 109
  "Percussion Discussion," 111–12, 115
  "Pithecanthropus Erectus," 112–13, 124
  "Prayer for Passive Resistance," 109
  "Work Song," 109
modernism, 22, 26, 46
  and Eliot, 26–28, 182n. 47
  and Marx, 183n. 59
  and Marxism, 20, 24, 28–30, 164
  and New Critics, 36
  and realism, 39
  Trilling on, 55
Monk, Thelonious, 202n. 27, 203n. 37
Moses, Robert (Parris), 194n. 15
Muhammed, Elijah, 79
music, popular, 176n. 32, 177n. 35
Muslims, black, 79
"My Back Pages" (Dylan), 144

Nash, Diane, 82
Nation of Islam, 204n. 52
naturalism, 39–40
nature, 6, 23, 35, 180n. 24
Neal, Larry, 86
New Critics, 21, 33–39, 167, 191n. 61
  similarities between New York Intellectuals and, 29, 50, 133–34
  Trilling on, 55–57, 61
  Robert Penn Warren, 64, 67, 184n. 82
New Left, 87, 163, 166
  and civil rights movement, 194n. 12
  on community, 1, 35, 168
  conception of politics, 75, 78, 80–83, 165
  and counterculture, 170, 220n. 10
  and Dylan, 126–28, 145, 151, 154, 161–62
  and jazz, 125
  and the self, 91
  Trilling's view of, 73
Newman, Paul, 218n. 119
New York Intellectuals, 3, 9–10, 20–21, 83, 163–64
  and "action painting," 214n. 42
  and Beats, 89, 133–34
  and communism, 20, 32, 40–41, 167, 175n. 23, 181n. 28
  and Communist Party, 21–22, 24–26, 29–31

and conservatism, 33, 37–38
decline in influence of, 74–75
differences among, 179n. 15
emphasis on experience, 25–26, 28–31, 134, 171
and "high culture," 33, 44–46, 179 n. 16
and liberalism, 20, 32–33, 38–40
and Marxism, 20, 21–26, 181n. 29, 182n. 47; postwar retreat from, 49–51; wedded to modernism, 24–26, 28–32, 164, 182nn. 37 and 46
on mass culture, 20, 31–33, 42–51, 188n. 154; and folk culture, 141; Clement Greenberg, 25; problems with, 167–68; and separation of art and politics, 77
on modernism, 20, 26–31, 179n. 16
and New Critics, 37–40
and political action, 20, 40–44, 77, 167
on Popular Front, 20, 21–22, 183n. 64
on proletarian literature, 20, 21–22, 25, 180n. 19
on psychoanalysis, 87–88
on realism, 20, 38–41, 179n. 16
on Rosenbergs, 44–48, 187n. 136
and Trotsky, 21, 24–25, 181n. 30, 182n. 36
Nietzsche, Friedrich, 142, 176n. 31
"No Particular Place to Go," 130
novels, 2, 38, 53–59, 68–75

Ochs, Phil, 150
Oglesby, Carl, 125
Olatunji, Michael, 104
Ong, Walter, 175n. 30
*On the Road* (Kerouac), 135
Ortega y Gasset, José, 48
Orwell, George, 39

Packard, Vance, 89
Parker, Charlie, 100, 107, 115, 133, 135, 202n. 28
*Partisan Review*, 11, 21, 24, 39, 41
Pateman, Carol, 174n. 7
Paz, Octavio, 146
People's Songs movement, 131
"Percussion Discussion" (Mingus), 111–12, 115
Perry, Charles, 90
Phillips, William, 25, 28, 43, 182n. 37
Pichaske, David, 219n. 134
"Pithecanthropus Erectus" (Mingus), 112–13, 123–24
Pitkin, Hanna, 173n. 5
Plato, 5, 205n. 57
pleasure principle, 88
Podhoretz, Norman, 197n. 52
Poirer, Richard, 218n. 111
political education, 3, 14
by artworks, 2, 11–12, 14, 21, 163–72, 219n. 7; according to Arnold, 17–20; in Dylan's music, 143–45; in early rock and roll, 128–31; in jazz, 101–25; proletarian literature, 25; realist novels, 40; three modes of, 8
defined, 5–6
*Politics* (journal), 48
"politics of experience," 83–84, 145
and Dylan's songs, 9, 149, 158, 162–63, 169
polyphony, 97–99, 111–16, 118–20, 122–23, 125, 200n. 10
Popular Front, 20, 21–22, 26, 30–31, 183n. 64
populism, 83
*Port Huron Statement, The*, 82, 127, 170
Pound, Ezra, 26, 50, 55, 184n. 75, 188 n. 159, 197n. 52
pragmatism, 25, 182n. 37
Pratt, Ray, 210n. 1, 212n. 28
"Prayer for Passive Resistance" (Mingus), 109
"Preacher, The," 100
prefigurative politics, 81
Presley, Elvis, 131, 211n. 9
"Pretty Peggy-O," 137
proletarian literature, 20, 21–22, 24, 25–26, 131, 180n. 19
and modernism, 29–30
Trilling on, 54
Proust, Marcel, 38, 55
psychoanalysis, 58, 87–88, 145
Puritans, American, 83

Radano, Ronald, 207n. 79, 209n. 99
"radical right," 21, 33, 47
radio, 129
Rahv, Philip, 25, 28–29, 31, 41
response to New Critics, 37–40
Rainey, Ma, 152

"Rainy Day Women #12 & 35" (Dylan), 154, 157–58
Ransom, John Crowe, 33, 36–37
rationalism, 54–56
rationality, 18, 42–43, 92, 146, 165, 167
  in bebop culture, 100
  and Dylan's works, 137, 150, 153, 169
  Marcuse on, 78
  and New Left, 128, 137
  New York Intellectuals on, 9, 20, 55
Ray, Johnny, 136
Reagon, Bernice Johnson, 97, 200n. 12
realism, 20, 38–41, 46
  in folk music, 133, 168
  "moral," 56, 70, 73
*Realist*, 91
reality principle, 87–88
reason. *See* rationality
*Rebel Without a Cause*, 89
record, 45 rpm, 129
recordings of music, 12
reflection theory, 13, 14
Reising, Russell, 36, 189n. 8
relativism, 165, 215n. 70
respect, 8, 9
rhythm and blues, 100, 116
Richards, I. A., 184n. 75
Richmond, Dannie, 114–15, 207n. 77
Riefenstahl, Leni, 15
Riesman, David, 131
Rimbaud, Arthur, 134, 147, 157–58
Rivera, Diego, 24
Roach, Max, 102–6, 111, 124, 203nn. 40 and 44
Rock, John S., 95–96
"Rock around the Clock," 130
rock music, 2, 89, 164–65, 175n. 24, 210n. 4
  Bob Dylan, 149–62, 171
  in fifties, 128–31, 211n. 12
  as "mass culture," 13
Rogin, Michael, 72, 89
Rolling Stones, 127, 170
Rollins, Sonny, 203n. 38, 208n. 93
romanticism, 55, 145, 153, 178n. 5, 182 n. 2
Ronk, Dave van, 136
Rosenberg, Harold, 214n. 42
Rosenberg, Julius and Ethel, 44–48, 187 n. 136
Ross, Andrew, 124
Ross, Bob, 135
Rousseau, Jean-Jacques, 175n. 20
Rubin, Jerry, 91–92

Sanders, Ed, 91
Sanders, Pharoah, 124
Santiago, Danny, 143
Savio, Mario, 80
"Say it Loud, I'm Black and Proud," 124
Schaar, John, 6
Schaub, Thomas, 189n. 8
Schiller, Friedrich, 23, 78, 92, 180n. 24
Schoenberg, Arnold, 171
"School Days," 130
Seeger, Pete, 131–32, 141
"See that my Grave is Kept Clean," 137
self, 54, 83, 91, 213n. 38, 216n. 82
  in Dylan's songs, 138, 140–43, 145, 150, 153
  in Trilling's work, 69–73, 192n. 78
self-expression, 77, 83, 87, 91, 125, 153
  in counterculture, 145
  Eliot's view of, 27
  in jazz, 97, 99, 104, 107–8, 120–21, 125; Coleman, 117–18; Mingus, 111, 114–15, 206n. 75
  in spirituals, 201n. 20
senses, 14, 23, 30, 87, 163, 166–67
sensibility, 7–8, 18
  encouraged by modernist art, 29
  necessary for democracy, 5, 8
  new, encouraged by artworks, 26, 149, 161, 170
"Sermon, The," 100
*Sgt. Pepper's Lonely Hearts Club Band* (Beatles), 218n. 111
Shepherd, John, 177n. 38
Shepp, Archie, 107, 209n. 98
sight, 11
Silone, Ignazio, 39
Silver, Horace, 100
Smart, Christopher, 145
Snyder, Gary, 213n. 38
socialism, 22, 24, 29, 34, 48
  New York Intellectuals' abandonment of, 32, 38, 88
solidarity, 205n. 57, 215n. 63
  and black power, 84–86
  and democracy, 8–9, 18
  and individuality in civil rights movement thought, 106, 164

in jazz, 98, 107–9, 111–25, 171
in spirituals, 201n. 20
"Song of the Underground Railroad," 122
"soul" style, 85, 196n. 35
sound, 11, 176n. 30
Southern Agrarians, 33, 36, 43
spirituals, 98–99, 201n. 20
Stalin and Stalinism, 21, 31, 179n. 15
Starobinski, Jean, 216n. 82
"status anxiety," 42
Stevenson, Adlai, 68, 80
"Strange Fruit," 100
Stravinsky, Igor, 202n. 28
Strong, George Templeton, 42
Student Nonviolent Coordinating Committee (SNCC), 79–83, 91, 106–7, 124, 204n. 52, 208n. 92
Students for a Democratic Society (SDS), 80–83, 125, 127, 135
"Subterranean Homesick Blues" (Dylan), 153–56, 166
Suchoff, David, 187n. 136
surrealism, 208n. 96, 216n. 83
and Beats, 134
and counterculture, 90
and Dylan, 9, 145–48, 155–59, 161–64
and Marcuse, 78, 87
and New Criticism, 36
and Yippies, 92
Szwed, John, 199n. 9

"Talkin' World War III Blues" (Dylan), 147–49, 160
Tate, Allen, 33, 35, 37, 50, 188n. 159
Taylor, Charles, 215n. 70
"Tears for Johannesburg" (Roach), 104
Teres, Harvey M., 179n. 15
*Theatre and Its Double* (Artaud), 92
Thoreau, Henry David, 83
"Time of Dyin'," 137
*Times They Are A-Changin', The* (Dylan), 137, 140, 153
"Times They Are A-Changin', The," (Dylan), 156
Tocqueville, Alexis de, 74
tolerance, 42–43, 83, 167, 172
and democracy, 8, 20
in Trilling's work, 9, 55–56
"Tombstone Blues" (Dylan), 157
"Tom Dooley," 132
totalitarianism, 32, 40, 47, 50, 89, 134
tradition, 41, 43, 129, 165
Trilling, Lionel, 41, 83, 154, 189n. 1
and Matthew Arnold, 178n. 1
on Beats, 197n. 52
on communism, 56, 61, 69–70
on ideas and emotions, 56–58, 134, 190n. 23
and Judaism, 192n. 70
on liberalism, 12, 55–56
on modernism, 55
on New Critics, 55–57, 61
on political power of literature, 9, 10, 163, 167
political vision of, 72–74
on psychoanalysis, 87–88
renunciation of action by, 59–64, 68–72
response to New Critics, 37–40, 56–57
works: "Freud: Within and Beyond Culture," 69–71; *The Liberal Imagination*, 55–59, 69–71, 189 n. 8; "The Meaning of a Literary Idea," 56; *The Middle of the Journey*, 60–64, 71
"Triptych: Prayer/Protest/Peace" (Roach), 104
Tristano, Lennie, 202n. 28, 205n. 64
*Triumph of the Will*, 15, 77
Trotsky, 181n. 32
and early New York Intellectuals, 21, 24–25, 48, 181n. 30, 182n. 36
and surrealists, 158
"Tutti Frutti," 137
Twain, Mark, 58
Tyner, McCoy, 99

*Union Maids*, 141

Vall, Tomas du, 105
Viorst, Milton, 194n. 15
Vonnegut, Kurt, 11

Wald, Alan, 179n. 15, 182n. 46
Waldron, Mal, 206
Walker, David, 95
Warhol, Andy, 4
Warren, Robert Penn, 33, 64–67, 184n. 82
Warshow, Robert, 43–47
Weathermen, 83
Weavers, 132
Weber, Max, 83, 195n. 28
Webster, Ben, 107

"Wednesday Night Prayer Meeting," 100
*Well Wrought Urn, The* (Brooks), 36
West, Cornell, 197n. 43
"What Love" (Mingus), 113–14
White, James Boyd, 8
Whitman, Walt, 145, 153, 216n. 80
"Who Killed Davey Moore?" (Dylan), 141–42
*Wild One, The*, 89
Wilkinson, Elizabeth M., 180n. 24
Williams, Cootie, 107
Williams, Hank, 136
Williams, Raymond, 8, 177n. 37, 178n. 5, 180n. 24
Williams, William Carlos, 197n. 52
Willis, Paul, 176n. 33
Willoughby, L. A., 180n. 24
Wise, Gene, 189n. 8
Wittgenstein, Ludwig, 6, 173n. 5
Wolin, Sheldon, 6, 171
Wordsworth, William, 54, 134, 190n. 23
"Work Song" (Mingus), 109
work songs, 98
Wright, Richard, 110

"Yakety Yak (Don't Talk Back!)," 130
Yippies, 87, 91–92, 170, 220n. 10